To
Utti
Best of health
[signature]

ETERNAL HEALTH

TILL
MIN KÄRA
SYSTER
MINNE FRÅN MIN
INDIENRESA JAN-FEB 2004
PUSS & KRAM
Lillemor

Dedicated to my honorable gurus

Vaidya Nanak Chand Sharma

and

Sri Haridas Shastri Maharaj

who shared their wisdom,
and inspired me to learn
the original principles of Āyurveda
and practice them in my life.

Ajñāna timirāndhasya jñānāñjana śalakayā
Cakṣurunmīlitam yena tasmai śri guruve namaḥ

I pay respects to my guru, who opened my eyes
and took me out of the darkness by giving me knowledge.

ETERNAL HEALTH

The Essence of Ayurveda

Dr. PARTAP CHAUHAN

JIVA

Jiva Institute
1144 Sector 19
Faridabad
Haryana
INDIA 121 002
Email: info@jiva.org

ISBN: 81-87153-25-3

Price: Rs. 295

Cover illustration:

Dhanvantari is the God of medicine. He manifested from the churning oceans, with a pot of nectar and bunch of herbs to heal sickness on Earth. The conch shell signifies harmony, peace and knowledge. He introduced the science of life (Āyurveda), and is considered the guardian of health and patron of Āyurvedic practitioners.

Artist: Nilesh Raste

This book is for information only and is not intended for medical diagnosis and treatment. It is not a substitute for medical consultation or advice from a registered health care professional.

Foreword

THE wisdom of Āyurveda is profound and eternal. It has healed mind, body and soul for millennia. Although the development of a body of supporting literature was impeded by foreign rule in India, Āyurveda has survived and continues to enlighten us today. The precepts of this health system treat millions of people in India, and increasingly around the world.

Āyurveda has recently been "re-discovered" in the pursuit of holistic healing and natural health. The globalization of Āyurveda offers evidence that the original theories still have much to offer to the modern world. With sincere effort and dedication on behalf of Āyurvedic practitioners, this method of herbal treatment may once again obtain the recognition it is worthy of.

The first step has already been taken. The word Āyurveda is becoming known around the world, and interest in it is increasing. It is now time for the second step, which is to demystify the original concepts and principles of Āyurveda at a deeper level. The translation of original texts, and presentation of that information in a modern, practical yet authentic manner is vital to maintain the integrity of this science.

Over sixty-five years ago, when I was a student of Āyurveda, it was emphasized that one should study the original texts (*saṁhitās)* from a genuine teacher (*guru*). That teaching style was essential to understand and practice pure Āyurveda. The situation today is very different. The increasing popularity of Āyurveda has meant that people have seized the opportunity to commercialize and exploit it.

We need to safeguard the heritage of this science by ensuring it is taught accurately, in order to benefit humanity. This book is written by a qualified Āyurvedic doctor, and is a valuable resource for those who wish to understand the original principles and apply them to their daily life. Dr. Chauhan is one of the few students I have encountered who is not only able to comprehend the subtleties of Āyurvedic theory, but also present it clearly and correctly.

His interest in accumulating more knowledge in this vast field has not waned in the fifteen years I have taught him. For five of those years he lived with me, and worked closely with me to learn the intricacies of herbal medicines and their preparation. I am proud of his efforts to now share this knowledge with you, and continue practicing Āyurveda in its original form. I commend this book, and trust you will enjoy learning about this wonderful science in your journey of achieving eternal health, harmony and happiness.

VAIDYA NANAK CHAND SHARMA
Kaya Maya Āyurvedic Hospital
Delhi, India.
August 2000

Vaidya Nanak Chand Sharma is a respected authority on Āyurveda, and is well known for treating incurable diseases. He has treated thousands of people since opening a private Āyurvedic clinic in 1935, and is currently the Director and Chief Physician at Kaya Maya Āyurvedic Hospital. He has held various positions in government health bodies and private Āyurvedic institutions. *Vaidya* Sharma is one of the few experts in the field of *Rasa Śastra* (*Vedic* chemistry), and is also an expert in *Jyotish* (astrology) and *Tantra.* He is the author of a commentary on *Ākāśa Bhairava Tantra*, and *Rasa Kāmadhenu.*

Contents

Foreword v

Preface xi

Introduction xiii

Part I: FUNDAMENTALS OF AYURVEDA

1 The Foundations of Ayurveda 3

Origin, Meaning and Scope of Āyurveda (Mind, Body, Senses, Soul); Objective of Āyurveda.

2 Principles of Ayurveda 17

Basic Principles: Theory of Creation; The Five Elements; Composition of Human Beings; Balance of Elements; Three Qualities; Modern Application of Āyurvedic Principles.

3 Physical Constitution 39

Tridoṣa; *Doṣa* Formation; *Doṣa* States and Balance; Evaluating *Doṣa* Type; *Doṣa* Characteristics; Reasons for Disturbance; Remedies to Alleviate.

4 Psychological Constitution 57

Triguṇa; Mind Types; Mind Balance; Diet and Nutrition; Lifestyle; Emotions.

5 Metabolism & Digestion 73

Four States of *Agni*; Digestive Process; Digestion, *Āma* and Disease; Wastes; Elimination of Wastes.

6 Physiology 87

Tissues; Formation and Imbalance of Tissues; *Ojas*; Channels; Function and Impairment of Channels.

PART II: HEALTH & AYURVEDA

7 Nutrition 101

Effects of Food; Principles of Food: Taste; Qualities; Potency; Digestive Effect; Special Action.

8 Diet 117

Dietary Guidelines; Quantities of Food; Digestive Power; *Sāttvic* Food; Other Considerations.

9 Complete Health 129

Spirituality; Lifestyle; Sleep; Sex; Exercise; Natural Urges; Hygiene; Daily and Seasonal Routines.

10 Disease 153

Causes of Disease; Role of *Doṣas*; Tendency to Disease; Identification of Disease; Patient Examination; Stages of Manifestation; Classification of Disease.

11 Therapies 177

Detoxification (*Panca Karma*); Rejuvenation Therapy (*Rasāyana*); Treatment for Addictions (*Madātya*).

12 Home Remedies 197

Home Remedies for Common Ailments: Anxiety and Depression; Arthritis; Asthma; Coughs and Colds; Fatigue; Headache; Indigestion and Constipation; Insomnia; Menopause; Menstrual Disorders; Obesity; Skin Problems.

PART III: APPENDICES

1 Reference Table of *Dosas* 227

2 Reference Table of Tastes 228

3 Instructions for Yoga Exercise 229

4 Common Herbs and their Uses 231

5 Basic Recipes 242

Glossary of Sanskrit Terms 247

Bibliography 256

❖—❖—❖

List of Tables

1. Elements and Senses 25
2. *Guṇa* Descriptions 30
3. Examples of *Guṇas* 31
4. *Doṣa* Characteristics 46
5. *Vāta* Divisions 50
6. *Pitta* Divisions 53
7. *Kapha* Divisions 56
8. *Guṇa* Characteristics 59
9. *Dhātu* Imbalance and Treatment 91
10. *Srota* Aggravation and Treatment 98
11. Tastes and *Doṣas* 106
12. Tastes and their Effects 108
13. Tastes and their Qualities 112
14. Tastes and Potency/*Vīrya* 114
15. Tastes and *Vipāka* 115
16. Misuse of Senses 158
17. Disease Manifestation and Treatment 170

List of Figures

1. *Suśrutā's* Surgical Tools 6
2. The Theory of Creation 18
3. Body Types 45
4. Location of *Doṣa* Divisions 56
5. The Seven *Dhātus* 88
6. Causes of Disease 155

Preface

ETERNAL HEALTH explains basic Āyurvedic concepts and lifestyle principles. It is a modern representation of the original knowledge, of which much has been overlooked. Authentic Āyurvedic teachings have been updated to take into account modern lifestyles, and presented with modern language and concepts.

The intention in providing you with this information is the same as that motivating the original Āyurvedic doctors. It is to enable you to understand how the body functions and how to maintain a healthy balance between your body, mind and soul. These aspects need to be in harmony internally and with the external environment, in order to maintain health, prevent sickness and reduce suffering.

Some modern books on Āyurveda have disregarded fundamental aspects of Āyurvedic theory, misinterpreted Sanskrit terms or not clearly explained basic principles. This book aims to clearly and accurately present the foundations of Āyurveda, and its practical applications, to enable you to adopt this philosophy in your life. Remaining faithful to the original texts and maintaining Āyurvedic values is essential in order to obtain the full benefits of this holistic life science.

You may be curious to know how this science developed and how it has survived for more than five millennia. The origin, scope and fundamental concepts of Āyurveda are explained in part I of the book. This also incorporates physiology and metabolism. The book has been structured specifically to build a step-by-step understanding of the composition of humans, our internal functioning and relationship to the surrounding environment. As you gain understanding of the body and environment, the lifestyle and health information contained in part II of the book will be much easier to comprehend.

The original Sanskrit terms are still used because they have a specific meaning, in the same way that Latin is used in modern medicine. As these words often do not have a direct translation in English, the original terms have been retained. These ancient terms (in italics) may be unfamiliar, so they are explained in the relevant sections. There is also a comprehensive Sanskrit glossary for quick reference on pronunciation and definition.

This book establishes the core concepts and terminology of Āyurveda, as a foundation for future publications that will further explore the complexities of this life-science. I hope you enjoy learning Āyurvedic wisdom and discovering the beauty of this timeless philosophy.

I would like to take this opportunity to recognize the assistance of others involved in the preparation of this book. I thank my students and patients for inspiring and encouraging me. Satyanārāyana Dāsa provided support and guidance; my assistants Dr. Mukesh Sharma and Dr. Sapna Bhargava helped check facts and looked after my clinic; Vijay Raina and Nilesh Raste worked long hours with total dedication on layout and illustrations; and Nic Haygarth proofread and offered valuable comments.

Finally, my special thanks to Brenda Foran, whose significant contribution to the content and structure of the book enabled it to be produced in its final form. She came here to work on the manuscript, and is now staying as my student.

Sarve bhavantu sukhina	*May all be happy*
Sarve santu nirāmayā	*May all be free from disease*
Sarve bhadrāṇi paṣyantu	*May auspiciousness come to all*
Ma kaścid dukhabhāg bhaveta	*May none ever suffer*

Dr. Partap S. Chauhan
Director
Āyurveda Division, Jiva Institute
Faridabad, India.
August 2000

Introduction

Āyurveda is the world's oldest known medical science, originating in India over five thousand years ago. The written source of this science is the *Vedas*. These ancient books of knowledge contain practical and scientific information on a wide variety of issues including philosophy, logic, engineering, agriculture, economics and politics. These areas are fascinating subjects in their own right, but this book explores only one of the *Vedic* branches, that of health—Āyurveda.

Vedic knowledge propounds the principle of natural balance within the body and harmony with the environment. People are seen as an integral part of their habitat and not as separate entities from the natural world. Obtaining and maintaining balance within the body and mind, and with the external environment, is one of the goals of this knowledge. Living in harmony with nature and according to natural principles ensures complete physical health and peace of mind.

Modern life often violates the principles of natural living. We work long hours in offices with artificial light and air conditioning systems. We rush from one mundane task to the next while being bombarded with advertising, constant noise and pollution. Pure water, air and food are becoming scarce resources, in an environment that is becoming increasingly toxic.

Our lifestyles are often as detrimental to our health as the environment. We don't have time to prepare breakfast, eat a fast food lunch at our desk and a pre-prepared dinner in front of the television. Coffee keeps us alert, alcohol "relaxes" us and drugs treat our ailments.

When the weekend arrives we are so exhausted that we often don't even have time to really enjoy it! And then it is Monday again with that familiar feeling of dread. We are back in the race of trying to make enough money to buy processed food, gadgets to save us time and amusements to distract us from the monotony of our lives. In our efforts to seek pleasure we are working hard to achieve personal suffering and poor health.

So why are people in modern times, with all the conveniences of technology to make life easier, finding that life has lost all joy? It is because we have lost contact with nature. People have forgotten the once instinctive ancient knowledge about the cycles and rhythms of natural living. As a result, we often feel empty and unsatisfied as well as physically sick, for reasons we can't really identify. We are overlooking the fact that humans are as much a part of Earth as all the other species.

Instead of being in harmony with Earth, we have adopted artificial practices that disturb the equilibrium of the mind and body. Despite the luxuries of modern times, people are anxious and depressed. We can't sleep, concentrate or relax. The imbalance in our lives manifests in addiction, disease and death much sooner than our anticipated lifespan.

This ancient knowledge has not been lost. It has just been ignored over generations and is now unfamiliar. People are raised without a basic education of how the body functions, what is beneficial and detrimental from physical and psychological perspectives, how to prevent illness and how to achieve peace and happiness. This is like buying a brand new car and instead of reading or understanding the manual, just jumping behind the steering wheel and taking off to see how fast it can go.

Without knowledge of how to check your new car's water, oil, tires or fuel, it will not be long before the car is not performing at its peak. Sooner or later it will begin rattling and jolting and eventually the engine will seize up and the car will be useless. It might look almost immaculate on the surface but ignoring the signs of rust, putting in the wrong fuel and not checking the basic systems will lead to irreversible damage.

The benefits of the car can then no longer be enjoyed unless you spend a lot of money fixing or replacing the parts. The car becomes a liability instead of an asset. It takes up space in your garage, drains your bank account and doesn't even take you to your destination safely. It is like a sick body that can no longer enjoy the advantages offered by life.

The human body is a far more complex and valuable vehicle than a car. You may be able to just sell or dump a car when it becomes a liability and buy a new one, but a body is irreplaceable. But some people seem more concerned with cleaning and checking their car than looking after themselves physically and mentally. Or they may think that their body and mind are the domain of experts and prefer to leave them to a doctor or psychologist.

Living naturally according to some simple principles can prevent the need for expensive medical treatment or suffering needlessly from debilitating conditions. Learning to listen to your body and read the signals of distress can help you maintain health, making you more productive as well as contented.

You may be pleasantly surprised to find out that these principles are easily learnt by anyone and can be adapted into your life starting from today. It does not require any fancy equipment or expert knowledge, and costs no more (and probably less) than what you already spend on groceries.

Maintaining your physical health is based on nothing more complex than understanding the characteristics of your body and qualities of the food you eat. Many of the remedies for common ailments can be simply and quickly prepared in your own kitchen with commonly available herbs.

The instruction manual of natural living for human beings is called Āyurveda, which is presented here in a simplified form. Understanding this philosophy of life enables you to become your own "healer". You learn about your body, how it functions and how to treat it through diet and herbal remedies. In fact, you also become your own dietician, personal trainer, psychologist, stylist and beautician! Āyurveda is a unified system that encompasses all these aspects. The magic of it is that it involves nothing more expensive or complex than adapting your diet and lifestyle.

This systematic approach includes gentle exercise, and daily practices that vary according to season. The purpose of these routines is to encourage longevity, vitality and physical and mental strength. As a bonus it also provides peace of mind and balanced emotions. With such perfect health, you are able to not only work more efficiently, you are also able to totally relax when you want to. You become the master of your body and mind, not the slave.

Āyurvedic applications can be used to explain and treat any physical or psychological ailment. There are no side effects or negative environmental impacts from the treatments, and the root cause of illness is treated rather than just the symptoms. All medicinal preparations used (herbs, plants, foods and minerals) are already found in the natural environment and are inexpensive.

Of course, just as your car may sometimes need to be looked at by a mechanic despite regular maintenance, you may still need to see a doctor occasionally for specialist treatment or guidance on health issues. However, these visits should become less frequent, and you will be more aware of what is happening to your body during treatment.

In society today it is difficult to avoid some things that disturb our natural balance. To follow the Āyurvedic principles, we don't need to reject modern life and live in a grass hut or on a deserted island. We often don't really have a choice, and we shouldn't have to forfeit the advantages of modern life simply because it has so many disadvantages.

Instead, we can utilize this discipline to learn how to identify imbalances in our body. We can also learn what to do in order to reverse such disturbances and stabilize our body and mind. This can be done prior to becoming seriously ill, uncomfortable and miserable. You can achieve total health, and this book will guide you in that quest.

Part I

FUNDAMENTALS OF AYURVEDA

Chapter 1

Foundations of Ayurveda

Modern science has allowed us to closely observe human anatomy and physiology. Many of the amazing secrets of our internal processes are being revealed with the assistance of technology. Despite that, much remains unknown about our nature. For all our technical knowledge, we are still grappling with fundamental aspects of human life. Āyurvedic theory may be ancient, but it was centuries ahead of its time with the unique conception of human beings as a combination of body, mind, senses and soul. The breadth and depth of this philosophy has yet to be surpassed, and it offers much to the contemporary health field as well as individuals seeking to enhance their well-being.

Origin of Āyurveda

It is difficult to date the origin of Āyurveda precisely due to the absence of written records. It is thought to have originated somewhere between 4000 and 6000 BC. Āyurveda forms part of the *Vedas*, which are the oldest known records of human civilization. As the *Vedic* manuscripts are dated in the same period, and refer to Āyurveda, it can be assumed that Āyurveda existed at that time. The knowledge contained in the *Vedas* existed in an oral form for at least several thousand years prior to the dated written records.

The history of this discipline is as interesting as its foundations. Only a brief outline can be provided here, despite such a remarkable evolution. When humans began to suffer from disease, a group of learned people (*ṛṣis*) became concerned and gathered in the foothills of the Himalayas. After lengthy discussion, they determined to elect one enlightened sage, named *Bhārdwāja*, to cure sickness and protect health through acquiring knowledge of "the science of life". Through divine inspiration, he obtained the wisdom of Āyurveda.

Bhārdwāja, in turn, taught the fundamental principles to a carefully selected student, *Punarvasu* (also known as *Ātreya*) and it was passed to successive generations in an oral form. This form of teaching is called *paramparā* or disciplic succession. The *paramparā* method of teaching emphasizes the necessity to teach the complete science in its original form, totally intact and without any modifications. It was a foolproof system to protect and pass on knowledge from one generation to the next. Therefore, the essence of this discipline remains unchanged even today.

Over time, most of the *Vedic* knowledge was recorded in written form in the ancient Indian language of Sanskrit. The Āyurvedic wisdom that was spread throughout the *Vedic* texts was extracted by Āyurvedic scholars and compiled into "*saṁhitās*". These are collections of relevant information, ordered according to subject by the author.

Three major ancient *saṁhitās* still exist today—those of *Caraka* (fundamental concepts, disease and herbal medicines), *Suśruta* (anatomy and surgery) and *Vāgabhaṭṭa*, who wrote *Aṣṭānga Hṛdaya* and *Aṣṭānga Sangraha*. The *Aṣṭāngas* offer an overview of the work of *Caraka* and *Suśruta*, and other Āyurvedic scholars. These core texts, and commentaries on them, are valuable sources of both theoretical and practical information.

Caraka Saṁhitā is considered one of the most authoritative texts on Āyurveda. It was based on the work of several authors and compiled by *Caraka* somewhere between 1000 and 500 BC. It is still studied by Āyurvedic students and consulted by practicing doctors today. The fact that these texts are still in use demonstrates the authors' remarkable insight and astuteness in providing information that would guide generations to come.

Āyurveda is so inclusive that eight specialized branches have been detailed. These are internal medicine (*kāya cikitsā*), ear, nose, throat and eye conditions (*śālākya tantra*), general surgery (*śalya tantra*), toxicology (*agada tantra*), mental health or psychiatry (*bhūta vidya*), pediatrics (*kaumārabhṛtya*) geriatrics and longevity (*rasāyana*) and procreation and reproduction (*vājīkaraṇa*).

Āyurvedic influence is widespread although often not acknowledged or recognized. The theoretical bases of these branches have provided guidance and inspiration for Chinese, Arabic, Greek and Roman schools of medical thought. Modern Western medicine has adopted Āyurvedic concepts, as well as many alternative health disciplines developed more recently such as homeopathy, naturopathy and aromatherapy. The global influence of its principles has meant that Āyurveda is sometimes referred to as the "mother of medicine".

Descriptions of many treatments and techniques used today are originally found in Āyurvedic texts. For example, the diagnosis and treatment for eye diseases including glaucoma, pterygium, trichiasis and uveitis as detailed in the texts of *śālākya tantra*, stand unaltered today. Therapies to detoxify and cleanse the body, like massage, sauna, fasting and colonic irrigation (enema) have their source in Āyurvedic theory and practice. The use of leeches as a natural method to drain blood has recently been revived in modern medicine, and was originally described in Āyurvedic texts.

Suśruta was a pioneer surgeon who developed the techniques for rhinoplasty (corrective nose surgery) and cauterization. *Suśruta* also performed successful amputations and skin grafts. He used herbal anesthetics, and plants with antibiotic properties after surgery to encourage healing and prevent infection. The surgical instruments he used are very similar in shape and function to the tools used today.

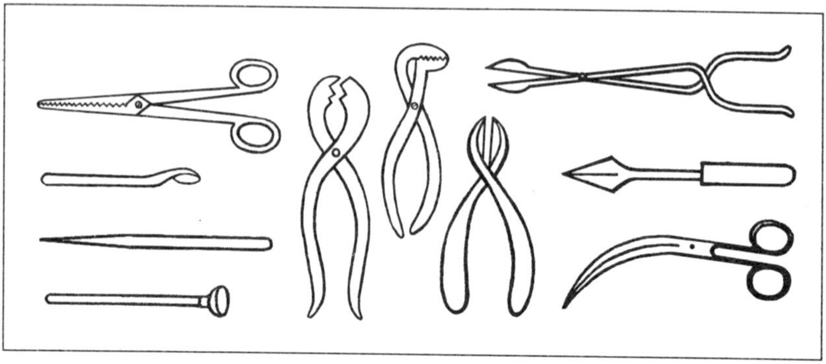

Figure 1 Suśruta's Surgical Tools

Toxicology (*agada tantra*) elaborates upon not only natural poisoning from insects, animals and plants, but also toxicity from mineral sources including lead, mercury and arsenic. Pediatrics and obstetrics (*kaumārabhṛtya*) describes human development from the time of conception to adulthood, the nutritional requirements during pregnancy to ensure healthy development of the fetus, in addition to the birthing process. This incorporates natural methods to assist labor, and manual assistance when labor is obstructed or prolonged.

The medical knowledge contained in all the branches is comprehensive and remains a rich source of wisdom even today. This information is not only about diseases, their symptoms and treatment, herbal properties and remedies, but also related aspects of health. Nursing and patient care, the qualities of a good doctor, ethics, methods to estimate lifespan, signs of imminent death, pharmaceutical preparation and even the construction of hospitals are encompassed.

Unfortunately, due to foreign occupation and domestic civil discord in India at various stages throughout history, many of these manuscripts and *saṁhitās* have been lost or destroyed. The chain of oral information between generations was also weakened and almost broken. Internal medicine (*kāya cikitsā*) was the main branch that survived as it was widely used on a daily basis, and some of this information is presented here.

We are fortunate today to retain the basis of this science, and can still marvel at the remarkable insight of the original sages, and their understanding of how humans function in relation to the world around them. In the last few decades there has been a revival of Āyurvedic education and research. Interest in the medicinal properties of herbs and remedies described in the ancient texts is increasing, along with the trend for natural health and healing. This has also been inspired by an increasing recognition of the limitations and deficiencies of modern medicine. In the coming decades, Āyurveda may reclaim an authoritative position in the health domain.

Meaning of Āyurveda

Āyurveda is derived from two words, *āyus* and *Veda*. Understanding the meaning of both words is necessary to fully grasp the philosophy of this discipline.

Definition of *Āyus*

> ***Śarīrendriya sattvātma saṁyogo dhāri jīvitam***
> ***nityagasca anubandhasca paryayai āyus uccayate***
>
> *Āyus is union of the mind, body, senses and soul. It is energy and vitality, and is eternal. (Caraka Sūtra Sthāna 1:42)*

The English translation of *āyus* is "life". In the Āyurvedic context, the definition of life is broader than simply chronological lifespan. It does not mean the age of a person; the number of years lived on Earth measured from birth until the present day. *Āyus* is much more than that, it is a combination of the:

- Body *śarīra*
- Senses *indriya*
- Mind *manas*
- Soul *ātmā*

Together, these four factors are responsible for sustaining the life air or force (*prāṇa*) in the body, and each must be present in order to produce *āyus*. If any one of the above factors is absent, we cannot say there is life/*āyus*. Everything on Earth has a physical body and a soul, but whether it also has a mind and senses determines whether it is alive. The reason why a rock is not alive (has no *āyus*) is that some of the factors mentioned above are absent (mind, senses). *Prāṇa* cannot be sustained in the absence of these factors.

Every species of animal has each of these four factors, so *prāṇa* can circulate and *āyus* is present. The senses and minds of animals are different to that of humans, but they still exist as living beings. Insects and animals may perceive things differently (such as colors, sounds, temperatures, odors) and the mind may not be as well developed as human beings, but the souls are alike. So *āyus* is the basis of distinction between inert objects and dynamic entities, or living beings.

Definition of *Veda*

Veda is a Sanskrit word which means "knowledge" or "science". *Vedic* knowledge is enshrined in fourteen sacred texts. There are four *Vedas* (*Rig, Yajura, Sama* and *Atharva*), six *Vedāngas* (auxiliaries), *Mīmāṁsa* (interpretations), *Nyāya* (logic), *Purāṇas* (philosophy) and *Sāśtras* (moral principles). There are also four *Upāngas*, which can be considered appendices to the *Vedas*. These are Āyurveda (health and medicine), *Arthasāśtra* (politics and economics), *Dhanur Veda* (martial arts) and *Gandarva Veda* (music).

Although *Vedic* knowledge originated in India, it does not mean this information is of relevance only to Indians. Knowledge is the universal asset of mankind—it is not the property of one region. *Vedic* information can be utilized by anybody, in any part of the world. If we, as Indians, think this wealth of information is our exclusive property and don't share it, we are not providing you with the chance to learn from the profound wisdom that has enriched our culture for centuries.

Scope of Āyurveda

Hitāhitam sukham dukham āyustasya hitāhitam
mānam ca tacca yatrokta āyurveda sa uccyate

Āyurveda is the knowledge of the entire span of life, including beneficial and detrimental ways of living, how to achieve happiness and how unhappiness is created. (Caraka Sūtra Sthāna 1:41)

As *Āyus* means "life" and *Veda* means "knowledge" or "science", the literal meaning of Āyurveda is "the science of life". Life is used in the Āyurvedic sense, incorporating the body, mind, senses and soul. It is apparent from this definition of life that Āyurveda is not a medical discipline limited only to the physical body. It also provides comprehensive knowledge about other crucial aspects of health.

Āyurveda is unlike any other medical science. It is not just based on medications, or treatment for symptoms experienced by the body. As a complete philosophy of life, it provides guidance on a whole range of activities and lifestyles beneficial in maintaining natural balance within the body, mind, senses and soul. The level of detail and practical application of this holistic life science is amazing.

It encompasses positive and negative aspects of living including eating, sleeping, working, relaxation and even conduct. These guidelines are designed specifically to achieve and maintain internal and external stability. The diet, herbs, exercises, therapies and lifestyles described in Āyurvedic literature aim to assist the individual to maintain and enhance all aspects of health—physical, psychological and spiritual. There are hundreds of botanical and mineral formulae used to assist in achieving a balanced physical and psychological state.

Adopting these concepts aims to benefit both the individual and society. If people are healthy and happy, then society as a whole functions much more effectively, efficiently and peacefully as well. Each aspect encompassed by Āyurveda (body, senses, mind and soul) is briefly considered in the following pages.

Body—*Śarīra*

The body is made up of a skeleton encased with various tissues, organs and muscles and covered with skin. Food, water and air sustain the physical body. The tissues and bones are supplied with nutrients through different channels and systems, which also remove toxins and wastes. Some of the systems are the respiratory, circulatory, endocrine (hormonal), digestive and nervous systems.

The human body is an amazing natural structure. It has 206 bones, which are five times stronger than steel of the equivalent weight. There are 639 muscles to carry out movements, which can contract to one third their size. The skin is waterproof, bacterium resistant and self-repairing. It has around 3 million pores to help regulate body temperature.

The brain contains around 15 billion nerve cells, and nerve impulses travel at speeds faster than 198 miles (320 kms) per hour. The lungs have over 300 million air sacs and a capacity to hold over a gallon (5 litres) of air. A person's heart beats around 37 million times per year to pump blood continuously around the body. If you laid all the blood vessels end to end, the line would stretch more than 99 000 miles (160 000 kms). We take our body for granted, but every day it performs feats of engineering and production that we are unaware of.

Senses—*Indriya*

Humans are unique animals. We have senses that work differently from any other animal on Earth. Āyurvedic medicine considers all of the senses in diagnostic and therapeutic practices. Awareness of the senses is a powerful tool in assessing and maintaining the state of our health.

Like the term "life", "senses" in the Āyurvedic context is broader than that used in common terminology. There are ten senses classified into two types—perceptual (or cognitive) and operative (or working). The perceptual senses include the organ as well as its function: taste (tongue) smell (nose), sight (eyes), hearing (ears) and touch (skin). These are all "knowledge acquiring" senses, used to gather, analyze and perceive information from our surrounding environment.

We use our sense of smell, sight and hearing, or the temperature receptors in our skin and so on to determine the quality and nature of our environment. These senses relay information to the brain, and provide it with the vital information it needs to transmit signals to the rest of the body.

For example, if something nearby smells offensive, or we are sitting too close to an open window on a hot day or the radio is too loud, our senses tell our brain and our mind decides to move our body away from this source of aggravation. Or the mind may decide to do something else, such as find the source of the odor, close the curtain, or turn the radio volume down. Or, depending on the context, the mind may decide not to do anything. Maybe the smell is coming from the passenger sitting next to you on the bus, and after looking around, you see there are no other seats available! Or maybe it is his radio and he is unaware of any disturbance.

There are also five "working senses". These perform the operative functions for the body and mind: mobility (feet), manipulation (hands), speech (voice), reproduction (genitals) and excretion (anus). These "working senses" operate in tandem with the "knowledge acquiring" senses to provide the action necessary to manifest the desires of the body and mind. The feet must be used to search for where the smell is coming from, and the hands must be used to close the window or curtain, or turn the volume control down.

So if the mind determines that the volume from the person's radio beside you is really too aggravating to tolerate, it may decide to ask (use the voice) for the radio to be turned down. That may only be after the eyes have determined that there are no other seats available, and the feet are already aggravated from too much walking and the ears are becoming very irritated!

Human beings use these ten senses in a complex pattern to monitor and direct their bodies. Every day you are noticing and responding to thousands of these signals, often as an automatic reflex without complete awareness of the interaction between the senses-mind-body. Your body and mind are constantly monitoring every aspect of your environment and reacting or responding in a way to obtain balance, through reducing aggravation or increasing stimulation.

For example, your skin is itchy and your hand scratches it, your nose is irritated and you sneeze, your eyes are hurting from the sun and they begin to water or blink excessively until your hands shade them or you put sunglasses on.

The detailed knowledge an Āyurvedic physician has of the senses means that a consultation may be very different to what you are familiar with. Your tongue may be examined, skin condition and color assessed, eyes and nails considered or you may be asked about your bowel movements. All these subtle signs yield vital clues as to how the internal systems are operating.

The therapies prescribed aim to balance all of the senses and the entire mind-body. This may involve massage using medicated oils, detoxification and internal cleansing, or herbal powders and infusions. Such therapies clean and soothe the senses and their associated organs. Similarly, the aim of the daily routine advocated is to keep the senses clean and operating at maximum efficiency. This enables us to assess our environment adequately, analyze information correctly and adjust to it promptly, before it distresses (unbalances) our body or mind.

Mind—*Manas*

You may have realized from the description of the senses that they assess and respond to external stimuli only with direct input from the mind. The mind is considered both a knowledge acquiring and working sense. It is considered a separate "master" sense, the eleventh sense that monitors all the others and keeps them operating cooperatively.

For example, in the case of eating, which is vital to maintain *āyus*, the mind acknowledges hunger. It guides the eyes and nose to identify food, the feet then take the body to the source, the hand selects the food that appeals to (looks and smells good) and satisfies the body and mind in the desire for nourishment. From there it goes to the stomach, which is considered in the section on metabolism and digestion (chapter 5).

It is now recognized by modern medicine that the mind and emotions have a direct impact on the physical body. For example, it has been determined through extensive research that those who are stressed in attitude are more likely to manifest certain physical conditions, such as heart attacks and depression. These diseases are different from those experienced and manifested in people who are relaxed by nature.

Similarly, those who remain optimistic and positive often overcome diseases that kill those who have lost faith in the healing process. It has also been noticed by modern medical researchers that these people have higher powers of immunity and rejuvenation. They don't get sick easily, and recover quickly if they do.

Āyurvedic science explained all of these factors that baffle modern medicine, long ago—with recognition of the power of the mind/*manas* and its interaction with the body. One of the fundamental pillars of Āyurveda is that the mind is inherently connected to the body and is ultimately responsible for its health. This is not only through the food it dictates the hand to choose, but also through the positive and negative feelings and messages it relays to the body about the environment and the self. It is the bridge between the external and internal environments.

When this is understood, you begin to see why it is just as important to maintain mental health as well as physical health. Sicknesses that originate in the mind, such as anxiety or anorexia, can be just as incapacitating and unbearable as physical ailments. Sometimes the pain and cost of these ailments are far greater than many physical conditions endured. For this reason, Āyurvedic practice enhances and maintains the health of body and mind equally, rather than one in isolation of the other.

This discipline recognizes that most diseases have both a mind and body component. Take obesity or being overweight for example. This can have a variety of root causes, but a common one is "comfort eating". You feel stressed or upset so you eat those foods that you think soothe the senses and somehow make you feel better, like chocolate, icecream, sweet drinks, cookies or those foods you remember from your childhood. The body then converts and stores all of the excess energy in various organs and limbs. Soon, you feel even more stressed because you can't fit into your clothes and you feel unattractive or awkward!

This example also illustrates why the senses are so vital. We need to learn to read our physical messages accurately and then control our senses accordingly so that we do not cause our body further distress. So, using the above example again, we can learn to identify when the signals for eating are for physical reasons (hunger or thirst) or psychological reasons (anxiety, loneliness, boredom). And then we can give our body and mind what it is really asking for rather than something that just makes it even more uncomfortable, or that may even be destructive and ultimately lethal.

Soul—*Ātmā*

The physical body is simply a shell for the soul. It is the physical outer layer, or material expression, of it. Every living entity has a soul/*ātmā*. Without the soul, there can be no life/*āyus*. To illustrate what this means in the Āyurvedic context, I may be morbid for a moment and ask you to consider a corpse. This will be the only occasion you will be asked to do so, as this book is about enjoying life to the fullest potential rather than dwelling on a dead body!

A corpse has a physical body including a heart, brain, lungs and legs. The sense organs all exist. But the body cannot see, walk or think. It has no soul/*ātmā* and therefore *prāṇa* (life air) cannot be circulated through the body via breathing.

The mind acts as the bridge between the external environment and the soul. Whatever objects the senses make contact with are ultimately perceived by the soul through the mind. It may be difficult to grasp exactly what the soul is, so the closest equivalent term is perhaps "conscience". The soul, although an essential aspect of the Āyurvedic philosophy, is a complex subject and is beyond the scope of this book. However, it will be touched on briefly later.

Objective of Āyurveda

Proyajanam cāsya swasthasya swāsthya rakśaṇam ãturasya vikāra praśamanam ca

The aim of Āyurveda is to maintain the health of the healthy and to cure the diseases of the sick. (Caraka Sūtra Sthāna 30:26)

There are two complementary aims of this discipline. The first is to **maintain the health** of those who are well. This entails specific diet and nutrition, hygiene, living habits, exercises and relaxation techniques. Following these guidelines enables a healthy person to maintain health and increase their life-span. The other is to **cure diseases** of the sick. This aspect relates to various diseases, their causes, diagnosis, remedies and therapies to cure and prevent relapses of illness.

Although both of these aims are connected and are comprehensive areas in their own right, the primary focus of this science is to maintain your health from the outset. This is done on a daily basis with attention to diet and lifestyle, helping the body and mind to be clean and stable. In this way, diseases do not find ground for establishment and growth.

A patient being treated with Āyurveda is considered a *puruṣa*, not merely a body. A *puruṣa* is the total combination of body, mind, senses and soul. The Āyurvedic doctor aims to achieve complete health for the patient, not just to suppress or alleviate troubling physical symptoms. The approach is to diagnose the root cause and eliminate it, allowing genuine healing to take place.

The basis of Āyurvedic healing is a personal relationship with, and compassion for, the patient. Healing is not possible without this personal connection between the patient and doctor. During treatment, the physician develops an intimate understanding of every aspect of the patient's physical, psychological and emotional nature to make an accurate diagnosis. The patient is treated with dignity, as a unique individual who has the ability to recuperate fully with caring support.

CHAPTER 2

Principles of Ayurveda

THE elements that make up the body and the physical environment are considered in this chapter. Understanding the nature of these elements is the key to understanding Āyurveda, and its explanation of the way humans interact with their surroundings. This chapter also covers other basic theories of the science of life. In conclusion, the modern application of Āyurveda is discussed. Although the scientific principles have remained unchanged over centuries, and remain as valid today as when they originated, the contemporary relevance of such tenets is often overlooked.

Basic Principles

Like all sciences, Āyurveda is based on certain basic principles. These principles are represented in figure 2 and explained throughout this chapter. They are:

- The theory of creation (*sṛṣti utpatti*)
- The elements that make up Earth and everything on it (*mahābhūtas*)
- The representation of the elements in human beings (*doṣas*)
- The fundamental character of all matter on Earth (*guṇas*)

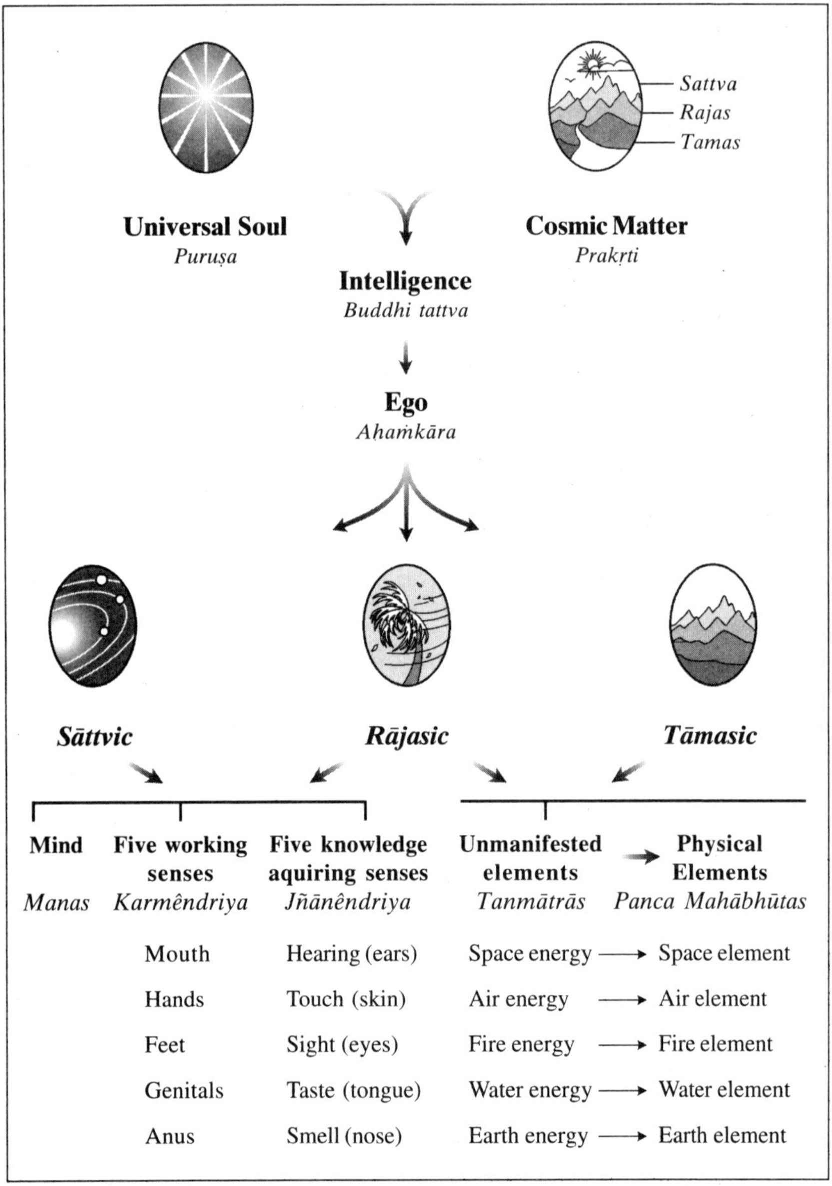

Figure 2 The Theory of Creation

The Theory of Creation—*Sṛṣti Utpatti*

The Āyurvedic theory of creation explains how the elements (*mahābhūtas*) were formed, and how they in turn formed Earth and all of the organic and inorganic entities on it. This theory is the practical basis of Āyurveda. There are five elements (*panca mahābhūtas*)—earth, water, fire, air and space. This may initially appear esoteric or irrational, but the theory is uncomplicated and completely logical.

Creation of the universe first involved the universal soul or pure consciousness (*puruṣa*) and cosmic matter (*prakṛti*) combining to form intelligence (*buddhi tattva*). Initially, *prakṛti* is inert and is made up of the three unmanifested qualities (*guṇas*)—goodness (*sattva*), passion (*rajas*) and ignorance (*tamas*). All the material necessary for creation is present in *prakṛti* but cannot be manifested without contact from *puruṣa*. Once they combine, a reaction in the three *guṇas* commences and intelligence (*buddhi tattva*), and then ego (*ahaṁkāra*), are created.

Intelligence and ego are a product of the three *guṇas*, so are of *sāttvic, rājasic* or *tāmasic* forms. The three types of ego combine with each other to form mind (*manas*), the five knowledge acquiring senses (*jñānêndriya*), five working senses (*karmêndriya*) and five unmanifested elements (*tanmātrās*). The five *tanmātrās* are the energy for, or "seeds" of, the five physical elements (*panca mahābhūtas*).

Some Āyurvedic books describe the development of the elements sequentially, as a chain of natural reactions. This is according to the manifestation of elements depicted in the *Taitreya Upanishad*. From universal soul or pure consciousness (*puruṣa*), simple *"aum"* sound vibrations created space/*ākāśa*. Once space was created, it began to swirl and move. This activity created the element of air/*vāyu*. The friction between air and space generated heat. The heat energy intensified and fire/*agni* was created.

As the heat intensified, part of the *ākāśa* and *vāyu* melted and combined, or became liquefied. This created the element of water/*jala*. Once water existed, some of it mixed with the space/*ākāśa*, air/*vāyu* and fire/*agni* elements and solidified, creating earth/*pṛthvī*. So from *ākāśa*, all the other elements were generated and Earth, as well as everything on it and the surrounding universe, were formed.

In humans, the five elements constitute three basic biological energies, which are represented in our physical and psychological nature. These are known as *doṣas*, and are termed *vāta, pitta* and *kapha*. As our intelligence and ego are products of the three *guṇas*, they may be of *sāttvic, rājasic* or *tāmasic* form. These terms and concepts may appear complex, so they are elaborated upon throughout the rest of this chapter. The concepts related to health: five elements/*panca mahābhūtas*, senses/*indriya*, biological energies/*doṣas* and the qualities/*guṇas*, are explained in more detail below.

The Five Elements—*Panca Mahābhūtas*

Earth, and everything on it, is the product of different combinations of the five basic elements: earth, water, fire, air and space. It should be noted that the names of these elements are actually representative categories. Everything found on Earth can be classified into one of these five categories, based on their innate characteristics. The word "element" is not used as a name or label for each individual natural element, in the manner that the modern scientific periodic table uses it.

Just as chemistry and physics use specific technical terms to classify matter, Āyurveda uses the characteristics of the five elements (*panca mahābhūtas*) to identify various objects. If something is classified as "fire" it does not mean that it is literally a fire. It means that the object displays the characteristics of fire, like combustion, heat and so on. Similarly, if an item is classified as "water" or "earth" it means it is moist, cool and sticky or heavy, solid and stable.

In Āyurveda, the place in which to determine the elements around us is not a science laboratory, but the human body. We use our senses of hearing, taste, touch, sight and smell to identify the surrounding elements and their qualities. The *panca mahābhūtas* theory may sound simplistic, but it is actually a very sophisticated method of classifying not only all the objects found on Earth but also its natural cycles like days, seasons and life itself. This is because the elements dominate at particular times, depending on the conditions experienced and observed.

For example, the human lifecycle is divided into childhood, where physical growth takes place (water and earth), adulthood where activity and change occur (fire), and old age where mobility becomes impaired and the body begins to weaken (space and air). The weather may be cold and rainy (water, earth), hot and dry (fire, air) or windy and cool (air and space), and so on.

Understood and applied correctly, such a system of classification becomes a powerful method for considering the way we interact with our environment. The elegance of this science lies in the simplicity of the basic concepts, and the powerful analytical tool they provide for internal (body-mind) and external (environmental) assessment.

Every natural element found in the periodic table of modern science can be divided into one of these five groups according to their innate nature. Everything on Earth can be classified accurately, unlike the periodic table system of categorization. For example, the periodic table lists a group of elements that defy classification due to their peculiar properties. They have been grouped together as a "transitional group" because their characteristics are unstable, and this volatility prevents any obvious and lasting classification.

Āyurveda has no "transitional" groups. Depending on the qualities displayed at a specific time, the object can be easily grouped under one of the five elements. The periodic table is continuously modified as a new compound is "discovered". In contrast, the Āyurvedic elemental categorization never changes because it already encompasses everything on Earth, regardless of whether it has been acknowledged ("discovered") or not.

Each element has particular tangible and intangible features that identify it. In terms of sensory qualities, space/*ākāśa* is linked to sound. Each of the elements that follow in the sequence of creation has its own unique sensory quality, in addition to the ones that preceded it. So air/*vāyu* represents sensation (touch) in addition to sound; fire/*agni* is light/form, sensation and sound; water/*jala* has taste, form, sensation and sound; and earth/*pṛthvī* has odor, taste, form, sensation and sound.

The elements (*mahābhūtas*) have certain qualities, attributes and impacts on the body and mind. All objects and substances are a mixture of the five elements, but they have one dominant element that allows them to be identified and classified. As food and herbs are the main substances discussed in this book, examples of these will be used to illustrate the elemental groups.

Characteristics of Elements

Space—*ākāśa*

Symbol	:	●
Qualities	:	soft, subtle, smooth and abundant
Action	:	provides room, looseness, openness
Facilitates	:	sound and non-resistance
Substance	:	anything that is light, porous or profuse
Example	:	hollow and light foods—popcorn, wafers
Intake	:	increases softness and lightness in the body

Air—*vāyu*

Symbol	:	——
Qualities	:	light, mobile, cool, dry, rough
Action	:	movement, evaporation, dryness
Facilitates	:	touch and vibration
Substance	:	anything dry and airy, or that creates gas
Example	:	toast, cookies, cabbage, beans
Intake	:	increases dryness, motion and circulation

Fire—*agni* or *tejas*

Symbol	:	△
Qualities	:	hot, sharp, dry, intense, subtle, light
Action	:	radiation of heat and light
Facilitates	:	form, color and temperature
Substance	:	anything combustible and spicy
Example	:	chillies, ginger, pepper, clove, cumin
Intake	:	stimulates digestion, metabolism, lustre of skin

Water—*jala* or *āpa*

Symbol	:	◡
Qualities	:	oily (unctuous), moist, cool, soft and sticky
Action	:	cohesion, lubrication
Facilitates	:	fluidity and taste (via saliva)
Substance	:	anything liquid, fluid or watery
Example	:	drinks, soups, melons, cucumber
Intake	:	smoothness, coolness, softness and flow of fluids

Earth—*pṛthvī*

Symbol	:	□
Qualities	:	heavy, hard, solid, stable, slow
Action	:	resistance, density
Facilitates	:	fragrance, odor and shape
Substance	:	anything solid and heavy
Example	:	fried foods, cheese, cakes, banana, pumpkin
Intake	:	heaviness, obesity and solidity in the body

Using the characteristics described above, every object around you can be considered and classified. This should be done with the basic understanding that everything is a mixture of different proportions of the elements, some of which may be manifested under different conditions.

For example, even the compound of water itself cannot be considered to have a single fixed elemental nature. When solid and heavy (ice, snow, hail), it is a representation of earth/*pṛthvī*. It melts due to the exposure of light and heat—fire/*agni*. So it returns to water/*jala*, then evaporates and creates steam due to contact with air/*vāyu* and disappears into space/*ākāśa*.

Another example from the five basic elements is fire/*agni*. It initially requires wood (earth/*pṛthvī*), paper or dry grass and wind (air/*vāyu*). Generated together they create friction and heat, which combusts to create fire/*agni*. As the wood or paper is burnt (*pṛthvī* engulfed by *agni*), the heat gradually diminishes and only ash (*vāyu* and *ākāśa*) remains.

These examples are intended to demonstrate that even the physical forms of the five basic elements themselves also may change in nature, as they also contain portions of each of the other elements. It is not meant to imply that everything transforms in a set or orderly sequence. Under some conditions or with certain combinations of elements, different elemental natures may dominate.

The balance and character of elements in the environment constantly fluctuates and is never static. The temperature (*agni*), humidity (*jala*), wind direction and strength (*vāyu*) and so on are in a natural state of flux, depending upon the combination and quantity of elements present. Sometimes severe weather conditions occur when this combination becomes volatile, unsustainable or extreme—electrical storms, cyclones or hurricanes, floods or drought.

Composition of Human Beings

Humans are one of the many living organisms present on Earth. People are physically made up of exactly the same elements that form all of the other entities that live on Earth. A person sustains the combination of elements already present in the body through breathing air and consuming food and liquids, taking in those elements found in the surrounding natural world. When we die, our bodies return to the earth, water, fire, air and space.

This ancient Āyurvedic concept has been acknowledged and adopted by leading nutritionists. Dr. Jenson, in his book *Foods that Heal*, states: "The only chemical difference between soil and human beings is that the...elements in our bodies are structured in a more highly evolved order than they are found in the topsoil of this planet. However, humans cannot assimilate or metabolize chemical elements from soil. Nature has dictated that we must obtain them from...plants." (1998:38)

Our five knowledge acquiring senses (hearing, touch, sight, taste, smell) are connected to each of the five elements (space, air, fire, water, earth) respectively. So each sense is linked to a specific element of the environment we live in, and is responsible for determining the quality or nature of that element. *Ākāśa* transmits sound, which is received (heard) by the ear. *Vāyu* enables touch, which is detected in the skin from movement (vibrations, weight and force).

Agni generates light, perceived by the eye through vision or sight in the form of shape and color. *Jala* allows taste, as saliva breaks down the compounds in the food eaten and comes in contact with the tongue. *Pṛthvī* provides odor (smell) through the particles it distributes in vāyu. These are identified with the nose.

Table 1: Elements and Senses

Element	Facilitates	Sense	Organ
Space—*ākāśa*	Sound	Hearing	Ear
Air—*vāyu*	Movement	Touch	Skin
Fire—*agni*	Light	Sight	Eye
Water—*jala*	Flavor	Taste	Tongue
Earth—*pṛthvī*	Odor/Fragrance	Smell	Nose

Using these senses enables people to interact with their environment safely. They provide us with a mechanism to assess our environment and protect the body by preventing the intake of toxic substances. If something smells or looks unpleasant, the tongue may refuse to taste it. Or it may do so reluctantly if the mind over-rides it by forcing it to do so! This may be in the case of medicines, foreign food, or particular vegetables in the case of children. Or if something feels rough, sharp or too hard against the skin, the body may want to move away. If the ears register a piercing sound, the hands may cover them.

The "five element" theory explains the similarity between humans and the natural world surrounding them. Humans are composed of combinations of the five elements. The universe and natural world (environment) are also composed of the same five elements. In this way human beings are simply microcosms of the universe surrounding them. That is why the theory of the creation of the universe and Earth parallels the creation of humans. The theory of creation describes the creation of not only the Earth, but also everything on it.

In our body, space/*ākāśa* is present wherever there is a cavity such as the nostrils, mouth, ears, throat, lungs, and stomach; air/*vāyu* in movement of the lungs, heart, stomach, intestines and joints; fire/*agni* in all metabolic activity, the eyes, intelligence and body temperature; water/*jala* in all plasma, blood, mucus, and saliva; and earth/*pṛthvī* in any solid structure like fat, muscles, skin and nails.

The basic elemental compatibility or similarity between Earth and humans clarifies why substances found in the natural world (plants, herbs, foods) are usually harmonious with the human system. They can be easily absorbed and cause no adverse reactions or side effects (if consumed in appropriate quantities) because they are fundamentally the same in character and composition. That is why foods and herbs are able to heal the human body. Vegetation can repair and restructure humans because we share a common elemental basis.

Humans display a unique combination of the elements/*panca mahābhūtas*, and a specific category is used to identify our disposition. The five elements in the human body constitute three *doṣas*. *Doṣa* is the biological energy of the combination of elements in the body, which is reflected or expressed in our physical nature. The *doṣas* are also responsible for various functions in the body, have particular physical locations and are influenced by different external factors. The *doṣa* classification recognizes three main groups or combinations of elemental natures—*vāta, pitta, kapha,* which is considered in chapter 3.

As distinctive animals, we actually have eight different groups of integrated components. In total, humans consist of:

1. Soul—*ātmā*;
2. Mind—*manas*;
3. Intelligence—*buddhi* or *mahad tattva*;
4. Ego—*ahaṁkāra*;
5. Five knowledge acquiring senses—*jñānêndriya*;
6. Five working senses—*karmêndriya*;
7. Five intangible elements—*tanmātrās*;
8. Five physical elements—*panca mahābhūtas*.

Initially, only the components based on the senses and the physical elements will be considered. The *tanmātrā*, soul, intelligence and ego are very subtle, complex and philosophical in nature. They are as important and essential for complete health as the others, but are vast concepts. The mind is covered due to the pivotal role it has with the body in obtaining health, but not in any depth due to the scope of this aspect.

Therefore, the senses and *panca mahābhūta* (in terms of the physical body and food/diet), which are more straightforward, are the main factors covered. The other components of a person have been elaborated upon in other publications by the Jīva Institute, and will be explored further in subsequent publications.

Balance of Elements

The body instinctively attempts to obtain a natural balance or equilibrium of the five elements/*panca mahābhūtas*. These elements are absorbed into the body through food, air, heat, sunlight and liquids. As humans generally favor those foods, environments and activities that reflect their own elemental composition, maintaining our internal systems is often intuitive.

We also have a natural tendency to balance them by taking in those elements inadequate in concentration, and excreting or removing those present in excessive amounts. For example, diarrhea, vomiting and sweating are some mechanisms that the body may employ to remove a toxic imbalance of elements.

ocuses on how to keep various elements balanced prevent constant discrepancies and the subsequent chological distress. Balance (harmony) of the mind, is considered the state of health, and imbalance is the state of disease.

When one of the elements is lacking, it can be increased by consuming herbs, minerals and foods that are dominant in that particular element. That is, you eat those things that display the qualities of the required element. On the other hand, you can reduce the intake of particular foods to decrease elements that have become aggravated. Instead, elements opposite in nature are consumed. So foods or herbs that display opposing qualities are eaten. This is the rule of "like increasing like" operating:

Sarvadā sarvabhāvānām sāmānyam vṛdhikāraṇam
hrāsahetu viśeṣasca pravṛttirubhayasya tu

What is similar always causes an increase, and that which is opposite causes a decrease. (Caraka Sūtra Sthāna 1:44)

For example, if there is an excess of water/*jala* in the body creating bloating or congestion, we can reduce the intake of juicy, watery foods, herbs and minerals. Instead, consuming substances that are dominant in the opposite element (fire/*agni*) balances the elements. So a person suffering from a cough or cold (congestion and phlegm in the lungs created from too much water/*jala* and earth/*pṛthvī*), can consume ginger juice mixed with honey. This is dominant in fire/*agni* and relieves the symptoms of excess water/*jala* and earth/*pṛthvī*.

Or, in order to reduce earth/*pṛthvī* in the body, one takes in compounds that are dominant in qualities opposite to those of earth/*pṛthvī*. So rather than heavy, solid and hard substances, those that are light, smooth, cool and porous in nature (air/*vāyu* or space/*ākāśa*) are consumed. The opposite pairings are:

- earth/*pṛthvī* and air/*vāyu* or space/*ākāśa*
- water/*jala* and fire/*agni*

Therefore the "five element theory" (*panca mahābhūta*) is the basis for maintaining balance and equilibrium in the body. The crucial factors to understand are the properties and characteristics of each element, as previously listed in the section on the five elements. This enables us to internally balance the combination of elements, whenever we detect an imbalance from physical symptoms experienced.

Sometimes we may crave a particular substance or food, which is not due to physical necessity or an inadequate concentration of elements in the body. The mind can be involved in this process through directing the body to consume foods or drinks for psychological reasons. For example, eating excessively or drinking alcohol when stressed is not physically necessary, and may even be detrimental. Āyurveda acknowledges the role of the mind in health, and this is discussed in chapter 4.

The Three Qualities—*Guṇas*

Guṇa is simply defined as character or quality, but has a broader meaning. A *guṇa* is also an influence or impulse. As discussed in the section on the theory of creation, cosmic matter (*prakṛti*) is made up of three *guṇas*. Everything on Earth also has a predominant *guṇa*, as well as the more specific qualities obtained from their elemental makeup. Just as our bodies contain all of the elements, our minds have each of the *guṇas*.

The three basic *guṇas*/qualities have no direct translation in English. They are *sattva* (knowledge, purity), *rajas* (action, passion) and *tamas* (inertia, ignorance). Each *guṇa* has a rightful place, role and function in our environment, despite some displaying more positive aspects and others negative. The *guṇas* can be described according to the typical characteristics listed in table 2.

Table 2: *Guṇa* Descriptions

	Sattva	*Rajas*	*Tamas*
Energy	Neutral or balanced	Positive or increased	Negative or decreased
Realm	Heaven, Cosmos	Atmosphere	Earth
Entity	Saints, God/esses, Wise	Human	Animal, Plant, Mineral
State	Intelligence, wisdom	Change, activity	Ignorance, delusion
Condition	Order, cleanliness	Chaos, turbulence	Waste, filth
Nature	Virtuous, ethical	Passionate	Inert, lazy, sluggish
Action	Light, luminous	Power, action	Dark, dull, heavy
Position	Harmony, balance	Dis-equilibrium	Obstruction
Direction	Inward, upward motion	Outward, self-seeking	Downward (gravity)
Result	Happiness, contentment	Fragmentation	Decay, disintegration
Quality	Clarity, understanding	Stimulation	Retardation, limitation
Effect	Peace, tolerance	Distress, conflict	Insensitivity, selfishness
Color	White—purity	Red—action, passion	Black—darkness, evil
Time	Daytime	Sunrise, sunset	Night, eclipse
Consciousness	Awake	Dreaming	Sleeping

To refer to a *guṇa* is to make reference to the qualities displayed by that entity or object, whether *sāttvic, rājasic* or *tāmasic*. In the human context, *guṇa* usually refers to the quality of the mind and character of a person. That is, whether they are calm, gentle, patient and tolerant (*sāttvic*), passionate, spontaneous, greedy and materialistic (*rājasic*), or ignorant, lazy, insensitive and deceitful (*tāmasic*).

All three types of *guṇa* are present in everyone, and each may be displayed in different contexts. Just as the five elements alternate in dominance depending on the environment, the various *guṇas* may dominate in particular circumstances. People can alternate between *guṇas* depending on the environment and their diet, as well as phase of life and other factors.

The relationship between mind *guṇa*, the *guṇa* of food consumed and the surrounding social or physical environment, means we can influence our state of mind through lifestyle choices. The quality of the food we eat, and our environment, are therefore crucial in maintaining mental and physical health. As human beings, our objective is to increase our *sattva guṇa* by choosing to eat and do those things that are also *sāttvic* in nature.

The characteristics listed in table 2 should not be interpreted literally. It does not mean that all plants or animals are *tāmasic* in nature, or that all humans are *rājasic*. It is an indication of the tendencies, or predisposition. Different animals, plants and humans or even activities may be considered *sāttvic, rājasic* or *tāmasic*, depending on the qualities they display, the senses they stimulate and their effect on the mind. The examples in table 3 demonstrate *guṇas* of various entities.

Table 3: Examples of *Guṇas*

	Sāttvic	*Rājasic*	*Tāmasic*
Plants	*basil (tulasī), sandalwood* Medicinal, calming, pleasant aroma	*chillies, garlic, onions most spices*—Stimulate senses, aid digestion	*mushroom, fungus* Grows in the dark Thrives on dung
Animals	*dolphin, elephant, cow* Intelligent, social, group based, highly communicative, gentle	*tiger, piranha, fox* Prowling, hunting, sense motivated, violent and aggressive	*vulture, pig, hyena* Scavenging, eats decaying matter, parāśitic, lives in filth, lazy
Foods	Freshly cooked or raw fruit & vegetables, salads, nuts, seeds, water, juice	Hot (spicy), fried and baked foods, sweets, cookies, carbonated drinks	Canned, frozen, preserved, fermented, processed, fast-food, left-overs
People	Wise, kind, helpful, patient, tolerant, generous, selfless	Passionate, greedy, materialistic, egotistic, seeks status and power	Ignorant, lazy, self-destructive, dependent, selfish, dull, insane
Activities	Calming—meditation, reading literature, chess, listening to peaceful music, gentle activity	Stimulating—competitive sports, loud music, dancing, parties, festivals politics, debating, gambling	Depressing—sitting idly, watching television, reading low quality literature, sleeping

Increasing our contact with, or consumption of, *rājasic* or *tāmasic* things ultimately creates an imbalance in the mind and distress in the body. This is followed by disease and sickness in a variety of forms. If your *doṣa* is unbalanced it can similarly disturb the mind *guṇa*. This link between the mind and body can often make diagnosis of the origin of some diseases difficult. Did it originate in the mind and then disturb the body, or vice versa?

Modern Application of Āyurvedic Principles

As already mentioned, the essence of this science remains identical to that elaborated upon thousands of years ago. All of the treatments and remedies used today are also indistinguishable from those prescribed at that time. The differences between modern Āyurveda and ancient Āyurveda are minor, and have no real impact on the original teachings or treatments.

For example, the tools and utensils used in ancient times were often made of bones or sharpened sticks. Today we have metal, glass and plastic. Some of the original doses were quite powerful and also have to be adjusted for modern human beings who have weaker immunity and digestive systems. All of these modifications are only made in accordance with the original philosophy, and do not distort the original teachings or principles.

Today we can also utilize modern technology, like the Internet, television and radio, to distribute information on health. Machinery and automated processes can be used to mass produce and package herbal remedies. In the era of the original sages, when even writing had not yet been invented, these modern applications would never have been considered possible.

Enduring Validity

Some people tend to think that such an ancient discipline cannot be practical in the modern world. To the contrary, modern medical research is only now demonstrating the value of many of the herbs and practices advocated by Āyurvedic doctors for centuries. Clinical medical research on traditional Āyurvedic herbal preparations is demonstrating the significance of many remedies. Some preparations are considered so valuable that companies are trying to patent their formula!

A few examples from the many herbs and foods or their properties that have been adopted in modern medical or cosmetic applications are *sarpagandhā, amalā,* and whey. The herb *sarpagandhā* has traditionally been used in Āyurvedic medicine to treat high blood pressure and is now a key ingredient in medication prescribed in the West to treat this condition.

The fruit *amalā* and derivatives of it are eaten for rejuvenation, to reduce the effects of aging and restore vitality. *Āmalā* is now known to be the richest natural source of vitamin C. The role of vitamin C as an antioxidant has recently been established, and this is a base ingredient of expensive cosmetics and formulations used to delay the aging process.

Caraka and *Suśruta* both mention the anti-viral and health-promoting properties of whey (a watery byproduct of yogurt production). Studies in the West have recently demonstrated that whey is a high source of protein, assisting iron absorption in the body as well as reducing the risk of cancers and tumors. Patients with cancers of the breast, pancreas or liver were fed whey concentrate daily for six months. All of the patients displayed tumor regression, normalization of hemoglobin in the blood and a decrease in the number of cancer-causing cells.

There are many other similar and commonly known examples that could be used—such as aloe vera to treat dry skin and burns, ginger for nausea or indigestion, and garlic for cholesterol, anti-bacterial and anti-fungal uses. A whole book could be devoted to this issue alone. However, the few mentioned illustrate the point adequately that the properties of natural substances and their role in the human body were clearly understood and applied by the original Āyurvedic doctors.

In addition to herbal remedies, many concepts originally found in Āyurveda have now been adopted in the West, with widespread and positive results. Detoxification, fasting, yoga, meditation, massage, aromatherapy, acupressure and the appropriate combination of foods are some practices which are an inherent part of Āyurvedic science. Music and color therapy, gemstone healing and emotions and health are other aspects of Āyurveda that have gained popularity in the West over the last couple of decades. It is often not realized that all these fields are fragments of one unified science—Āyurveda.

Application to New Substances

It is true that many objects and compounds now found in our environment did not exist in 4000 BC. This does not mean the principles of Āyurveda are redundant, and cannot be applied to modern life. There is much to learn from Āyurvedic knowledge, despite our environment and lifestyles being starkly different from that of our ancestors who devised this science.

In fact, the ancient wisdom and guidance of Āyurvedic practitioners can prove more valuable when we are confronted with a constantly evolving environment on Earth. It just requires an appreciation of the basic and universal concepts, in order to see how everything around us is still governed by the fundamental theories the ancient sages understood so well.

The basic principles and foundations can be applied to any new compound that human beings have manufactured over the centuries using substances found on Earth. These have all been manufactured using the basic five elements. They are only new combinations of these elements—not entirely new elements in themselves.

This issue can be considered further through some examples. The basic principles of Āyurveda include:

- Natural substances are best for human health and development. They have no side effects (if consumed in appropriate quantities), have powerful healing properties and are readily assimilated into the body.
- Each organ, internal system and sense has a unique role in maintaining our body and mind balance.
- Equilibrium is the ideal state of health—our senses and physiology should not be too stimulated or aggravated by internal or external elements.
- Balance is the key—abundance and shortage should be moderated so that the senses are neither deprived nor overwhelmed (over-gratified).

Knowing and understanding these four simple concepts can help us evaluate everything around us today, to determine whether it has beneficial or adverse impacts on the body and mind. Substances or activities that did not even exist when Āyurvedic knowledge originated can be considered in relation to these four principles. These principles can provide an indication of how to maintain complete health, even in our rapidly changing world. The examples of coffee and chocolate, infant formula and the recreational drinking of alcohol are considered using these principles, below.

Coffee and chocolate

Coffee and chocolate are fairly recent inventions compared to the history of human beings. The base ingredients of these substances (coffee and cocoa beans, sugar) can be found in the environment. But humans have formulated these ingredients to create products that are far stronger than a few beans in the raw form. The naturally occurring caffeine in these substances is concentrated during the manufacturing process. It is ingested in far greater quantities than could have been physically possible without this processing.

Such unnatural quantities stimulate and irritate the nervous system and metabolism. You may have experienced some of the symptoms of excess caffeine including rapid heartbeat, shaking and insomnia. This is not to say you cannot have a cup of coffee or eat some chocolate occasionally, but you need to moderate your intake to maintain equilibrium.

Occasionally you may indulge if you have the desire, but with the awareness that these substances are concentrated and are disturbing the natural balance of your body. If you hanker for these acquired tastes, you may want to explore totally natural alternatives like carob or chicory based drinks. That way your senses do not feel deprived and your body maintains a balance.

Infant formula

Another modern dilemma about whether or not to use a new product can be clarified with the application of these principles. Modern mothers are faced with many choices of what to feed their infant if they think that breastfeeding presents difficulties. They may feel inconvenienced by breastfeeding their baby on demand, it may seem painful initially, or any number of other reasons.

Human milk contains all the nutrients that are essential for the growth of a human baby. Breast milk also provides the infant with antibodies required for immunity and strength. It is the natural source of nourishment for the child, and the function of the breast. Such feeding by the baby completely satisfies its hunger and thirst, as well as the senses—such as the need to touch, look at and hear the mother.

This feeding also stimulates and stabilizes the internal hormonal system of the mother, in order to return the body to the pre-pregnancy state. The natural balance is achieved effortlessly. Milk can easily be extracted and stored for use if the mother is unable to be personally present at feeding time, or occasionally formula may be used if circumstances demand it.

Compare it to a formula based on another species' milk. It not only has the wrong balance of nutrients for a human infant's growth, but also needs to be mixed with water (which may be impure), heated to the right temperature and fed through a sterilized bottle. The baby is deprived of the sensory pleasure of the mother's contact, and is often left to feed itself while she is busy tending to other domestic issues.

The mother misses out on this vital aspect of her child's growth, while the baby may suffer from allergies or digestive imbalances. It fails to thrive, as the emotional bond and psychological connection between mother and child is weakened. Denying breastfeeding, which is the natural expression of love and affection from the mother, can have both short and long-term emotional and physical consequences for the child.

Alcohol

I would like to discuss one more substance that has caused so much sickness in the modern world due to excessive consumption—alcohol. Āyurvedic practice recognizes the use of alcohol only for medicinal, not recreational or social purposes. It is a highly valuable substance when used therapeutically, and was originally obtained from naturally fermenting plant sources. Āyurvedic medicine actually uses over eighty different types of herbal wines to treat specific diseases and conditions. But this is in very small quantities of no more than a couple of tablespoons twice per day after meals.

We already know that alcohol causes disease and distress, but perhaps you can think about it in the context of the four points mentioned above. Humans have taken a naturally occurring drug and overdosed on it. Is it natural to consume alcohol in quantities that creates numerous physical and psychological side effects, such as loss of memory, dehydration, vomiting and ultimately complete unconsciousness (or "black outs") in the short-term?

Does it allow all your organs to function according to their proper role? The kidneys and liver cannot cope with its processing and elimination. Does it enhance the appreciation and operation of all of your senses? You may have heard the slurred speech of someone who is drunk, or noticed their lack of co-ordination, coherence, appetite or alertness. Or you may have experienced enough intoxicated evenings and hangovers the next morning to already know exactly what I am talking about! Again, if alcohol consumption cannot be eliminated from lifestyle and diet, it should at least be moderated for the benefit of health.

You may now be able to see clearly how Āyurveda works in the modern world just as validly as it did five thousand years ago. You can consider any other example and apply the principles above to see what an Āyurvedic perspective on it would be. Processed, packaged and frozen foods, genetically modified foods and carbonated beverages are other revealing examples. This approach will become useful in guiding you in your daily life, or when deciding whether to replace something natural with an artificial source.

- Does it naturally occur in this form in my environment?
- How does it affect the relevant organ and its functions?
- Does it aggravate or stimulate my senses or soothe them?
- Is my intake or association with this substance excessive or too limited?
- Does using this substance pollute my body or my environment?

Āyurvedic medical theory and science, although ancient, has enduring relevance and wisdom for human beings in any age. It has been used to treat millions of people worldwide over centuries, and will continue to offer insight well into the 21st century—that is, if we choose to appreciate the core messages that the original practitioners chose to impart for our benefit.

Chapter 3

Physical Constitution

THERE are two distinct, yet inter-related, classifications of a person in Āyurveda. The first relates to the body, and the second to the mind. Your nature is determined by this combination of body and mind types, and is known as your *prakṛti*. *Prakṛti* means "nature". When referring to the theory of creation, it is the unmanifested nature of cosmic matter. When referring to humans, *prakṛti* means the unique physical and psychological nature displayed.

The body *doṣas* are discussed in this chapter, followed by a consideration of mind *guṇas* in chapter 4. Knowing your *doṣa* and *guṇa* provides you with an understanding of your basic physical and psychological nature, and helps you tailor a personal diet and lifestyle that maintains optimum health and peace of mind. Each person has a unique *doṣa* with unique nutritional needs. Establishing your *doṣa* enables you determine suitable diets, exercise and lifestyles to maintain balance. This is the key to maintaining health.

Tridoṣa

The five elements (*panca mahābhūtas*) combine in different proportions to form three basic biological energies. These elemental combinations are reflected in your physical and psychological constitution, and are sometimes referred to as "biological humors." The Āyurvedic term for the biological energy of the elements is *doṣa*. The three *doṣas* roughly correspond to the ectomorph (thin); mesomorph (medium) and endomorph (large) body categories of Western medicine, but are far more detailed and complex.

In Āyurveda, they are known as *vāta, pitta* and *kapha*. *Vāta* represents a predominance of the elements of space/*ākāśa* and air/*vāyu*, *pitta* is fire/*agni* and *kapha* is water/*jala* and earth/*pṛthvī*. These main energies are identified by certain physical characteristics, as well as temperament and a variety of other factors.

As there are three basic energies reflected in constitution, this section of the discipline is called *tridoṣa* (*tri* meaning three). All humans have varying proportions of the three *doṣas*. Although all of the concepts of Āyurveda are important, the concept of *tridoṣa* (elements in the body) is central. All other aspects of this science, such as dietary advice, diagnosis of disease, treatments and therapies, health maintenance, exercise and so on, are explained with direct reference to the three *doṣas*. Without an understanding of *tridoṣa*, it is difficult to comprehend a diagnosis or remedies prescribed.

An imbalance of *tridoṣa* is the root cause of all physical sickness and disease. If your *doṣa* is unbalanced, sickness and disease follow. This is because *vāta, pitta* and *kapha* are the three pillars on which the body is based. If any one of these pillars is weak, the body cannot remain stable and will become diseased. It may take months or years for disease to manifest in chronic physical symptoms, if early warning signs of *tridoṣa* distress are ignored.

If illness arises due to an imbalance in the *tridoṣa,* it will first affect the body, and then the mind. Although there are only three *doṣas*, the manifestation of physical illness from their disturbance is countless. Due to the vital importance of the *doṣas*, many texts describe them in great detail.

Āyurvedic teachers consider it of greater importance to be able to locate the unbalanced or aggravated *doṣa* and treat it appropriately, rather than knowing the specific name of the disease itself. Although Āyurveda has a complete section on disease, understanding the *doṣas* is emphasized for this reason. Once the root of the disease is understood (that is, which *doṣa* is disturbed), prescribing therapies and herbal remedies to balance that *doṣa* is relatively straightforward in most cases.

Definition of *Doṣa*

It is difficult to translate the precise meaning of *doṣa*. It is often translated as "biological type" or physical constitution. This definition allows a simple and easy understanding of the concept. However, the original definition of *doṣa* is more complex. In Sanskrit, *doṣa* is defined as "*dūṣyati iti doṣa.*" The literal meaning of this is "that which contaminates is called *doṣa*." So *doṣas* may be considered the pathogenic factors, or disease-causing agents in the body. Imbalance of *vāta, pitta* and *kapha doṣas* cause disease in the body.

Doṣa only refers to the three biological energies of *vāta, pitta* and *kapha*. As an imbalance of these elemental combinations is the direct cause of physical disease, they are the prime disease causing factors (the "contaminants"). Secondary factors in the disease process, like body tissues (*dhātus*), toxins (*āma*) and waste materials (*malas*) are actually the product of, or dependent upon, an imbalance in the *doṣas*. The disease process is discussed in chapter 10.

Attributes of *Doṣas*

Each *doṣa* has exclusive attributes. Each general category of *doṣa* is further divided into five divisions, referred to by some authors as *sub-doṣas*. The *doṣas* have particular:

- Qualities
- Dominant elements
- Definitions
- Locations
- Roles
- Related senses
- Related emotions
- Reasons for aggravation
- Symptoms of disturbance
- Disorders and diseases
- Remedies to balance them
- Divisions, or types

The information in this chapter on each *doṣa* is summarized in tabular form in appendix 1 (p. 227).

Doṣa Formation

The *doṣa* combination you have is determined at the time of conception in the womb. At fertilization, the sperm and ovum unite to form a new human being. The sperm carries the elements from the father, and the ovum the elements from the mother. When combined, they produce another human being, which is a unique combination of both parents' elemental natures. The five elements are therefore present in their unique proportions from the time of conception.

Almost every human has varying degrees of *vāta, pitta* and *kapha*. In most people there is a natural uneven distribution of the *doṣas*, but very rarely, a person may have a completely even distribution. As the sperm and ovum are unique, and fertilization takes place under different psychological and environmental conditions, it is difficult to obtain a "perfect match"—where the sperm and ovum unite to create a perfectly equal distribution of each doṣa. It is not impossible, and the reproductive branch of Āyurveda (*vājīkaraṇa*) specializes in that field.

Although we have characteristics of *vāta, pitta* or *kapha* to different degrees, one of these elemental natures will dominate and that is our "main" *doṣa*. The secondary *doṣa* is the one present in the next highest proportion. Every *doṣa* type or combination is acknowledged in Āyurveda, which lists seven separate physical constitution types based on the basic three: (1) *vāta*, (2) *pitta*, (3) *kapha*, (4) *vāta-pitta*, (5) *vāta-kapha*, (6) *pitta-kapha* and (7) *vāta-pitta-kapha.*

Doṣa States

The *doṣas* operate in either a natural (normal) or an unnatural (abnormal) state. In the natural state, the *doṣas* function in equilibrium and therefore good health is maintained. In this state, the *doṣas* nourish, sustain and maintain the body, protecting it from disease. In the unnatural state, the *doṣas* are aggravated or unbalanced, and give rise to numerous disorders.

Under different environmental conditions and diets, where the elements in the body have become unbalanced, the *doṣas* are aggravated. If the *doṣas* are disturbed, your inherent nature may be obscured. For example, if *vāta* is aggravated, you may display *vāta* characteristics even if you are predominantly *pitta* in nature.

Depending on the proportion of the *doṣas*, there are three main states of functioning or operating:

- The increased state refers to a particular *doṣa* (element/s) being present in greater than normal or natural quantity. It is also known as aggravated;
- The balanced state is when all three *doṣas* (element/s) are present in the normal quantity and natural proportion, sometimes referred to as equilibrium; and
- The decreased state is when a *doṣa* (element/s) is present in less than the normal quantity or is in a reduced state.

Of all the possible states of *doṣa*, it is the increased (or excess) form that creates disorders. The remedies mentioned in this chapter are for balancing a *doṣa* through diet and lifestyle, when it is increased and showing symptoms of aggravation. Being aware of your *doṣa*, and symptoms of its disturbance can assist in maintaining harmony and therefore good health.

Doṣa Balance

There is a simple formula to obtain balance and alleviate an aggravated *doṣa*: consume those substances that are the opposite in elemental nature. Eating foods similar in nature to the aggravated *doṣa* will only increase it further. For example if *vāta* is disturbed, eating foods that share the elements of air/*vāyu* and space/*ākāśa* (foods that are dry, porous or gas promoting) will only increase *vāta* aggravation. Instead, foods that are solid, heavy, watery or spicy should be consumed (fire/*agni*, water/*jala* or earth/*pṛthvī*). One way of determining the elemental nature of foods is by taste, which is discussed in chapter 7.

When you are healthy, you are generally instinctively attracted to foods and activities similar in elemental composition to your own body. When you are sick and the elements are unbalanced, you are attracted to those foods opposite in nature. For example, if you are suffering from a cold, or chest congestion (due to an imbalance in *kapha*), you usually choose to avoid those foods that are *kapha* in nature such as dairy products, or heavy and oily foods.

A "balance" of the *doṣas* does not mean ensuring each *doṣa* is present in even proportions, or in equal amounts. That is impossible, as the inherent balance of *doṣas* is determined in the womb and cannot be modified after birth. Obtaining "balance" means the *doṣas* are in their original proportions as determined before birth, and maintaining that intrinsic elemental nature.

It should always be kept in mind that you cannot change your elemental nature or *doṣa*. So if you wish to acquire *kapha* qualities, you cannot do so by eating a lot of food high in the *kapha* elements of water/*jala* and earth/*pṛthvī*. You will only disturb your primary *doṣa*. Changing your nature through acquiring positive qualities, and minimizing negative temperamental characteristics, is the role of the mind.

Evaluating *Doṣa* Type

To determine your primary and secondary *doṣa*, consider the characteristics listed in table 4, on the next page. Variations of these attributes are commonly used to identify *doṣa*, and are listed in most Āyurvedic texts. The column that lists the majority of your characteristics indicates your primary *doṣa*. As mentioned, most people will display a mixture of these characteristics, reflecting the varying proportions of *vāta, pitta* and *kapha*.

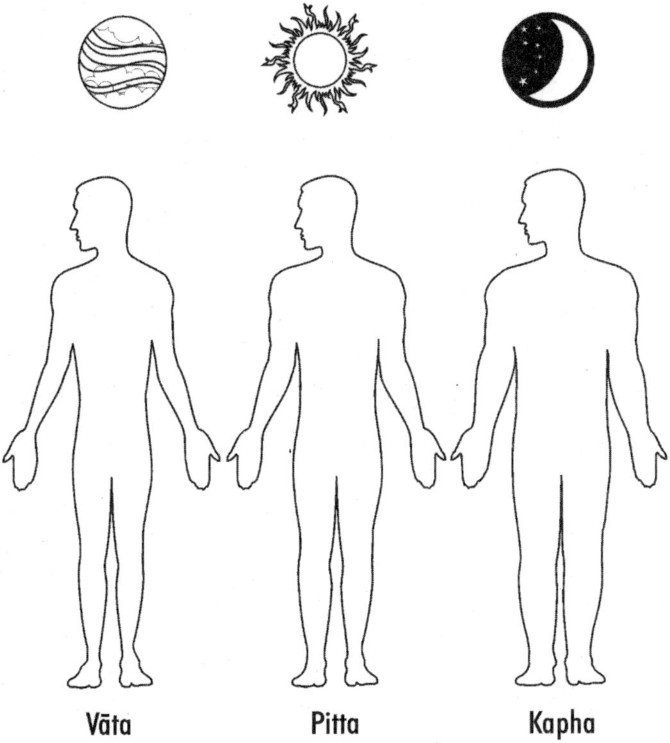

Figure 3 Body Types

Table 4: ***Doṣa* Characteristics**

	VĀTA	*PITTA*	*KAPHA*
		Physical	
Body Frame	Thin, bony, tall or short	Medium, balanced	Large, broad
Weight	Low	Moderate	Heavy
Skin	Dry, rough, cool, dull	Soft, oily, warm, ruddy	Thick, moist, cold, pale
Hair	Dark, dry, curly	Soft, oily, fair or red	Thick, oily, wavy
Teeth	Protruding, big, uneven	Moderate, yellowish	Strong, even, white
Nails	Rough, dry, brittle, bitten	Soft, pink, strong	Soft, large, white
Eyes	Small, dull, dry, nervous	Sharp, penetrating	Big, thick lashes
Appetite	Variable, small	Good, regular	Slow and steady
Food	Simple, sparse, snacks	Requires regular meals	Gourmet, luxury, fatty
Thirst	Variable	Excessive	Minimal
Elimination	Dry, hard, constipated	Soft, oily, loose	Thick, heavy, slow
Urine	Frequent but sparse	Yellow, copious	Infrequent, average
Sweat	Minimal	Profuse, pungent in odor	Slow to begin, heavy
Pulse	Weak, erratic, fast	Stable, strong	Slow, smooth
Circulation	Variable, poor, sluggish	Good	Moderate
Sleep	Light, disturbed, minimal	Sound, moderate	Heavy, excessive
Speech	Rapid, high or hoarse voice	Sharp, cutting, loud	Slow, harmonious
Libido	Varies, directed in fantasy	Passionate, excessive	Slow but strong, loyal
Immunity	Variable, poor	Moderate	High
Activity	High, restless, mobile	Moderate, directed	Minimal, slow
Endurance	Minimal	Moderate	Excellent
		Psychological	
Mind	Restless, curious	Aggressive, clever	Calm, slow
Memory	Short term	Sharp, good	Long term
Routine	Dislikes	Enjoys planning	Adaptable, tolerates
Faith	Erratic, changeable	Fanatical	Steady, devoted
Opinions/Moods	Variable, fluctuate	Expresses forcefully	Changes slowly
Finances	Poor, spends rapidly	Moderate, buys luxuries	Rich, thrifty
Hobbies	Travel, art, philosophy	Sports, politics, luxuries	Serene, leisurely types
Creativity	Original, fertile	Technical, scientific	Entrepreneurial
Sensitivities	Cold, wind, dryness	Heat, sun, fires	Cold, damp, humidity
Temperament	Nervous, insecure, shy	Determined, motivated	Conservative, resilient
Dreams	Frequent, fearful	Fiery, violent, vivid	Romantic, calm
TOTAL	***Vāta*:**	***Pitta*:**	***Kapha*:**

Doṣa Descriptions

Characteristics of *Vāta*

Elements	: Space/*ākāśa* and air/*vāyu*
Definition	: "That which moves."
Location	: *Vāta* is mainly present in the lower part of the body—colon, rectum, bladder, urinary tract, spine, thighs and legs. It governs the neuro-hormonal system and nerve impulses, respiration, movement, circulation of fluids, excretion, stimulation of digestive juices and movement of the digestive tract.
Role	: Transportation of fluids, air and food within the body, movement.
Related senses	: Hearing and touch.
Related emotions	: Fear, tension, anxiety and impatience.
Qualities	: Rough, dry, light, mobile, cool and subtle.

People with a predominantly *vāta doṣa* display physical and emotional characteristics linked to the elemental qualities of space/*ākāśa* and air/*vāyu*. They are very active, mobile, restless and energetic. They have fast metabolisms, so are often thin with little muscle development and protruding joints that may make cracking noises. Their skin is dry, rough and thin with visible veins.

Sleeping, eating and personal habits are irregular and erratic, with appetite and sexual desire varying between extremes. They sleep lightly, are easily disturbed and prone to insomnia. Their speech and movement is usually fast, and they are talkative and enjoy all forms of communication. Their pulse is fast, weak and irregular. They dislike cold, windy or dry environments and feel chilled quickly or shiver easily. Extremities (hands and feet) are often cold, or become cold easily.

Mentally and emotionally they are rapid. They gather information or display emotions quickly, or determine swiftly whether they like or dislike something. While they learn quickly and are usually intellectual, their retention is poor. Money is spent quickly and impulsively. They demonstrate high creativity, innovation and sensitivity.

Individuals with this nature are introspective, shy, modest and lacking in confidence. They are often unsettled and impatient, but very flexible and adaptable to change. People with *vāta doṣa* often feel anxious, worried or stressed—especially in unfamiliar, cramped or noisy environments. They are most likely to be loners, or non-conformists.

Reasons for *vāta* aggravation

- Eating large quantities of foods that share vāta elements (space/*ākāśa* and air/*vāyu*)—dry, light, airy and gas forming: fruits and vegetables such as cabbage, broccoli, cauliflower, beans, lettuce, mushroom, parsley, peas, bell pepper (capsicum), spinach, corn, lentils, white or rye breads, soya products, yeast based spreads, smoked foods and dried fruit. Very cold foods or drinks also disturb *vāta.*
- Eating while anxious or depressed increases *vāta.*
- Indulging in activities that are similar to *vāta* in nature, including traveling, watching too much television, exposure to high levels of noise, late nights and excessive physical, mental or sexual activity.
- During periods when conditions are naturally high in *vāta* such as when it is cold, dry or windy, just prior to sunrise and sunset, and during middle to old age, *vāta* can become more easily disturbed.

Symptoms of *vāta* disturbance

There are eighty types of disorders or diseases caused by *vāta* imbalance. Any condition caused by dryness (lack of fluids), problems with mobility or movement or excess air is usually *vāta* related. Disorders like dry skin, dandruff, premature aging, constipation, joint pains, paralysis, dizziness, delirium, headache, heart palpitations, insomnia, anxiety, depression, muscle stiffness and loss of memory are associated with excess *vāta*.

Remedies to balance *vāta*

To alleviate aggravated *vāta*, consuming substances opposite in nature is recommended. Therefore, rather than eating light, airy, dry and cold foods, those which are hot, oily, dense and heavy are substituted. Food that is sweet, sour or salty in taste is also beneficial.

Foods that are mainly *pitta* (salty, spicy) or *kapha* (dense, sweet) should be included in the diet. This includes most fresh fruits, pasta, rice, dairy products, avocado, brown breads, nuts in moderation, spices and lots of fluids (especially warm drinks). Salads should have a creamy or oily dressing.

Warming colors, gems and aromas are useful. For example: orange, yellow or crimson shades of color; ruby, beryl, yellow-sapphire or cats-eye gems; and cinnamon, basil or sandalwood essential oils.

Avoiding activities that stimulate *vāta* is suggested. A regular routine and adequate rest and relaxation is necessary. Oil massage (*abhyanga*) and steaming (*svedana*), as well as detoxification of the colon (*basti*) are also of assistance to balance disturbed *vāta*. These therapies counteract dryness, increase circulation and reduce stiffness of muscles, as well clean the main location of *vāta* (the colon).

Table 5: *Vāta* Divisions

Doṣa Type	Location	Functions	Disorders	Remedies
Prāṇa	Heart, chest, ears, nose, throat	Breathing, sneezing, spitting, swallowing	Hiccough, cough, bronchitis, asthma, colds, hoarse voice	Chest/back massage, ginger, honey, cloves
Udāna	Throat, navel and chest	Speech, voice, singing, mind, memory, enthusiasm	Diseases of the eye, ear, head, nose and throat	Head massage licorice, herbal gargles
Samāna	Stomach, duodenum, small intestine, intestinal tract. Near the digestive fire	Digestive enzymes, assimilation of food and its separation into tissue elements	Indigestion, diarrhea, and inadequate nutritive assimilation	Asafoetida, mint, ginger, cumin, turmeric, *yoga,* fasting
Apāna	Colon, anus, urinary tract and bladder, navel, genitals, organs near the pelvis	Elimination of body wastes, semen, fetus, menstruation, pregnancy	Diseases of bladder, anus, testicles, renal stones, urinary tract infections, diabetes	Water, garlic, *basti*, hot fomentation on pelvic area
Vyāna	Heart and all over the body	Functioning of circulatory system and channels, sweating	Impairment of circulation, fever, diarrhea, tuberculosis	Basil, sesame oil massages, *basti,* proper sleep and diet

Characteristics of *Pitta*

Element : Fire/*agni*

Definition : "That which digests."

Location : Pitta is mainly located in the middle portion of the body—stomach (gastric juices), liver, spleen, duodenum, gall bladder, bile, pancreas, small intestine, skin and blood.

Role : Controls conversion processes such as digestion, metabolism and enzyme activity.

Related Sense : Sight

Related Emotions : Anger, jealousy, courage, willpower.

Qualities : Hot, sharp, acidic, intense, oily.

People with a *pitta doṣa* display an inherent fire/*agni* elemental character. They are of medium build, with greater muscular development than that displayed by *vāta*. Their skin is soft and warm, and they have a lot of body heat and often perspire excessively. Their hair is thin and often reddish or blond, and they may experience premature graying, baldness or excessive hair loss. Their skin flushes easily and they often have many freckles and moles. They develop acne, rashes, bruises or sunburn easily.

Their desires (appetite, sex) are strong in nature. Sleep is moderate and not easily disturbed. The pulse is strong and stable. Individuals with a *pitta doṣa* speak loudly and passionately, and often dominate the conversation. They have an aversion to hot weather, sunlight and heat, and their eyes are sensitive.

In temperament, they are extroverted and love to be the focus of attention. Although they can usually control their emotions, they may become irritable, angry and judgmental under stress. Money is prudently managed. They are decisive, aggressive, ambitious and determined, often aspiring to positions of leadership. They enjoy competitive sports and games, either as spectators or participants. Their intelligence is high, and they have good insight and a keen sense of discrimination.

Reasons for *pitta* aggravation

- Eating foods that share the elemental fire characteristic of *pitta* (pungent, sour, acidic, spicy, salty and hot) such as chillies, most spices, fried and greasy food, aubergine (eggplant or brinjal), beetroot, tomato, carrot, onion, garlic, apricot, plums, cherries, citrus fruit (grapefruit, lemon, lime, orange), peach, papaya, pineapple, rhubarb, strawberries, most nuts, chutneys, sauces, pickled food, mustard and vinegar.
- Eating while angry, or experiencing anger frequently, drinking excessive amounts of tea, coffee, alcohol or smoking are *pitta* aggravating.

- Engaging in activities that are *pitta* in nature, such as having a sauna, competitive sports, debating or anything that arouses passionate emotions can stimulate *pitta*.
- The naturally occurring *pitta* aggravating factors include exposure to heat and sunlight, midday and midnight, and adulthood.

Symptoms of *pitta* disturbance

There are forty types of disorders and diseases caused by *pitta* imbalance. Conditions involving excess heat and acidity such as hyperacidity, skin diseases, burning sensations or heartburn, liver disorders, hepatitis, gastric or duodenal ulcers, gastritis, hair loss, baldness, urinary tract infections, gall bladder disorders or kidney stones, mouth ulcers, excessive sweating often with a pungent odor, excessive thirst and fevers are *pitta* related.

Remedies to balance *pitta*

To balance *pitta*, foods and herbs opposite in nature are consumed. So rather than pungent, acidic, salty and hot foods being predominant in the diet, those that are sweet, cold and watery are eaten (*kapha* or *vāta*).

Foods that should be included are grains, rice and pasta, beans, breads, dairy products (except those salty or sour in taste), sweet drinks and foods. The use of spices should be reduced. Intake of coffee, tea, alcohol and smoking should be minimised or eliminated.

Cooling colors, gems and aromas are beneficial. For example: blue, purple or white colors; amethyst, pearl, moonstone or emerald gems; and rose, jasmine and lavender essential oils.

Avoiding those activities that stimulate *pitta* is recommended. Purgatives or laxative treatment (*virecana*) is considered the best therapy for excess *pitta*, as it is mainly located in the small intestine.

Table 6: *Pitta* Divisions

Doṣa Type	Location	Functions	Disorders	Remedies
Pācaka	Stomach, duodenum, small intestine	Digestion of food and separation of wastes	Indigestion, swollen abdomen, formation of toxic wastes (*āma*)	Black pepper, coriander, buttermilk, walking after meals
Rañjaka	Liver, spleen, stomach	Blood formation from digestive juices	Anemia, jaundice, hepatitis	Cabbage, apples, carrot, beet, dates
Sādhāka	Heart	Memory, mental functions, emotions	Psychological and emotional disorders	*Brāhmi, ghī, yoga*, meditation, *prāṇāyama*
Ālocaka	Eyes	Maintaining normal vision	Diseases related to sight and vision	Almond, white pepper, honey, washing, resting and exercising eyes
Bhrājaka	Skin	Color and lustre of the skin, absorption of oils massaged into the skin	Skin diseases—rashes, dryness, psoriasis, and eczema	*Neem, āmalā*, Aloe vera, turmeric, eggplant, early morning sun

Characteristics of *Kapha*

Element : Earth/*pṛthvī* and water/*jala*

Definition : "That which binds."

Location : *Kapha* is mainly located in the upper part of the body—head, nose, throat, chest, lungs, joints, fatty tissue, connective tissues, ligaments, tendons, mouth.

Role : Provides moisture, connection and solidity.

Related senses : Taste and smell.

Related emotions : Love, patience, forgiveness, greed, attachment and possessiveness.

Qualities : Dense, heavy, firm, stable, slow, thick, sticky, wet, clear, cold.

People with a mainly *kapha doṣa* tend to have a heavy and solid, or large build. They are often overweight, gain weight easily and have high muscle development (plump and round). Their skin is thick, smooth and moist with few wrinkles. Their complexion is usually clear, fair or pale, and hair is oily, thick and wavy. Their teeth are strong, white and well formed.

Kapha types have a moderate or low appetite and slow digestion. They enjoy eating gourmet or luxury foods (that appeal to taste and smell) or buying and preparing food. In movement and activity, they tend to be slow and methodical, with a lot of endurance. However, they are sluggish and lethargic or difficult to motivate. They are prone to sleep heavily and excessively. Their pulse is slow, steady and regular. They have a pleasant appearance and voice. Those with *kapha doṣa* dislike damp conditions.

In temperament, they prefer familiar surroundings and tradition. They learn slowly, but have excellent memories. Money is hoarded (or they are thrifty) and they are good, stable providers. Typically, they are serene and tranquil and their emotions are slow to become excited or aroused.

Kapha individuals can be sentimental, nostalgic and romantic in nature. They are highly tolerant and forgiving, with medium intelligence. They prefer to belong to a group, club or community and cling to their family or familiar associations.

Reasons for *kapha* aggravation

- Eating a lot of food that is *kapha* in nature (heavy, oily, sweet, dense) such as foods high in sugar and fat content including meat, dairy products (milk, butter, yogurt, cheese, cream, ice-cream, chocolate), nuts, avocado, banana, mangoes, melons, pasta, rice, breads, cakes, custards and puddings, watery foods and consuming a lot of liquids.
- Eating while feeling grief or sadness, or being greedy.

- Engaging in activities that increase *kapha* include overeating, sleeping excessively (especially during the day) or being sedentary and engaging in limited physical activity.
- The natural conditions that aggravate *kapha* are cold and damp climates, early morning (after sunrise) and evening (after sunset) and childhood.

Symptoms of *kapha* disturbance

There are twenty types of diseases caused by aggravation of *kapha*. Those conditions with symptoms of congestion, heaviness and lethargy such as asthma, coughs and colds, nausea, mucus in the throat or lungs, congestion in the chest, sinus conditions, obesity, laziness, excessive sleep, heaviness in the body and indigestion are related to excess *kapha*.

Remedies to balance *kapha*

To balance excess *kapha*, foods and drinks opposite in nature are consumed. So foods that are *vāta* or *pitta* in nature (light, dry, spicy, acidic, hot) should be eaten. Those foods that are bitter and astringent (sharp) in taste should be increased in the diet.

Cauliflower, broccoli, spinach, carrots, beans, lettuce and most spices can be included. Dairy products, pasta, rice, potatoes, nuts and oils should be avoided, and less water and fluids consumed.

Vivid and stimulating colors, aromas and gems are recommended. For example: red, saffron and gold tones; clove, basil and sage essential oils; and agate, garnet, topaz or opal gems.

Avoiding activities that stimulate *kapha* is beneficial. Heating therapies (*svedana*) and increased physical exercise (mobility and movement) alleviate *kapha*. Emetic therapy, or supervised vomiting (*vamana*), is the prime therapy for severely disturbed *kapha*, as the main physical location is the stomach and upper body.

Table 7: *Kapha* Divisions

***Doṣa* Type**	**Location**	**Functions**	**Disorders**	**Remedies**
Kledaka	Stomach	Moistens food, helps in digestion	Indigestion and diseases related to digestion	Ginger, lemon, buttermilk, salty, sour and bitter foods
Avalambaka	Heart and chest region	Protects heart from excessive heat and gives energy to limbs	Laziness, lethargy weakening of heart and limbs	Camphor, *prāṇāyama*, *yoga*, meditation, walking in the morning
Bodhaka	Tongue	Perception of tastes, activates salivation	Abnormality in perception of tastes	Sweet foods, vegetable soup, asafoetida, cumin seeds, papaya
Tarpaka	Head, brain and sense organs	Nourishment of the sense organs	Memory loss and impairment of sense organs	Head massage *rasāyana* meditation
Śleṣaka	Joints	Lubrication of the joints, function of the joints	Pain in the joints, abnormality in the function of the joints	Oil massage, *Yoga* postures, garlic, aloe vera, fasting

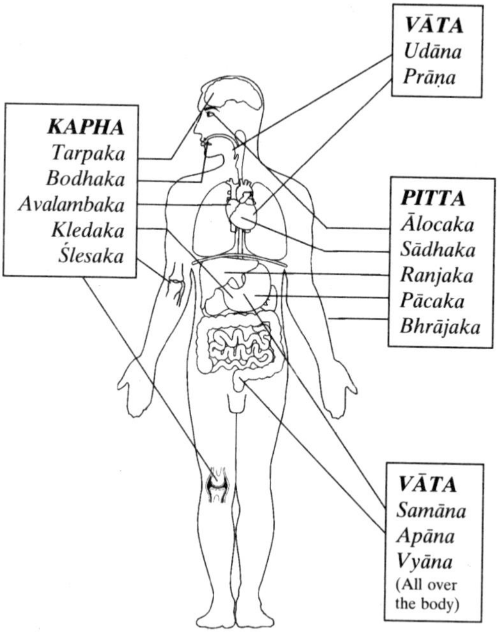

Figure 4 Location of Doṣa Divisions

CHAPTER 4

Psychological Constitution

THE mind is a partner to the body in achieving health and happiness. Like the physical constitutions, there are three mind constitutions that vary in nature. These are the *triguṇa* of *sattva, rajas* and *tamas*. The mind constitution/*guṇa* prevailing provides subtlety and further character to the dominant *doṣa*.

Triguṇa

As mentioned in chapter 2, the three types of *guṇa* (*triguṇa*) are present in all of us to varying degrees and each may be displayed in different contexts. The *guṇa* is not determined at birth, unlike a *doṣa*, but is molded by environment and influenced by nutrition. So a person's mind *guṇa* reflects their social and physical environment and their diet.

Some modern authors on Āyurveda have linked specific mind *guṇas* with body *doṣas*. They have assumed that each *doṣa* type has a tendency towards a particular mind *guṇa*. For example, *pitta* types are considered to have a tendency towards *rajas* or *kapha* towards *tamas*. Others believe that each *doṣa* has a psychological equivalent, in the form of a *guṇa*.

This approach confuses two discrete principles within Āyurvedic theory. At different stages of the lifecycle different *guṇas* may predominate, and each *doṣa* has different psychological characteristics and tendencies. However, it does not necessarily follow that human physiology is inherently connected to a predetermined *guṇa*. Each body *doṣa* may display any of the mind *guṇas*.

The relationship between *guṇa* and *doṣa* is more subtle. The predominant *guṇa* influences the nature of the doṣa displayed. When *sāttvic* in nature, the *doṣa* will be positively expressed (balanced), when the mind *guṇa* is predominantly *rājasic,* the *doṣa* will be unstable and when *tāmasic*, the *doṣa* is negatively expressed (obscured).

There are seven different mental states based on combinations of the mind *guṇas*. These are (1) *sāttvic*, (2) *rājasic*, (3) *tāmasic*, (4) *sāttvic-rājasic*, (5) *sāttvic-tāmasic*, (6) *rājasic-tāmasic* and (7) *sāttvic-rājasic-tāmasic*. It is very rare to find a person who displays the characteristics of only one *guṇa*, but for the purpose of illustration, the descriptions of each *guṇa* in this chapter are of the "pure" or "complete" types.

Mind *guṇa* can be identified by behavior and preferences. To determine the balance of your mind *guṇa*, consider the table on the following page. This can assist you to identify various *sāttvic, rājasic* and *tāmasic* tendencies.

Table 8: *Guṇa* Characteristics

	SĀTTVIC	*RĀJASIC*	*TĀMASIC*
Diet	Vegetarian, fresh, light	Some meat, spicy	A lot of meat, fast food
Appetite	Regulated	Moderate	Excessive
Drugs/stimulants	Never	Regularly, on occasions	Often, frequently
Sleep	Minimal, refreshing	Moderate, disturbed	Excessive, lethargic
Sexual desire	Low	Moderate	High
Hygiene	Excellent	Reasonable	Poor
Health	Robust, strong immunity	Inconsistent	Poor, weak immunity
Environment	Peaceful, serene, fresh	Noisy, colorful, chaotic	Dirty, boring, unkempt
Speech	Calm, clear, serene	Excitable, excessive	Dull, dreary
Sensory control	Good, strong	Variable	Weak
Concentration	High, extended	Medium, distracted	Poor, unable to
Memory	Excellent, clear, realistic	Moderate, patchy	Poor, distorted
Intelligence	High	Medium, average	Low, ignorant
Money	Unattached	Likes to accumulate	Greedy, selfish
Work	Selfless, devoted	For personal gain/goals	Avoids when possible
Discipline	Strong	Moderate, lapsing	Weak
Activities	Creative, productive	Competitive, passionate	Minimal, passive
Pride	Modest	Some ego	Conceited and vain
Violence	Never	On occasion, or cruel	Frequently, excessive
Anger and Fear	Rarely, never	Occasionally	Regularly
Depression	Never	Sporadically	Often
Forgiveness	Easily, totally	With effort	Holds grudges
Generosity	High, unconditional	Medium, expects returns	Never, greedy, selfish
Creativity	High	Moderate	Low
Honesty	Always	Usually	Seldom
Spirituality	Strong, daily	Wavering, occasionally	None, disregards
Love	Unconditional, universal	Personal, selective	Unable to experience
TOTAL	***Sāttvic:***	***Rājasic:***	***Tāmasic:***

The Mind Types

Sāttvic

People of a *sāttvic* nature are intelligent with a good memory. They are instinctively clean and ordered, take good care of themselves and are health-conscious. They are calm, gentle and considerate of others—polite and helpful to all, with good manners. They seek to improve themselves, even though already knowledgeable, and are focused on work, self-improvement and intellectual or spiritual pursuits.

They are highly positive in nature, demonstrating generosity, kindness, openness, fairness (equity) and forgiveness. They readily share what they have and enjoy doing so, but expect no reward in return. *Sāttvic* people see life as a productive learning experience and do not begrudge their position, nor hold grudges.

They do not seek to accumulate wealth or status, to dominate others or impose their will. Their mind is clear and peaceful, and they are honest, humble and quiet. They are spiritually inclined and have a strong faith and belief in God, often engaging in selfless service or charitable activities.

Those with a *sāttvic nature* express happiness, enthusiasm and joy. They are flexible, moderate, regular and balanced in habits and activities. Sleep is minimal, yet deep and refreshing. Food that is fresh and not extreme in terms of preparation or taste is preferred (not heavily spiced or very sweet).

There are seven types of *sāttvic nature*:

- *Brahma* respectful, sincere, discriminating;
- *Mahendra* studious, courageous and learned;
- *Varuṇa* attractive, tolerant, kind, pleasant;
- *Yāmya* shows initiative, leadership, timely action;
- *Kubera* virtuous, patient and diplomatic;
- *Gandharva* wealthy, cultivated, enjoys music and art; and
- *Ārśa* self-controlled, clever with good memory.

Rājasic

Those that are *rājasic* in temperament are dynamic and seek to control and dominate others. They are medium in intelligence and have a variable memory. Those with a *rājas guṇa* value prestige and authority and so seek power, status, fame, wealth and recognition.

Rājasic people are never satisfied with their position or possessions—they always seek to accumulate more and enjoy flaunting what they have. In addition, they seek continual gratification of desires (sex, food), stimulation of the senses (music, color, fragrance) and entertainment (parties, functions, festivals). However, they are often distracted or quickly bored.

Generally, they are very ambitious as well as highly active and industrious. They can be brave and courageous, but often display jealousy, maliciousness, cruelty and egotistical behavior. Those with this temperament can be extremely determined, manipulative, selfish and proud. They can often be rude, arrogant and angry and usually respond with irritation to external stimulus. In terms of spirituality, they are doubtful and questioning. A negative, sometimes cynical attitude is prevalent.

Those of a *rājasic* nature rarely give unconditionally. It is always done with some reluctance and to demonstrate generosity (or with some expectation) rather than genuine altruism. Relationships are therefore based mainly on their own needs and desires rather than on reciprocal interest and regard. Sleep is disturbed or troubled by intense dreams, so is not refreshing. Food that is strong and excessive in flavor (spicy, hot, salty) is preferred. Stimulants such as coffee, tea, alcohol and tobacco are consumed regularly.

There are six types of *rājasic nature*:

- *Asura* — proud of achievements and possessions, self-praising, brave but ruthless;
- *Rākśasa* — cruel, intolerant, eats, drinks and sleeps excessively;

- *Paiśācika* — unclean, abnormal or irregular diet and routine, weakness for the opposite sex;
- *Sarpa* — cowardly, deceptive, envious, fearful;
- *Preta* — greedy, spiteful, lacks discrimination; and
- *Śākuna* — passionate, unstable, ruthless, excessive appetite.

Tāmasic

Those demonstrating a *tāmas guṇa* are ignorant, lazy and fearful with poor memories. They are usually apathetic and insensitive in nature. They show little consideration or regard for others, and are coarse, brash, immoral or violent. They may be stubborn or obstinate, and inattentive to those around them. *Tāmasic* people show little or no desire to improve physically or mentally, or lack the will power and discipline to do so.

Tāmasic individuals do not engage in anything that is physically or mentally taxing, and will avoid any work at all if that is possible. They seem almost to be entirely engaged in (or thinking about) eating, drinking, sleeping, sex or idleness. They are dishonest, unclean in habits and have no regard for their health. Often, they show no initiative and minimal interest in, or understanding of, spirituality. They have little or no faith in God. People with a *tāmasic* nature are frequently sorrowful or depressed.

Those predominantly *tāmasic* in nature demonstrate no love except that based on the own sensory gratification, so relationships are totally exploitative. They rarely give, instead preferring to take or even obtain through deception. Often, they complain about their job or position in life although show no motivation or take no action to change it.

Tāmasic people sleep heavily and are not easily roused from sleep, and are usually sedentary. They overeat, and consume food that is overcooked, sweet and heavy or stale, cold, preserved and processed. "Fast food" or "junk food" and meat constitutes a large part of their diet.

There are three types of *tāmasic* nature:

- *Pāśava* — low intelligence, animalistic behavior, excessive indulgence in sleep and sex, disobedient;
- *Matasya* — unstable and changeable in character, cowardly, consistent desire, excessive intake of liquids; and
- *Vānaspatya* — excessive consumption of food, no interest in education or learning about other people and the surrounding world.

Mind Balance

The human system (body-mind) has a tremendous capacity to heal itself when in a balanced condition. Many diseases or disorders can be easily healed once the body and mind have been brought into balance. For example, a person may have digestive problems due to improper diet, and as a consequence the digestive tract is irritated and damaged. First, physical discomfort can be treated with dietary modifications. Then once diet is modified, the body and mind can begin to naturally repair any damage that may have been caused by the unhealthy diet.

The power of a positive and balanced mind is crucial at this stage. Through bringing our internal physical and psychological systems into balance, we remove the cause of disease, cure its symptoms and then allow the damage to heal itself.

The mind is considered balanced when it is not agitated, and is clear and stable. For example, if somebody abuses you and you remain calm, this indicates no agitation. If the mind is agitated by outside stimulus or actions, it is not independent and detached. It is dependent on and reactive to those external triggers.

Each of us wants to be independent, but we are actually slaves to our body and mind. This can be illustrated with a story about Buddha, considered a great master of his mind and senses.

One day a person abused and spat on Buddha. He wiped off the spit, saying, "Do you have anything else to say?" The man was surprised and replied "I've just abused you, why aren't you angry or upset?" Buddha replied, "I am not your slave. Whether I become angry or not is my decision. My mind is not the slave of your actions."

Most people do not act (that is, behave independently) but instead react, based on the actions or desires of other people. As long as we only react, we are dependent on others and our mind is neither balanced nor controlled. Āyurvedic lifestyle principles ultimately aim to avoid sickness and disease, as well as achieve contentment, happiness and peace through complete body-mind balance and control.

Research in the West has recently established that people who can tolerate and deal effectively with stressful situations or chronic diseases share particular mind characteristics. They are clear and focused, remain positive and optimistic and often have a deep spiritual faith. They heal quicker, require less medical intervention and suffer fewer relapses or recurrences of sickness. These mind qualities are termed *sāttvic* in Āyurveda, and can be acquired through attention to diet and nurition, lifestyle and emotions.

Diet and Nutrition

Āhāriyate iti āhāra. *Whatever enters the body is food.*

Anything that is consumed by the body or nourishes it is considered food (*āhāra*). This includes anything absorbed by the senses, or that enters into the body through the mouth, nose, ears, skin or eyes. Everything that enters the body in either a tangible or intangible form is therefore a part of the diet.

As everything on earth has a primary *guṇa*, diet/*āhāra* may be classified into the categories of *sāttvic, rājasic* or *tāmasic*. Anything we hear, smell, watch, taste or touch may be divided into one of these three groups (see table 3, p. 31 for further reference).

Mind balance in Āyurveda means modifying the mind *guṇa* from *tāmasic* or *rājasic* to *sāttvic* through modifying diet/*āhāra*. That is, choosing those foods and activities that are *sāttvic* in nature in preference to those that are *rājasic* or *tāmasic*. With consistent and dedicated attention to diet, environment and sensory experiences (*āhāra*), total mind balance can be achieved.

A predominantly *sāttva guṇa* is usually preferred, but it is often human nature to display *rājasic* or *tāmasic* qualities. It may initially take strong discipline and effort to become *sāttvic*, but the peace of mind, health, strength and immunity that is obtained from this mind *guṇa* makes it worthwhile. However, *rajas* and *tamas* still have a role in our lives and are needed for existence. Some *rajas* and *tamas* qualities are required for action and motivation to achieve our goals (*rajas*) and inaction, sleep or rest (*tamas*).

According to Āyurveda, a deranged and undesirāble mental state results from an excess of *rajas* or *tamas*, or domination of the mind by these *guṇas*. Mental illness and physical disease are created from, and are stimulated by this state. In order to be balanced, cheerful and calm in disposition, we should therefore emphasize *sāttvic āhāra* in our lifestyles and minimize *rājasic* or *tāmasic āhāra*.

In terms of nutrition, this includes:

- Increasing the amount of fresh fruits and vegetables, grains, salads, pure fruit juices, herbal teas, water and milk, nuts, seeds and honey. Food should be eaten freshly prepared.
- At the same time, foods that are processed, pre-prepared, preserved, fermented, canned and packaged, frozen, microwaved, fried or barbecued, high in sugar or spices, or containing artificial flavors or colors should be minimized.
- Mushrooms, onions, spices and garlic should be avoided, as they are *tāmasic* and *rājasic*. Consumption of alcohol, caffeine and meat should be moderated or eliminated for the same reason.

Clinical studies in India have demonstrated that increasing *sāttvic* foods increases *sāttvic* qualities. For example, animals fed mostly vegetarian food in laboratories became calm, peaceful and alert. In contrast, those fed stale or frozen foods, meat and other *tāmasic* or *rājasic* food became violent, restless and agitated (Joshi 1998:138). The hypothesis that food creates behavioral and mood changes has been replicated in studies in the West, where dietary links to behavior (body-mind) have been observed in controlled studies of children.

These studies have shown that a high consumption of foods that are artificially colored, flavored, excessively sugary and fatty or processed and refined results in hyperactivity, irritability, lack of concentration, aggression, violent or emotional outbursts and anti-social behavior. Although these studies may not have used the categories of *sāttvic, rājasic* and *tāmasic* foods, the results indicate the same conclusions and corroborate the findings of the Indian studies cited by Joshi (1998).

The role of the diet in influencing the mind is extremely complex and is an area that will benefit from further clinical research. For example, recent studies considering depression, anxiety, insomnia, alcoholism and bulimia have found links between diet and the chemicals in the brain that regulate moods and sleeping patterns. These brain chemicals also stimulate desire for carbohydrates and sugars, triggering cravings for food or drinks that a person feels unable to control.

Research into foods and psychology are intriguing in their implications, as well as concerning. Many foods we eat today have only recently been manufactured, and the long-term implications of such wide scale dietary changes may not be known for some years. For example, caffeine and chocolate have been considered in research into mental health conducted in Britain. They were found to have a detrimental impact on psychological problems such as anxiety, phobias, eating disorders, schizophrenia and depression.

The link between body-mind is not straightforward, and is still being clarified with modern scientific studies. The exact nature of the links between diet, mind and body is still not clearly understood despite such extensive studies. For example, the reasons for differences in results based on sex, age or ethnicity have not yet been fully explained.

However, the link between diet and psychological and emotional states is now conclusively recognized. What you eat or drink can, and does, ultimately influence your emotional state and mind balance. This can be in the short-term (alcohol, sugar, caffeine) or long-term (fats, refined and processed foods). Āyurveda has understood and taught about the relationship between mind and diet for centuries.

Lifestyle

Just as the state of mind can be enhanced with diet and nutrition, lifestyle factors also exert a major influence on mind equilibrium. Lifestyles that are stressful, erratic, excessively active and unbalanced can have a very negative impact on the mind *guṇa.* Activities and routines that are *sāttvic* in nature encourage the development of *sāttvic* qualities.

Sāttvic activities are calming, quiet, inspiring and mentally invigorating. They may include meditation, *yoga* or other forms of gentle exercise, listening to peaceful and classical music, enjoying nature and the outdoors, gardening, creative or artistic pursuits, or reading good quality literature. Meditation is calming and helps balance emotions, so passion, anger, fear and extreme emotions are minimized.

Dealing effectively with stress and anxiety is the role of the mind. Stress is a subjective experience—the mind interprets the external stimulus and the body responds. Accelerated heart beat, increased respiration or perspiration, a clenched jaw or fist, muscle tightness and digestive disorders can be physical responses to a perceived threat or stressful situation. The physical stress response eventually harms the body if it is frequently activated.

The skin, brain, heart, circulatory system and intestines can all show symptoms of chronic stress.

Managing stress with classic Āyurvedic concepts such as meditation, gentle exercise and breathing or relaxation exercises that control and calm the mind are now accepted as scientifically valid. Such practices stop the flow of hormones associated with stress, lower the heart rate and blood pressure and increase immunity. All of these factors have a significant positive effect on health.

The long-term impact of stress on the body and physical health has been studied extensively. Dr. Peeke, of the University of Maryland, asserts that the human body was not designed to deal with the prolonged stress associated with modern living or negative mind states like anxiety and frustration.

The first known study into stress and the response of the body considered immunity and resistance to viruses. This study, conducted less than a decade ago, showed that people who ranked highly on anxiety and stress were much more likely to develop symptoms of a cold or influenza when exposed to a respiratory virus. Studies done since then have refined the results to demonstrate that chronic, or on-going stress can at least triple the likelihood of contracting such illnesses.

Research by a Stanford psychiatrist, Dr. Spiegel, found that people who were naturally resistant to stress were able to maintain a remarkable peace of mind through spiritual faith and positive emotions such as optimism. The physical benefits of learning to adopt this balanced state of mind have been demonstrated clinically. For example, psoriasis sufferers who meditated during the course of conventional therapy healed in only around forty-six days, in comparison to double that time for the normal healing process.

In 1978, clinical research demonstrated that meditation retards and even reverses the aging process. Two groups of people were medically examined and tested by physiologists. One of those groups had meditated for more than five years. The results found that those who had mediated were biologically much younger than their chronological age. The long-term meditators were on average twelve years younger physically than their chronological age.

Another study in America, undertaken in 1986, may partly explain this. This study found that meditators produced a particular hormone associated with anti-aging and anti-cancer properties (DHEA or de-hydroepiandrosterone) in far greater quantities than those who did not meditate (Chopra 1991:175). The production of DHEA usually peaks around the age of thirty, and then begins to decline. Meditation seems to stimulate the continuing production of this hormone.

Having a balanced, calm and gentle approach to life is positive for both physical and mental health and only involves a change in attitude and routine. It involves being kind to your body and mind, through balanced and ethical behavior. Learning to reduce and deal with stress is a crucial aspect of this lifestyle approach. This can be achieved with a daily routine that includes meditation, massage and regulated sleeping and eating habits. These are all aspects of a *sāttvic* lifestyle, and are discussed further in chapter 9.

Emotions

The impact of positive and negative emotions and attitudes on health is also being analyzed and explored further by modern medical science, with some surprising clinical results. For example, the first study conducted into domestic arguments found that couples who fight frequently are damaging not only the relationship, but also their health. Scientists at the University of California found that arguing with your spouse suppresses the response of the immune system.

During an argument, the body releases cells into the blood stream that are meant to protect it in times of threat from the attack of viruses, infection and disease causing toxins. Emotional conflict results in such antibodies being released in large quantities. When an authentic physical threat to the body actually arrives, there are not enough cells to fight off the health hazard. People who argue frequently therefore have a greater risk of contracting disease and sickness.

Other studies have clarified the association between emotions and physical health. For example, a study conducted in California and reported in the *Journal of the American Medical Association* demonstrated that anger or hostility damages the arteries even in young adulthood. Hundreds of people between the ages of 18 and 30 were examined over a ten-year period. Those who displayed hostility, or an attitude of "cynical distrust", had up to 2.5 times the risk of developing hardening of the coronary arteries.

The impact of depression and anxiety on heart disease and other physical illnesses is well documented. Nevertheless, this is still being explored, often with alarming results. *The Archives of Internal Medicine* recently published a study that found that people suffering from depression had more than a 70% greater risk of suffering heart attacks and other heart diseases.

The profound nature of the mind-body link has only been superficially considered by modern medicine. However, it is already clear that mental health is an essential aspect of physical health.

The basis of Āyurvedic nutrition and lifestyle guidance is not only to balance the *doṣas*, but also to increase *sāttvic* temperament. This includes avoiding conflict, aggression, hostility and other negative emotions that have a detrimental impact on physical and mental health. Such a lifestyle is stress-resistant. It is serene, peaceful, patient and tolerant and avoids extremes of emotion.

Focusing on maximizing *sāttvic āhāra* and enhancing *sāttva guṇa* ultimately creates a pure and lasting happiness with total peace of mind. In Indian philosophy, happiness is divided into three types according to which mode or guṇa it was achieved in. Happiness that "tastes like poison in the beginning but in the end is like nectar" is said to be happiness obtained from the mode of *sattva*, or goodness.

Happiness that is derived from gratification or stimulation of the senses "appears like nectar in the beginning but is poison in the end" and is obtained in the mode of *rajas*, or passion. And happiness which is obtained with "delusion from beginning to end" and that arises from oversleeping, laziness and fantasy is achieved in the mode of *tamas*, or ignorance.

A *sāttvic* attitude not only benefits the individual, but also contributes to a more peaceful and productive community. Starting on an individual level by adopting Āyurvedic principles in your lifestyle can work towards peace and harmony in your family and community. Regardless of your faith, ethnic or economic background, modifying your diet and developing *sāttvic* qualities may seem a small step, but it is one in the right direction. The impact on your health, attitude and peace of mind will be remarkable.

The main factors involved are related to diet, lifestyle and emotions. In terms of diet, eat freshly prepared food, eat more plant based foods and decrease consumption of alcohol, caffeine, processed food and meat. Lifestyle should be balanced (between work, family and social concerns), with gentle exercise and regular routines to minimise stress. In relation to emotions, conflict, aggression and hostility should be minimised, and a positive and optimistic outlook adopted. Meditation to help you detach from and balance emotions is recommended.

Specific lifestyle and dietary considerations to achieve a *sāttva guṇa* and maintain health are discussed in more detail in part II of the book.

Chapter 5

Digestion & Metabolism

Good health depends upon the adequate digestion and assimilation of food. Undigested food will be harmful to the body, even it is nutritious and fresh. The digestion of food is carried out in the stomach (*jaṭhar*) by what is referred to metaphorically as a "fire" (*agni*).

In addition to the "stomach fire" (*jaṭharāgni)*, twelve other *agnis* operate in the body with responsibility for various metabolic activities. The *agnis*/fires are descriptive categories for types of enzymes, or conversion processes. There are seven *dhātu agnis* for the formation of tissues (*dhātus*) and five *bhūta agnis* responsible for the integration of the elements (*panca mahābhūtas*).

Of the thirteen *agnis*, the most important is the digestive fire/*jaṭharāgni*. The concept of *jaṭharāgni* is significant due to its central role in the digestive process, and the importance of digestion in the formation of nutritive fluid (*āhāra rasa*), the physical elements (*doṣas*), tissues (*dhātus*) and wastes (*malas*). It is vital to maintain the balanced functioning of *jaṭharāgni*, as the body depends on it in order to receive the proper nourishment.

Prior to starting a systematic treatment for any disease, defects in *agni* function are considered and investigated by the Ayurvedic physician, and efforts are made to correct them using herbal remedies that stimulate their functioning. Once the particular *agnis* are stimulated, they become more effective. This enhances the formation of tissues/*dhātus,* assists in the elimination of wastes/*mala* and prevents the formation of toxic deposits/*āma.*

Four States of *Agni*

When *doṣas* are aggravated, the functions of all the internal systems and *agnis* are affected. Four different states of *agni* exist in the body. Of these various states, three are due to the aggravation of each doṣa respectively (*vāta, pitta, kapha*) and the fourth state is considered the balanced state.

Viṣamāgni

This is an erratic and unstable agni state, arising due the influence of *vāta.* The functioning of the *jaṭharāgni* is variable—sometimes it digests food normally, and at other times slowly. This type of *agni* is often found in people with a *vāta doṣa* or when *vāta* is aggravated. Symptoms of *viṣamāgni* include constipation, distension or swelling of the abdomen, dysentery, colic type pain and wind, gas or gurgling sounds in the intestines.

Tikśṇāgni

The function of *agni* becomes too fast or strong in this state, which is due to an aggravation of *pitta.* It is often seen in people with a predominantly *pitta* constitution, or when *pitta* is disturbed. The *jaṭharāgni* becomes hyperactive, and can digest even large quantities of food in a very short amount of time, leaving the person feeling constantly hungry. Symptoms of this state of *agni* include a dry mouth and palate, a burning sensation in the stomach and excessive thirst.

Mandāgni

The *agni* begins to function at a minimal rate in this condition, which is often found in people with *kapha* aggravation or constitution. The *jaṭharāgni* cannot digest even a small quantity of food. Symptoms including nausea, vomiting, heaviness in the stomach, laziness, coughing, coating of the tongue and excessive salivation may be experienced when *agni* is in this condition.

Samāgni

The functioning of *agni* is normal and stable in this state, reflecting the balanced state of the three *doṣas* in the body. *Jaṭharāgni* can easily digest the normal diet and extract adequate nourishment. All the tissues/*dhātus*, cells and organs receive sufficient nutrition and a condition of good health is maintained.

Digestive Process

In the mouth, food is tasted with the tongue and chewed with the teeth. Salivary glands provide moisture and help break down the food. These actions are all enabled by the action of *prāṇa vāta*. When the food reaches the stomach it is kneaded into a dough-like consistency by *kledaka kapha*, and then exposed to *jaṭharāgni*, the digestive fire.

The *jaṭharāgni* heats the food and, with the assistance of *pācaka pitta*, forms the nutrient fluid—*āhāra rasa*. *Pitta* is a vital part of the entire digestive process, as it is responsible for heat, energy, acidic actions (such as gastric activity) and all conversion functions, such as those undertaken in the stomach and liver.

The nutrient fluid nourishes and forms the seven tissues/*dhātus*. This nutrient fluid/*āhāra rasa* is carried to the *dhātus* by *samāna vāta*. The portion of food with no nutritive value is termed *mala* or waste material. The waste/*mala* is transported by *apāna vāta* to the colon and rectum to be eliminated.

Importance of Good Digestion

Food is responsible for building the *dhātus*, maintaining the body, forming *ojas* (vital fluid), and increasing immunity. It provides energy to *prāṇa* and is responsible for generating willpower, determination and enthusiasm. Although food is necessary for these functions, the *jaṭharāgni* enables the food to be converted into a form that is useful for the body.

If *jaṭharāgni* is weak or defective, it is not able to digest food adequately. The *āhāra rasa* produced will be poor in quality or quantity, or both. Therefore, the *dhātus* and *ojas* will not receive proper nourishment and will inevitably become unbalanced. In addition, all the other metabolic processes and activities, which are dependent upon the *jaṭharāgni* for fuel and nourishment, will become ineffective.

If *jaṭharāgni* operates in a balanced way, the person stays in good health and enjoys a long life. If the function of the digestive process is impaired or unbalanced, the person becomes unhealthy and disease is generated, as a weak *jaṭharāgni* leads directly to an imbalance of *dhātus, malas* and *doṣas*. If it is totally destroyed, death results.

Kāya cikitsā is one of the eight branches of Āyurveda. *Caraka Saṁhitā* defines *kāya* as a synonym for *agni* (or *jaṭharāgni*) and *cikitsā* as "treatment." Internal medicine, or *Kāya cikitsā* basically means treatment of the digestive fire. This indicates the central role of *jaṭharāgni* in maintaining health and the impact of digestion on the disease process.

When treating people who are sick, an astute Āyurvedic physician usually prescribes some herbal medicines to improve the strength of *jaṭharāgni*, even if there are no visible symptoms related to a weak or disturbed digestive process. If the *jaṭharāgni* is impaired in any manner, the patient will not be able to digest and absorb the remedies provided.

Digestion, *Āma* and Disease

If the *jaṭharāgni* is not robust enough to digest food thoroughly, or becomes overwhelmed with food that it cannot process, *āma* is created as a toxic by-product. *Āma* is the material arising from any undigested food, and can develop in two ways.

- **Due to a weak *jaṭharāgni***: If the functioning of the digestive fire is weak, all the food consumed is not fully digested. Some food remains in an undigested form, and transforms into *āma*.
- **Improper eating**: Even if the *jaṭharāgni* is normal in strength and function, it may not be able to digest food adequately if excessive amounts are consumed, and *āma* results. Eating appropriate foods according to the strength of the digestive fire, as well as following basic eating guidelines, is necessary for complete digestion. Eating food prior to the last meal being fully digested, or consuming inappropriate combinations of food, also produces *āma*.

Āma mixes with circulating fluids (mainly *rasa*/lymph and *rakta*/blood) and travels to different parts of the body. While traveling around the body, the *āma* is deposited at those locations or in those systems with a weak immunity. As it builds up at those sites, it begins to block the *srotas* (channels) or unbalance the *doṣas*, instigating the related diseases that follow such imbalances.

Āma impairs the functioning of the organ or system it gathers in, and causes different diseases depending on the location of its accumulation. For example, when *āma* collects in the lungs, it may cause congestion, coughs or asthma. When located in the joints, it leads to arthritis. In the intestines, *āma* affects absorption of *āhāra rasa* and creates illnesses such as dysentery, diarrhea, irritable bowel syndrome and so on.

Āma is therefore a significant factor in the disease process, and is becoming an increasing problem in modern society. One reason for the increasing creation of toxicity in the body is that people do not establish regular habits or follow eating routines.

In addition, many of the basic eating rules are ignored or overlooked. These guidelines are covered in chapters 7 and 8.

A high proportion of foods commonly consumed today encourage *āma* production. This includes fast foods, packaged and processed foods, fried foods, white flour and sugar products, and animal and dairy products. All of these foods are heavy in nature and difficult to digest. Whenever possible, these foods should be avoided to prevent excessive production of *āma* in the body.

Symptoms of *Āma* Production

If symptoms of *āma* begin to appear, it is a sign that either the *jaṭharāgni* is not strong or eating habits are inappropriate. These are the two main factors involved in the formation of *āma*. General symptoms caused by the presence of *āma* in the body are:

- Laziness, lethargy or weakness
- Depression, irritability
- Slight fever
- General pain in the body
- Loss of appetite
- Heaviness in the stomach
- Constipation
- Formation of gas or wind
- A coating on the tongue
- Bad breath
- Excessive perspiration
- Pungent perspiration
- Dull skin and eyes
- Cloudy urine
- Mucus in the stool
- Stool that does not float

Āma cannot be removed naturally from the body, as there are no *srotas* (channels) for its elimination. Mucus on the tongue or in the stool, cloudy urine or strong perspiration may expel some *āma* by chance, but these are symptoms of excessive *āma* toxicity rather than routine methods of removal. The *panca karma* techniques (chapter 11) eliminate built-up waste materials and *āma,* stabilize the *doṣas* and clean the *srotas*/channels. Taking Āyurvedic herbal remedies can also neutralize or destroy *āma*. When the channels are clean, the *agnis* work more efficiently and *āma* production is more easily prevented.

Measures to minimize *āma*

As discussed, improper digestion of food is one of the main causes of āma formation. To minimize the production of *āma*, complete digestion of food needs to be achieved. In order to enable complete digestion and maintain good health and longevity, you should establish a regular eating routine, follow the basic principles for eating and choose a diet that can be easily digested. To assist the *jaṭharāgni* digest food:

- Select a diet that is light, fresh and mainly plant based. Decrease the consumption of fried and processed foods, white flour and sugar products, caffeine and alcohol.
- Increase intake of fruits, boiled or steamed vegetables, bitter foods, vegetable soup, vegetable and fruit juices and buttermilk (recipe in appendix 5).
- The quantity and type of foods consumed should not weaken or overburden the *jaṭharāgni*, leading to symptoms like heaviness or drowsiness after eating, gas or indigestion.
- Certain herbs can also act as a tonic for the *jaṭharāgni*, including *citrak*, mint and ginger. A homemade tonic that can stimulate digestion consists of peeled and finely chopped fresh ginger and lemon juice. A small glass container is half filled with the ginger, and then the remaining half is filled with lemon juice and a pinch of salt. Eat half a teaspoon of this mixture before meals.
- The use of particular spices in cooking, including turmeric, cumin, cayenne, asafoetida, and coriander assist digestion.
- Regular exercise, oil massage, and occasional fasting (one day every two weeks) contribute to cleansing and maintaining the strength of the digestive system. On days of fasting, foods such as fruits and light vegetable soup can be eaten, and drinks can include juices, herbal tea and water with lemon juice.
- Some Āyurvedic herbal preparations can be used when the *jaṭharāgni* has become impaired. The most popular and common remedies include *Lavaṇa Bhāskar* powder and *Citrakādi* tablets.

Symptoms of weak *jaṭharāgni* and some illnesses, such as indigestion, loss of appetite, dyspepsia and flatulence, are relieved or cured through following the above dietary recommendations. Within two or three weeks, a noticeable difference in general health and well-being can be observed. To determine a more personalized diet, an Āyurvedic physician can be consulted.

The daily and seasonal routines, dietary guidelines, massage therapy (*abhyanga*), and detoxification therapies (*panca karma*) all aim to enhance and keep the *jaṭharāgni* in a balanced state. Maintaining a healthy digestive system avoids the development of many painful and disturbing disorders. This is the secret of good health and longevity.

Like a new car, a person up to the age of forty years is generally in good health with all senses and internal systems functioning. High immunity and swift recuperation from illness is enjoyed. After the age of forty however, one needs to be more careful in maintaining a proper diet and lifestyle, as many chronic diseases may occur if these matters are neglected.

It is even better to begin at an earlier age than this, and take undemanding preventative measures through some basic dietary precautions. This attention to health can assist in avoiding many of the problems associated with growing old. Eating fresh, good quality food helps in the prevention of common diseases and disorders. These are usually considered an inevitable part of aging, but can be prevented with awareness of the body and its needs.

Waste Products—*Malas*

Another basic constituent of the body is waste material, known as *mala*. A general definition of *mala* is "*malinīkaraṇa mala*", which means those materials that, when accumulated internally, cause impurity or disease. **Feces, urine** and **sweat** are the three main *malas*. If they gather in the body beyond a certain limit, they will cause the organs, *dhātus* and *doṣas* to become impure and lead to physical disorders.

They are also considered wastes/*malas* because they are excreted from the body through specific channels/*srotas*, purely as a by-product of the digestive process. "*Malinīkarṇāda āhāra malatvānmala*" explains this further, meaning "wastes arise from the process of digesting food and they make the body impure—that is why they are wastes" (*Vāgabhaṭṭa, Aṣṭānga Sangraha*).

As food is processed, and *āhāra rasa* is transformed into various *dhātus*, wastes are also created. The by-products of metabolic processes are eliminated at each step of *dhātu* formation, as they have no further use in any system or structure of the body. The fact that they have no further physical function means that their removal is required through various outlets or passages designed for that purpose. If this normal excretory process is disturbed or blocked, they will increase in quantity internally. Their build-up beyond a certain limit causes *malinīkaraṇa* or poisoning of various organs, systems or functions of the body.

Classification of Wastes

The three types of wastes/*mala* mentioned above (feces, urine and sweat) are the main types of *mala*. Waste materials created from *dhātu* production are collected through various channels, combined with the *malas* mentioned and then eliminated. Minor types of *mala* include earwax, and discharge from the nose, eyes and throat. Body hair and nails (wastes of bone tissue/*asthi dhātu*) are also in the minor *mala* group. These *malas* usually do not create disease, even though they are wastes. Therefore, feces, urine and sweat are only considered when discussing *malas*.

Doṣas or *dhātus* may also cause impurity or imbalance, when present in excessive amounts. Under certain conditions, they may also be considered *malas* according to a general application of the definition. However, the definition provided above by *Vāgabhaṭṭa* explains some specific attributes of *mala*. One of these is *malinīkaraṇa*—"making impure." This is listed as the main attribute of *malas*. In the case of *doṣas* or *dhātus*, *malinīkaraṇa* is not their main attribute, although they do create impurities under certain conditions. They may be considered as temporary *malas* in those cases. As they have different primary functions and attributes from *mala* they are not generally classified in this category.

Āma is also not classified as a *mala* due to the specific qualities ascribed to the waste materials. *Malas* are a normal by-product of the digestive process and metabolic activity, and have particular excretory channels for elimination. Up to a certain quantity, mala is also necessary for healthy functioning. Food is automatically transformed into both *mala* and *āhāra rasa* in order for the body to assimilate nutrients. In contrast, *āma* is the toxic product of undigested food and has no excretory channels for elimination. It represents unassimilated nutrients. It is not required for the healthy functioning of the body and therefore has a separate category of its own.

Wastes and Health

Proper elimination of *mala* is one criterion for good health, as accumulation leads to various diseases created from impurities within the body. As *mala* naturally occurs as a result of metabolic processes, they are not harmful to the body within certain limits. It is probably more appropriate to call them "metabolic end products" rather than "waste products" as they actually have a legitimate function in maintaining health, and are not simply "body garbage."

A certain quantity of *mala* is necessary to sustain the body. For example, many nutrients stay in the stool or feces after digestion of food in the stomach, and are absorbed through the large intestine. If a person expels feces without the proper processing through the large intestine (diarrhea), it is considered an illness. The person becomes physically weak, as nutrients are lost from the body. Similarly, if too much urine is passed (a condition known as polyuria), it is classified as an abnormality and results in physical weakness.

If there were no value to the body in any of these wastes, the person experiencing these conditions should instead become healthier and stronger—due to the ability to pass them from the body rapidly and in large quantities! It is the accumulation above a certain limit that causes disease, as well as excretion above a certain limit. Within this range, the presence of mala is normal and an indicator of proper internal processing.

Elimination of Wastes

Improper elimination of wastes/*malas* creates particular imbalances, depending upon the type of *mala* and the nature of the incorrect discharge. If *malas* are not evacuated from the body in a timely manner, they can be reabsorbed and then circulated within the body. In addition, suppression or blockage of the elimination process causes discomfort, irritation, and pressure in the relevant channels/*srotas* as well as surrounding organs.

Poor or impeded excretion of *malas* has a link with tissue/*dhātu* disorders. This is because the by-products of *dhātu* creation are combined with feces, urine and sweat for elimination. If the *malas* are not eliminated, then the *dhātu* wastes also accumulate within the *dhātu*. This explains why constipation, for example, usually indicates problems elsewhere in the body, as well as in the channel/*srota* for elimination. Unusual perspiration or urine (such as abnormal quantity, color or odor) are also indicative of *dhātu* irregularities.

The role of urine and feces in revealing the internal operations of the body is acknowledged in Western medical science as well. Examinations to check the various constituents of *malas* are standard practice when considering the state of health or the nature of the physical disorder.

Wastes should always be eliminated from the body when the natural urge for this is experienced. One should not try to forcefully stop the urge to pass out *malas*. Some of the common symptoms experienced due to not allowing the wastes to be expelled from the body are headache, pain in the genitals, colon, or lower legs, feeling of nausea and drowsiness, distension in the bladder or stomach and formation of wind.

In particular, if the natural urge to pass stool is not attended to, then after a period of time that urge is lost. When the urge to do so returns, the feces have become hard and dry because most of the water has been absorbed. Regular suppression can affect the functioning of the intestine and lead to chronic constipation.

Stool or feces—*purīṣa*

Feces are the solid waste from digestion, incorporating waste products from *dhātus* creation. Due to this relationship with *dhātus*, treating constipation is often an effective treatment for a range of seemingly unrelated illnesses such as bronchitis, asthma, lumbago and rheumatoid arthritis. These conditions involve wastes accumulating in the joints and lungs, as *malas* have built-up in the *dhātus* or have been reabsorbed and deposited within the body. This accumulation may prevent remedies prescribed operating effectively, unless the wastes are first removed.

This is also the rationale for an Āyurvedic physician inquiring about bowel movements—to ascertain whether any health conditions experienced have a link with the bowel movements of the patient. A healthy person should have a bowel movement at least once a day. Passing stool twice a day is also normal. If a history of constipation is established, then herbal remedies to treat that condition are also prescribed when treating the related *dhātu* disorder.

If there is diminished elimination, and a person does not pass stool at least once a day, it is known as constipation. As a result of this condition, the waste products stay in the intestine. This puts pressure on the nearby organs, causing painful symptoms. It can aggravate and block the channel/*srota*, creating difficulty in moving the bowel, or feces may be passed in very small fragments over a long period of time.

The consistency of the stool can alternate between being loose and watery and very hard. There is an urge to pass the feces very often and hemorrhoids may result. Colic type symptoms, flatulence and wind formation, distension of the abdomen, drowsiness and headache are other symptoms experienced from constipation. Diseases related to the colon or lower intestine and rectum are associated with constipation. Treatment of constipation is discussed in the home remedies section (chapter 12).

Diarrhea occurs when an excessive amount of loose, watery stool is passed. In this case, the person is losing nutrients, as stool is passed before it is adequately processed by the intestine. The nutrients required to nourish the tissues and other organs are expelled instead of being circulated for absorption. Liquids which are vital for the functioning of systems and tissues/*dhātus*, are not absorbed sufficiently, leading to dehydration.

Symptoms of diarrhea include pain in the chest region, colon, stomach and lower back. A lot of gas may be mobile in the intestines, creating gurgling sounds and causing discomfort. The patient becomes weak and dizzy. It is imperative in these situations that sufficient water is consumed, which can be mixed with sugar and salt. There are various home remedies that can be used to reduce symptoms such as eating bananas, apples, boiled rice and natural yogurt, or boiled rice mixed with natural yogurt. In severe cases, medicines may be required to bind the feces and prevent continuing expulsion.

Urine—*mūtra*

A healthy person usually passes urine between four to six times during the waking hours (approximately 50 ounces, or 1.4 litres). If a person is passing markedly more or less than this frequency, it should be considered cause for concern as it may indicate a symptom of developing disorders, or a disease.

Suppression of the necessity to pass urine can lead to infections in the urinary tract, bladder or the urethra. The symptoms caused by suppressing the urge to urinate include painful urination, pain in the thighs and sometimes burning sensation when passing urine.

If the quantity of urine passed is diminished, there is often pain in the bladder and urinary tract, painful and burning urination, change in the normal color of urine, and swelling in feet, ankles and face. The treatment for such condition is to increase the consumption of liquids, particularly diuretics that have sweet, sour and salty tastes, juices and water. Barley water, coconut water and sugarcane juice are very beneficial. If the quantity of urea excreted in urine is less than normal, it will remain in the body causing damage to the kidneys.

When the quantity of the urine eliminated is excessive, the urge to pass urine is experienced frequently, along with pain and distension in the bladder, weakness and pain in the legs, and excessive thirst and dryness in the mouth.

Sweat—*sveda*

Regular sweating is also necessary to clean out toxins from the body. It is very healthy to engage in regular exercise for this purpose. Therapies like saunas and steam baths (*svedana*) are also useful to encourage perspiration. Certain herbs or Āyurvedic medicines are beneficial in inducing sweating, and are frequently used in the treatment of fevers. In these cases, sweating provides immediate relief through removing the toxins that are causing disturbance in the body.

Excessive perspiration can lead to an accumulation of bacteria, creating unpleasant body odor. Fungal infections in locations that are consistently moist, such as between the toes or folds of skin can also occur. Diminished elimination of sweat creates blockage of the pores of the skin, which becomes dry and may crack. Skin sensation is reduced and body hair may fall out. It also has an impact on the internal temperature regulating system.

Chapter 6

Physiology

Physiological aspects of the body are prime indicators of our health. Tissues like skin, muscles or fat readily display symptoms of internal malfunction or disease. Channels within the body that are responsible for transporting oxygen, blood, food and wastes also have a significant role in our physical condition. Tissues (*dhātus*) and channels (*srotas*) are the primary features of our biology considered in this chapter. Together, they contribute to our immunity, strength and longevity (*ojas*).

Tissues—*Dhātus*

The body is built with *dhātus*. They are the basic tissues that maintain and nourish the body, and are cellular matter in either solid or fluid form. The meaning of *dhātu* in Sanskrit is "*dhāraṇāta dhātu*"—"That which sustains or nourishes is called *dhātu*." As sustenance of all organs and systems is the primary function of *dhātus*, their proper formation and balanced functioning is very important for good health.

The *dhātus* are formed in the body in a sequential order, and each has a particular relationship to the one preceding it and following it. As there are seven *dhātus* in total, they are known as *saptadhātu* (*sapta* meaning seven).

- *Rasa* plasma or lymph
- *Rakta* blood
- *Māṁsa* muscle
- *Meda* fatty tissue
- *Asthi* bone
- *Majjā* marrow
- *Śukra* reproductive fluid

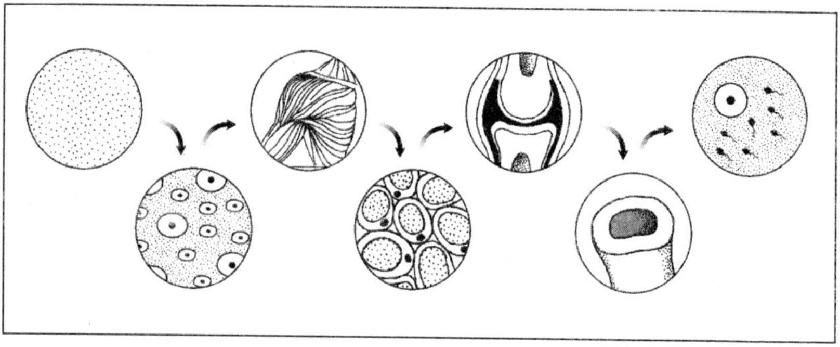

Figure 5 The Seven Dhātus

There is another group of tissues in the body that sustain the body, but do not nourish it. They are known as "sub" or "supplementary" *dhātu* (*upadhātu*). They are similar in nature but do not perform identical functions, and include tendons and skin.

Formation of *Dhātus*

Like the three *doṣas*, the *dhātus* are made up of the five elements. The food we consume is the main component in their formation. During digestion, food is separated into two portions. One part is waste (*mala*) and the other is the nutrient portion in a liquid form, known as *āhāra rasa*. This is the "essence" of the food, and is transported to the heart by the action of *samān vāta*. From the heart, *vyāna vāta* circulates the *āhāra rasa* all over the body where it is transformed into various *dhātus*.

The transformation of *āhāra rasa* into *dhātus* is performed by metabolic processes *(dhātu agnis)*. Just as there is a special type of digestive fire (*jaṭharāgni*) for the digestion of food, each *dhātu* has a special metabolic fire (*dhātu agni*) to process *āhāra rasa*. If food is not digested properly in order to create an effective *āhāra rasa*, the formation of all of the *dhātus* will be negatively affected. If there is an inadequate supply of *āhāra rasa*, there will be insufficient nutrients to form healthy *dhātus*.

The formation of *dhātus* by *dhātu agnis* involves a transformation similar to the digestive process, which converts food into two parts (food essence/*āhāra rasa* and waste/*mala*). As āhāra rasa is transformed into dhātus, some nutritive fluid remains which provides nutrition for the next *dhātu*, and a by-product is generated (*mala*). The waste products generated at each stage of *dhātu* formation are ultimately disposed of via different excretory channels.

Each *dhātu* receives nutrition from the previous *dhātu*, and provides nutrition to the next. So the quality and quantity of each *dhātu* affects the quality and quantity of those subsequently formed. If a *dhātu* is deficient in nourishment (quality) or formation (quantity), it will absorb the required nutrients from the preceding *dhātu* to try to make up for this deficiency. For example, if too much *śukra dhātu* is released from the body, then to make up for the deficiency, nutrition from *majjā dhātu* will be absorbed which in turn will take nutrition from the *asthi dhātu* and so on.

According to the original Āyurvedic texts, three basic rules relate to the formation of *dhātus*:

- ***Kedārikulyā***: *Dhātus* are formed consecutively from one primary source (the same *āhāra rasa*) until all *dhātu* formation is complete.
- ***Khale kapot***: Each *dhātu* has its own transportation channel to deliver the *āhāra rasa*, known as the *srota*. The channel/ *srota* is proportionate in length to the order of that *dhātu* in

the hierarchy of creation. That is, the first *dhātu* formed (*rasa)*, has the shortest channel and the last one (*śukra)*, the longest.

- ***Kśīra dadhi***: The *āhāra rasa* is taken to the different locations of *dhātu* formation by the action of *vyāna vāta*. On reaching the destination, the *āhāra rasa* is directly transformed into the respective *dhātu*.

Imbalance of *Dhātus*

The *dhātus* are present in specific proportions, and any imbalance in this proportion can create disease. *Dhātus* do not create imbalance or disease independently of aggravated *doṣas*. Once a *doṣa* is aggravated, it disperses throughout the body and relocates in a *dhātu*. When disturbed by a *doṣa*, the *dhātu* is termed *dūṣya*, which means "the location of an aggravated *doṣa*". The disturbed *dhātu* (*dūṣya*) manifests in a variety of physical ailments.

In all chronic diseases, there are usually symptoms related to *dhātu/s* disturbance. This is because the aggravated *doṣa* relocates in one or more *dhātu/s* and creates an imbalance in that tissue. Consideration of the *dhātus* themselves is therefore very important when diagnosing disease. There are many diseases related to deficiencies, excesses or improper formation of certain *dhātus* in the body. For example, muscular dystrophy is a disease caused by the improper formation of muscle/*māṁsa dhātu*.

According to modern medicine, this disease is difficult or even impossible to treat, but Āyurveda has remedies for muscular dystrophy, and many other conditions related to *dhātu* irregularities. Sometimes the disease is related to the metabolic process (*dhātu agni*), or the *srota* carrying the nutrients. In other cases, it may be the *āhāra rasa*, which is not rich enough to adequately nourish the *dhātu*. Identifying the *dhātu* deficiency and its source is therefore essential to determine the appropriate treatment.

When the *dhātus* are unbalanced, various symptoms are displayed. The following table lists some of these symptoms, with natural remedies to assist in balancing them.

Table 9: *Dhātu* Imbalance and Treatment

Dhātu	Symptoms	Treatment
Rasa/plasma upadhātu Menstrual blood Breast milk	Anorexia, lethargy and drowsiness, nausea, fainting, yellowing of skin (jaundice), graying of hair, wrinkled skin, impotency, indigestion and coating of the tongue	Fasting Fruit, vegetable juices, aloe vera, seaweed (kelp and agar agar), apples, bananas, potatoes, beans, wholegrain cereals, nuts
Rakta/blood upadhātu Blood vessels Tendons	Skin problems including acne, pimples, leucoderma, bruising, black moles, rashes, scabies and ring worms, menstrual disorders, abscesses, mouth ulcers and disorders in which the blood flows out of the body, (e.g. epistaxis)	*Prāṇāyama*, fasting *Virecana* (laxatives) *Rakta mokśaṇa* (blood letting) Iron rich foods—green vegetables, whole grains, nuts, apricots, wheatgerm, peanuts, dried fruit
Māṁsa/muscles upadhātu Skin Body oils	Swelling in throat (uvula), gangrene, tumors, abscesses, cysts, tumors in muscles, tonsillitis, muscular dystrophy and weak muscles, postural problems	*Yoga*, oil massage Surgery or cauterization Protein rich foods—grains, legumes, milk
Meda/fat upadhātu Ligaments Sinews	Numbness, increased discharge of strong smelling fluids from the body (sweat, urine), dryness of mouth and throat, burning sensation, indigestion, sweet taste in the mouth	Exercise *Svedana* (sweat therapy) *Vamana* (supervised vomiting) Wheat germ, lecithin, flax seeds, milk, cheese
Asthi/bones	Pain in the bones, teeth cavities and weakness, various hair and nail disorders, osteoporosis and atrophy of the bones	*Basti* (enema) Calcium rich foods—milk, yogurt,cheese, cream, sunflower and sesame seeds
Majjā/marrow	Giddiness, deep abscesses, numbness, fainting, impairment in the formation of blood cells and pain in the joints (especially fingers)	Detoxification, *Svedana* Exercise Vitamin B rich foods—grains, beans, milk, nuts, sesame seeds
Śukra/semen-ova	Impotency and infertility, negative effects on the health of children produced (including under-developed organs)	Detoxification *Rasāyana, Vājīkaraṇa* Exercise Bitter food

Ojas

Ojas is the "essence" of the seven *dhātus*. In the original texts, *ojas* is described after the seven *dhātus*. For this reason, some authors consider it the eighth *dhātu*. *Suśruta Saṁhitā* describes the prescence of *ojas* in the body: "As *ghī* (clarified butter) is present in milk but cannot be seen, in the same way, *ojas* is present in all of the *dhātus* in a very subtle form." Although *ojas* is present throughout the body, the heart is its specific location and seat.

Like the *dhātus, ojas* obtains nutrition from *āhāra rasa* and a *sāttvic* lifestyle. *Ojas* gives stability to *dhātus* and is responsible for the immunity of the body. As *ojas* is a vital energy giving fluid that provides power and strength, in some texts the words "strength" or "immunity" have been used as synonyms for it.

The function of *ojas* is to sustain the vital force of the body. As long as *ojas* is present, strength, energy and immunity are high. All mental and physical activities, as well as sense functioning, are directly or indirectly carried out by *ojas*. When the supply of *ojas* is exhausted, death results. *Caraka Saṁhitā* notes that even if the *tridoṣa* are functioning at their maximum vitality and are in a balanced state, a person dies when the supply of *ojas* in the body finishes.

Types of *Ojas*

Ojas is either of the *para* or the *apara* type. The *para ojas* is in a fixed proportion, and if even a minute fraction of this is lost, the person dies immediately. This has led some Āyurvedic doctors to deduce that the *para ojas* is inherently connected to the soul/ *ātmā*, or that it directly nourishes the consciousness. As it is situated in the heart, if there is sufficient damage or shock to the heart disturbing the *para ojas*, death is instantaneous. For example, any wound to the heart from shooting, stabbing or a severe heart attack usually results in a swift and unavoidable death.

In contrast, the *apara ojas* circulates throughout the body and is present in larger quantities than *para ojas*. It varies in proportion depending upon the state of health. If *apara ojas* is in the proper proportion and quality, mental, physical and spiritual health is excellent. Any disturbance of *apara ojas* creates physical symptoms, disease and ultimately death.

If the *apara ojas* is displaced (not located in the proper *dhātus)*, the *doṣas* become disturbed and symptoms of *tridoṣa* imbalance appear. Physical, mental and verbal activities become inconsistent, irregular or unstable. Loose joints, fatigue and lack of mental or physical energy are evident. If it is poor in quality or quantity, symptoms of heaviness in the body, stiffness in joints, edema or swelling, excessive lethargy and diminished vitality of the skin are apparent.

If the *apara ojas* is decreased, the *dhātus* become weakened and contracted. Muscle/*māṁsa* and fat/*meda* is lost and the body becomes emaciated or skeletal, while the senses become less effective. Hearing, vision or taste may become impaired, and the mind may be clouded, confused and weak. Skin becomes dehydrated and dull. The person becomes delirious, fearful and anxious, and lapses into a coma or loses consciousness before death occurs.

Maintaining *Ojas*

To maintain good health, or when undergoing any form of treatment, one primary aim should be to increase *ojas*. There are many kinds of activities, foods, diets, herbs in Āyurveda prescribed for this purpose. *Ojas* is increased when a happy and relaxed frame of mind is achieved. Meditation and conserving *śukra dhātu* assist in sustaining *ojas*. Milk, *ghī* and the rejuvenating herbs (*rasāyanas*) increase *ojas*, as do all the foods and activities that enhance *sāttva guṇa* (see chapter 4).

Ojas is destroyed through harmful diet and lifestyle. Experiencing negative emotions (anger, anxiety, stress, grief), hunger or excessive fasting, over-indulgence in sexual activity and overwork all deplete the *ojas* and therefore should be avoided if possible. Eating *tāmasic* food, intense activity, lack of sleep and an irregular lifestyle are further factors that may diminish the quality or quantity of *ojas* available to the body. Chemicals, pollution, extreme weather conditions and chronic sickness also play a role in *ojas* destruction.

When *ojas* becomes low, the immunity of the body weakens and the person becomes mentally and physically fragile or sick. Some contemporary Āyurvedic experts have compared these symptoms with the modern disease of AIDS, or Acquired Immune Deficiency Syndrome. This is because most of the symptoms experienced by people suffering from AIDS are very similar to those caused by diminished *ojas* mentioned above.

It is very important to monitor the status of *ojas* in the body when healing a patient, or while trying to maintain good health. In any treatment, the physician should always include an *ojas* increasing diet, regimen and herbs. This diet/*āhāra* will increase immunity and assist in recovery from illness.

Channels—*Srotas*

The channels/*srotas* also perform particular functions and have a role in the disease process. The definition of *srota* in *Caraka Saṁhitā* is "*sravaṇāta srotansi*" meaning "that which carries things." They are the transportation channels, responsible for carrying various materials around the body. Like all other aspects of physiology, the *srotas* also consist of the five elements. The element of space/*ākāśa* is the dominant *mahābhūta* responsible for their construction.

Srotas vary widely in size, shape and structure. Some are round, large and wide, whereas others are very small, long, and in the form of a web-like net. They are either visible or invisible channels. The *srotas* include all the larger conduits within the body such as the intestinal tract, lymphatic system, urinary tract and the reproductive organs. The microscopic channels such as blood capillaries are also *srotas*.

Function of Channels

The main function of channels/*srotas* is transportation of all materials. They transport physical elements (*doṣas*), tissues (*dhātus*), wastes (*malas*), food (*āhāra*), nutritive fluid (*āhāra rasa*), air (*prāṇa*) and nerve impulses and signals from the senses (*indriyas*). All the bodily functions therefore depend on *srotas* in one way or another. Their crucial role of transportation of bodily fluids and materials makes their proper functioning vital for health.

Blockage of *srotas* prevents the efficient transportation of nutrients and fluids necessary for optimum physical and mental operation. Often, the blockage of *srotas* is a significant factor of the disease process. The blockage is usually caused by *āma*, the toxic material that arises from incomplete or poor digestion. To avoid *āma* blocking the *srotas*, it is necessary to maintain good digestion (see chapter 5).

Fasting helps clear the channels, as it removes *āma* and increases the strength of digestion/*jaṭharāgni*. If the *jaṭharāgni* is strong, *āma* will not be formed to accumulate in *srotas*. Timely excretion of waste materials/*malas*, and regular physical exercise are also important in order to keep the *srotas* clean and operating efficiently.

Impaired Channels

The ultimate cause of the diseased state is an imbalance of *doṣas*. Relief from pain and physical distress may be obtained by balancing the *doṣas*, but a permanent cure will not be achieved unless any malfunctioning *srotas* are also identified and treated. If the *srotas* are normal, then *doṣas, dhātus* and *malas* receive proper nutrition and transportation, and thus are able to function in equilibrium. As a result of this equilibrium the body is healthy. If the function of *srotas* is disturbed, there will be an imbalance in *doṣas, dhātus* or *malas* and disease may be manifested.

The disturbance or impairment of the normal functioning of *srotas* is termed "*sroto duṣṭi.*" There are several causes of *sroto duṣṭi*. Diets and lifestyles that are very similar in nature to the dominant *doṣa* of the person will aggravate the *doṣa* and ultimately lead to *srota* disturbance. So a *kapha* person with a highly *kapha* diet and lifestyle may eventually suffer from *sroto duṣṭi*. A diet that decreases the *dhātus* also causes imbalance in the functioning of *srotas*. Improper diet and lifestyle create an imbalance in the *doṣas*, which in turn aggravates the *dhātus*, and from this arises *sroto duṣṭi*. *Āma* may also block the channels/*srotas*.

When *srotas* become abnormal, their functioning is impaired. The affected *srotas* also influence the functioning of neighboring *srotas*, as they are inter-related. For example, in the case of a common cold, initially the *srotas* located in the nose are affected causing mucus blockage and loss of smell. Then the neighboring *srotas*, those in the throat, are affected and cause irritation and coughing. The *srotas* of the ear may also become affected, causing pressure, pain or difficulty in hearing. From there, the *srotas* in the head become disturbed, leading to headaches or migraines.

When *doṣas* and *dhātus* are aggravated but the function of *srotas* is normal, symptoms of sickness will be created throughout the body. This is because the *srotas* spread the aggravated *doṣas* or *dhātus* throughout the body. For example, fever results in high temperature and sore muscles all over the body.

If the function of *srotas* is abnormal, then the transportation of aggravated *doṣas* or *dhātus* is not possible. In that case, they will remain localized and cause disease in one location only. Arthritis and swelling, for example, may result. Various types of tumors or cysts result from *sroto duṣṭi*. These are caused when the *doṣa, dhātu, mala* or other fluids are blocked in one place.

Srota duṣṭi should be very carefully considered when making a diagnosis and prescribing treatments. If only the *doṣas* or *dhātus* are involved, therapies to balance them are considered appropriate. However, if there is *sroto duṣṭi* (*srota* obstruction), the removal of this blockage also needs to be a factor of treatment.

One of the ways to tell whether the disease is caused by *sroto duṣṭi* as well as by aggravation of tissues/*dhātus*, is to observe the symptoms of the disease closely. If the symptoms are spread all over the body there is no *sroto duṣṭi*, as the *srotas* have been involved in transporting the disease and its symptoms. If the symptoms are localized (present only in one place), *sroto duṣṭi* must be involved.

Symptoms of *sroto duṣṭi*

In cases of *sroto duṣṭi*, the disturbed *dhātu/s* and *srota/s* will show symptoms similar to the attributes of the aggravated *doṣa*. For example, in a case of *sroto duṣṭi* due to *vāta*, there will be *vāta* like symptoms such as dryness and spasm of the *srotas*. The symptoms of the *sroto duṣṭi* help in diagnosing which *doṣa* or *dhātu* is aggravated. Once that is determined, the treatment is clear: the aggravated *doṣa* or *dhātu* simply needs to be balanced. Symptoms of *sroto duṣṭi* include:

- Increase in the quantity of the fluids or materials flowing in the *srotas*, such as diarrhea, excessive perspiration or urination, swelling or water retention.
- Obstruction in the *srotas* due to inadequate elimination of toxins and wastes, such as constipation or arteriosclerosis. This impediment to efficient transportation prevents materials and fluids from reaching their required destination.
- Formation of tumors in or on the *srotas*, creating pressure on the *srotas* and blocking the flow of circulation. In some cases the size of the tumor is so large that the flow is blocked completely. In these cases, the materials or fluids in the *srotas* will seep out into the surrounding tissues or organs and cause *sroto duṣṭi* in the neighboring *srotas* as well.
- Flowing of fluids or material in the opposite or wrong direction in the *srota*, such as vomiting where there is a reverse flow of food in the esophagus, or hyper-acidity where the stomach acid sometimes rises into the mouth.

Table 10: *Srota* Aggravation and Treatment

Srota	Transports	Aggravated by	Remedies
Prāṇa-vaha	*Prāṇa*—life air respiration	Excessive exercise or physical work, hunger, dehydration	*Prāṇāyama* Chest massage
Udaka-vaha	Bodily fluids—water, lymph	Alcohol, exposure to heat and sun, indigestion, eating dry foods, thirst	Fluid intake Diuretic herbs
Anna-vaha	Nutrition—food and drinks	Weak digestion, over eating, eating in conflict with season/constitution	Fasting Ginger
Rasa-vaha	*Rasa dhātu*—Plasma, lymph	Heavy, cold, oily or greasy foods, anxiety, stress and worry	Massage, Meditation Anti-*kapha* regime
Rakta-vaha	*Rakta dhātu*—blood	Hot, spicy, sour foods and drinks, tea, coffee, alcohol, exposure to heat/sun	*Rakta Mokśaṇa* Anti-*pitta* regime
Māṁsa-vaha	*Māṁsa dhātu*—muscle nutrients	Fried foods, oils, fats and meat, sleeping in the day or after meals	Massage, *Vamana* Surgery or cauterization
Meda-vaha	*Meda dhātu*—fat tissue	Lack of physical work or exercise, greasy or oily foods, sleeping during day, alcohol	Massage *Svedana* Exercise
Asthi-vaha	*Asthi dhātu*—bone nutrients	Excessive exercise, high intake of *vāta* aggravating foods, lack of *kapha* foods	*Basti* Anti-*vāta* regime Dairy products
Majjā-vaha	*Majjā dhātu*—bone marrow	Injury to the bone marrow and crushing or compression of bone	*Virecana, Svedana* Detoxification
Śukra-vaha	*Śukra dhātu*—reproductive fluid	Over-indulgence in sexual activity, suppressing natural urge for sex	*Rasāyana, Vājikaraṇa* Exercise
Mūtra-vaha	Complete urinary tract—urine	Intake of *pitta* aggravating foods, suppressing urge to pass urine	Anti-*pitta* regime Increased water
Purīṣa-vaha	Lower intestinal tract—feces	Eating food when there is undigested food in stomach, constipation, suppressing urge for defecation	*Virecana* *Basti* High-fibre foods
Sveda-vaha	Sweat glands—perspiration	Excessive exercise, exposure to alternate heat/cold, excessive heat, anger, grief, anxiety, stress and fear	*Svedana* Meditation Cooling foods
Ārtava-vaha	Menstruation	Hormonal imbalance, intake of *pitta* aggravating foods (sour, salty, pungent)	Blood purification, oil massage, *uttara basti*
Stanya-vaha	Breast milk, lactation	Emotional disturbance (anger, grief, depression), poor diet	Internal *snehana* *Virecana*

Part II

HEALTH & AYURVEDA

Chapter 7

Nutrition

Prāṇā prāṇabhṛtāmannam tadayuktyā nihantyasan viṣam prāṇaharam tacca yuktiyuktam rasāyanam

Food is life. When taken properly, it enhances youthfulness and longevity. Improper intake of food creates toxins and ultimately takes one's life. (Caraka Sūtra Sthāna 27:3)

In Āyurveda, food (*āhāra*) is the prime preventive medicine. Proper diet and eating habits are considered the source of both physical and mental health. You may have heard of the proverbs "You are what you eat," or "You are digging your grave with your knife and fork." In Āyurveda, these sayings are not just figurative; they are the practical basis of the science of life. The first step to good health is an appropriate diet. This is not just eating the right foods, but also eating them in the correct combination and quantity.

Eating is the main method of maintaining the internal balance of elements. Health is maximized and sickness can be treated with knowledge of the properties of food, and the application of dietary guidelines. Once these principles are understood, they can be applied to your daily diet as well as on those occasions when you feel unwell. There are dozens of remedies that can be prepared easily in your own home using common foods and herbs.

At home, the pharmacy is really no further than the kitchen cupboard or the refrigerator.

Not following a proper diet or eating routine inevitably creates an imbalance of *doṣas*, with symptoms experienced in the *dhātus, agnis* and/or *malas*. Most diseases can be traced to an inadequate diet and improper eating. Poor nutrition or eating habits also disrupt any treatment or therapies undertaken. This essentially works against efforts made to retain a balanced state. Therefore, following dietary advice is an important aspect of any treatment for sickness and disease.

When discussing food and nutrition, terms such as calories or kilojoules, carbohydrates, protein value, vitamins and minerals are usually used. These measurements are complex and difficult to understand, let alone to apply on a daily basis. The nutritional science of Āyurveda is based on the tastes (*rasa*) of food and the qualities (*guṇas*) they display. The nutritive value of particular foods, and their internal effects, can be determined by their taste and qualities. Obtaining and maintaining a normal weight becomes quite simple when these factors are taken into account, and the basic dietary guidelines are observed.

Effects of Food

Food eaten has varied impacts on the body-mind. You may have noticed this yourself, and wondered why consuming one type of food leaves you feeling much different physically or mentally than others do. Differences in elemental nature, processing and so on, give substances different internal effects. According to *Caraka Saṁhitā*, the effects or benefits of food are determined by the following eight qualitative factors:

Nature (*prakṛti*): By nature, some foods are heavy and others are light, or some are moist while other items are dry. Foods that are heavy, greasy or oily have a much different effect than foods that are light and dry. Heavy foods (fried foods, cakes, yogurt and cheese) should not be eaten in as large a quantity as light foods (soup, salads and fruits).

Processing (*karaṇa*): Processing or preparation of food alters its internal influence. Different processing and preparation methods include cooking (frying, steaming, baking), flavoring with herbs, sweetening, diluting, drying and crushing. For example, raw foods become easier to digest when processed by cooking with various spices. Fresh food has a higher nutritive value than packaged, canned, frozen or stale food.

Combination (*saṁyoga*): Combining foods may produce a completely different quality than those of the individual foods alone. For example, mixing milk (sweet) and orange juice (sour) can produce a bitter or curdled taste. Adding salt or spices, which may be unpalatable individually, to something bland can enhance flavor and intensity of taste.

Quantity (*raśi*): The total quantity, as well as proportion of different foods eaten is important. The impact of a food can depend on the quantity consumed. For example, eating a large quantity of sweet, heavy foods can result in indigestion, sour foods can create hyperacidity, or an excessive intake of salty foods can cause vomiting.

Habitat (*deśa*): The region and climate in which a particular food is grown are also significant. A particular food grown in different places or environments will have different qualities. Soil type, temperature, rainfall and humidity can be determining factors in nutritional value and taste. Herbs and vegetables grown in watery environments are harder to digest (heavy) than and those grown in arid environments (light).

Time (*kāla*): *Kāla* refers to the time of the year or the season in which a particular food is grown. It also refers to the time of eating a food—the time of day, the length of time after preparation or the time of year. For example, eating hot foods during summer and cold foods during winter conflicts with good health. The benefit of a particular food can depend on the state of health (the timing of the disease process) of the person consuming it.

Consumer of the food (*upyoktā*): The person who eats the food is an agent in the effect of the food. The internal effects are dependent upon the specific constitution of the person, age, digestive power, dietary habits and emotional state. Different foods aggravate or alleviate different *doṣas*. Hot, spicy food may be good for a *kapha* type, but may create problems for *pitta* type. A certain food may be good for a young person, but may disturb an older person's digestion. For example, heavy foods are not good for weak or older digestions.

Dietary guidelines (*upyog-saṁsthā*): The same food has different effects when eaten with or without following proper eating rules. The eating guidelines are described throughout this chapter, and in the following chapter.

Understanding these factors, which determine the relative benefits of different foods, becomes easier when the principles of food are described. These principles are related to the combination of the elements/*panca mahābhūtas* present in the food item.

Principles of Food

In food, herbs and herbal remedies, the five elements are represented in the form of:

- Taste (*rasa*);
- Qualities (*guṇas*);
- Potency (*vīrya*);
- Post digestive effect (*vipāka*); and the
- Unique impact (*prabhāva*).

Food is commonly classified by taste (*rasa*) and qualities displayed (*guṇas*). Herbs are considered in terms of their *rasa*, but more so by their potency (*vīrya*), the digestive effect (*vipāka*) and unique impact (*prabhāva*). These factors and categories can produce countless combinations and variations.

Taste—*Rasa*

Rasa has a very prominent place in the science of Āyurveda. Just as an understanding and analysis of the *tridoṣa* is necessary for diagnosis of disease, an understanding of the tastes (*rasa*) is necessary for treatment of disease. A physician who has a thorough knowledge of *doṣa* and *rasa* will always be successful in treating even the most chronic disease.

Āyurveda classifies vegetation into two main groups—food and herbs. To understand their action in the body, it is necessary to understand their elemental composition, which creates their taste. The tastes are composed of different combinations of the five elements (*panca mahābhūtas*), with the element of water/*jala* (saliva) being necessary for their perception.

The qualities of the herb or food and its internal effect, are determined by its unique *rasa*. For example, whether a certain food will increase *pitta* or decrease *kapha* can be determined exclusively by its *rasa*. Due to the importance of taste/*rasa* in both food and herbs, it is considered in some detail. The information in this section is summarized in appendix 2 (p. 228).

Six tastes

The authors of the original texts discussed the qualities and classification of tastes at length. In ancient times, Āyurvedic scholars and schools of thought had diverging views on the actual number of tastes. *Caraka Saṁhitā* describes a conference held among these scholars to discuss *rasas*, and resolve the differing opinions to form a consensus. During the discussion it was determined that only six tastes existed, which have formed the basis of Āyurvedic practice ever since: sweet, sour, salty, pungent, bitter and astringent.

Every food item and herb contains varying proportions of these six tastes, providing a unique identity. When we identify an item as "sweet", all six tastes are present in different proportions but the sweet taste (*rasa*) is dominant. The other tastes are termed *anurasa* (not dominant).

Despite being a mixture of the *panca mahābhūtas*, each taste/*rasa* has two predominant elements. They have differing effects on the *doṣas*, due to the interaction between their elemental combination and that of the body (*rasa* and *doṣa*). For example, a sweet *rasa* is mainly earth/*pṛthvī* and water/*jala*. Sweet foods aggravate (increase) *kapha doṣa*, as it is also predominantly earth/*pṛthvī* and water/*jala*. Salty, sour and pungent foods have the fire/*agni* element, so aggravate *pitta*. *Rasas* containing air/*vāyu* (pungent, bitter, astringent) aggravate *vāta*, as it shares air/*vāyu* as a dominant element ("like increasing like").

Table 11 explains the relationship between each *rasa* and *doṣa*. In decreasing order of strength (in terms of energy provided to the body), the tastes are:

Table 11: Tastes and *Doṣas*

Taste: *Rasa*	**1. Sweet** *Madhura*	**2. Sour** *Amla*	**3. Salty** *Lavaṇa*	**4. Pungent** *Kaṭu*	**5. Bitter** *Tikta*	**6. Astringent** *Kaṣāya*
Elements: *Mahābhūtas*	earth/*pṛthvī* water/*jala*	earth/*pṛthvī* fire/*agni*	water/*jala* fire/*agni*	fire/*agni* air/*vāyu*	air/*vāyu* space/*ākāśa*	air/*vāyu* earth/*pṛthvī*
Aggravates:	*Kapha*	*Kapha* *Pitta*	*Kapha* *Pitta*	*Vāta* *Pitta*	*Vāta*	*Vāta*
Alleviates:	*Vāta* *Pitta*	*Vāta*	*Vāta*	*Kapha*	*Kapha* *Pitta*	*Kapha* *Pitta*
Examples:	Sugar, bread, honey, rice, milk, melon, potato,	Lemon, cheese, yogurt, vinegar	Salted nuts, sauces, salt, processed foods, kelp	Ginger, onion, garlic, pepper radish, chilli, most spices	Turmeric, rhubarb, barberry aloe, *neem*	Unripe fruit, tea, alfalfa raspberry, quince, plums

Tastes and health

Once the nature of food has been determined, according to its taste/*rasa* and predominant elements, this knowledge can be used for balancing the *doṣas, dhātus* and *malas*. This is because of the direct relationship between *rasa* and *doṣa* explained above. The tastes that share a common element with a *doṣa* serve to increase (aggravate) it, whereas those tastes contrasting with the elemental nature of the *doṣa* decrease (alleviate) it.

A balanced intake of all six *rasas* is necessary for the proper functioning of organs and systems. A diet containing proportions of all the six tastes is considered to be one of the objectives when choosing food, as this provides the necessary nutrients to all *dhātus, doṣas* and the other body constituents.

Excessive intake of a *rasa* can irritate a particular organ or *doṣa*. Allowing one *rasa* to dominate the diet, excluding one totally, or consuming them in the wrong combination, leads to an aggravation and imbalance of *doṣas*. When the aggravation of a *doṣa* is caused by an excessive intake of one *rasa*, including tastes in the diet that are opposite in elemental nature to the aggravated *doṣa* can assist in balancing it.

Combining tastes in the right mixtures can prevent any negative impact on the *doṣas*. For example, a sour taste increases *pitta*. If a bitter taste is also included (*pitta* alleviating), this neutralizes (balances) the effect of the sour *rasa* on *pitta*.

However, if a *doṣa* has been aggravated by causes other than diet, using only taste/*rasa* to balance it may not be sufficient. For example, if *pitta* is aggravated due to external factors (such as excessive exposure to heat and sun), reducing sour, salty and pungent tastes and increasing sweet, bitter and astringent tastes may not be sufficient. Additional remedies may be required, such as taking a cool shower and applying a paste of cooling herbs (sandal, rose). These remedies offer relief to externally aggravated *pitta* and are beneficial when combined with the internal remedies of selective *rasa* consumption.

The relationship between *rasas* and *doṣas* can also be utilized to maintain a state of good health. Selecting foods according to your constitution is one aspect of preserving internal balance. Another is choosing a diet that represents all tastes. This assists in nourṣing each of the *dhātus* and *doṣas*, and there will be neither a deficiency nor an abundance of any bodily constituent. This is essential in disease prevention.

The treatment of sickness and disease (balancing the *doṣas*) is based on including or excluding certain tastes/*rasa* in the diet. For example, a person suffering from a *pitta* related disorder should not eat sour, salty or pungent tastes in excess. For this reason, an Āyurvedic doctor will provide advice about diet, and tastes to avoid or increase during treatment. When prescribing herbal remedies, a physician requires a detailed understanding of the tastes and their complex interaction with *doṣas*. The specific diet recommended should support the treatment and remedies prescribed and not contradict it.

If the nature of the *rasas* and their relationship to the *doṣas* and the disease in question are overlooked, symptoms may be aggravated and worsened rather than alleviated. For example, *avipattikar* powder is commonly used for the *pitta* disorders of hyper-acidity and ulcers. However, it contains sugar (sweet/*madhura*) and may disturb symptoms of diabetes, as it increases the blood sugar level. So it should not be prescribed to a diabetic, even one experiencing *pitta* related conditions.

Foods of certain *rasa* may also stimulate specific emotions, often associated with the *doṣa* of the same elemental composition. Table 12 provides details of *rasas* and their effects.

Table 12: Tastes and their Effects

Taste *Rasa*	**Sweet** *Madhura*	**Sour** *Amla*	**Salty** *Lavaṇa*	**Pungent** *Kaṭu*	**Bitter** *Tikta*	**Astringent** *Kaṣāya*
Action *Karma*	+ weight + strength + toxins	+ appetite +acidity – libido	+ digestion + elasticity – *śukra*	+ metabolism + thirst/temp – *āma*	+ coldness – fever – toxins	+ stiffness + emaciation + contractions
Organ Affected	Pancreas	Liver	Kidneys	Lungs	Heart	Colon
Disorders	Diabetes Cough Asthma	Hyperacidity Jaundice Ulcers	Infertility Baldness Wrinkles	Weakness Vertigo Joint pains	*Dhātu* growth Dehydration Immunity	Stomach ache Colitis Angina
Emotions	Love Attachment Satisfaction	Envy Irritation Pessimism	Greed Self-pity Obstinacy	Hatred Anger Resentment	Grief Sorrow Despair	Fear Anxiety Asceticism

Impact of tastes

Sweet (*madhura*)—builds all seven tissues/*dhātus*, gives strength and immunity to the body, provides lubrication, improves complexion and satisfies the senses. It is especially necessary for children, aged people and pregnant and nursing mothers. *Madhura rasa* increases *kapha doṣa* and reduces *vāta* and *pitta*. If taken in excess, it leads to *kapha* related conditions such as heaviness, lethargy and obesity. It is a factor in many degenerative diseases including diabetes, arthritis, heart disease, tumors, headaches and urinary system diseases.

Sour (*amla*)—induces appetite, acts as a heart tonic by regulating the function of heart, increases the digestive fire/*jaṭharāgni*, assists in elimination of wastes/*malas* and gas. It aggravates *pitta* and *kapha doṣa*, and alleviates *vāta*. If taken in excess, symptoms of *pitta* disturbance may occur such as impurities in the blood, itching, skin problems, infections, fever, thirst, iron deficiency and swelling.

Salty (*lavaṇa*)—increases appetite and digestion, assists in building new cells and removes blockages in channels/*srotas*. *Lavaṇa rasa* increases *pitta* and *kapha*, and decreases *vāta*. If taken in excess it causes skin disorders such as leucoderma, burning and itching sensations, baldness and wrinkles. Excessive salt intake also makes one susceptible to poisons, creates swelling and uterine disorders.

Pungent (*kaṭu*)—decreases swelling, helps to reduce fat, cures nasal and chest infections, opens up blocked channels/*srotas*, acts as an appetizer and mouth purifier. *Kaṭu rasa* is helpful in many allergies. It increases *vāta* and *pitta*, and decreases *kapha*. If taken in excess, it destroys connective tissue in the joints, breast milk, *śukra* and fat deposits. It can create tremors, pelvic pains and emaciation. *Kaṭu rasa* should be taken with *ghī* (clarified butter) or oil, as it may irritate the stomach and intestinal walls and destroy the positive bacterial flora in the intestines.

Bitter (*tikta*)—decreases swelling and fluid retention, kills parāśites, neutralizes poisons in the body and purifies the blood. It helps cure burning and itching sensations, skin diseases and controls nausea and vomiting. It is used as a tonic for a weak liver. *Tikta rasa* purifies breast milk and is beneficial for nursing mothers. It is also useful in fevers and throat infections. *Tikta rasa* increases *vāta*, and decreases *pitta* and *kapha*. If taken in excess, it dries out the body fluids leading to dehydration of *dhātus* and reduction of body strength.

Astringent (*kaṣāya*)—purifies the blood, aids digestion, cleans toxins from the skin and is useful to control diarrhea. It aggravates *vāta* and alleviates *pitta* and *kapha*. If taken in excess, it creates wind, distention of the abdomen, heart pain (angina), constipation, emaciation, thirst and impotency.

Improper utilization of tastes

Using the sense of taste incorrectly causes imbalance in *doṣas*, and symptoms may consequently appear in the *dhātus*. There are three main methods of inappropriately using taste:

- **Excessive utilization** of certain tastes: The aggravation of a *doṣa* by the intake of tastes is only possible if a specific taste is used in excess, continuously and over a long period of time. The occasional excessive use of a certain taste will not cause undue aggravation. For example, when it is stated that an excessive intake of sweet/*madhura* rasa aggravates *kapha*, it means an excessive intake of sweet foods over an extended period.

  The excessive intake of one *rasa* creates an imbalance because when there is an interaction between two substances, the one with the stronger nature always dominates over the weaker. One element will become stronger than another if one *rasa* is eaten excessively over a long period, due to the sheer quantity consumed. Thus, the dominant element in the *rasa* will increase the proportion of that element/*doṣa* present in the body. The principle of "like increases like" is operating.

The same principle of weaker and stronger elements is operating when a substance decreases or alleviates a *doṣa*. An excess of *kapha* is reduced by pungent (fire/*agni* and air/*vāyu*) tasting food, when it is consumed in quantities that allows it to dominate the *kapha* elements water/*jala* and earth/ *pṛthvī*. To allow the fire and air to dominate water and earth, it needs to be taken in sufficient quantities over time.

- **Non-utilization** of certain tastes: Excluding particular tastes or consuming them in insufficient quantities eventually creates physical disorders. For example, lack of salty foods can lead to muscle cramps, or lack of sweet *rasa* may create hypoglycemia.
- **Incorrect utilization** of certain tastes: Consuming *rasa* in the wrong combination, by mixing incompatible food items and tastes, can disturb the balance of elements and aggravate the *doṣas*. For example, eating salty snacks and drinking sweet milk is a contradictory combination.

Qualities—*Guṇas*

When considering the attributes (*guṇas*) of foods and herbs, ten descriptive pairs of adjectives are used. These *guṇas*, which total twenty characteristics, have varying physical and therapeutic impacts on the body-mind. The ten *guṇa* pairs are opposite in nature and may be used to classify all edible items.

1.	Heavy *guru*	Light *laghu*
2.	Hot *uṣṇa*	Cold *śīta*
3.	Moist (oily) *snigdha*	Dry *rūkśa*
4.	Dull *manda*	Sharp *tīkśṇa*
5.	Smooth *slakśaṇa*	Rough *khara*
6.	Solid *sāndra*	Liquid *drava*
7.	Soft *mṛdu*	Hard *kaṭhina*
8.	Firm *sthira*	Flexible *sara*
9.	Subtle *sūkśma*	Gross *sthūla*
10.	Clear *viśada*	Viscous *picchila*

Of all the *guṇas*, the first three pairs listed are the most significant, and therefore commonly used, when describing foods. These are explained below. The *guṇa* does not simply refer to the physical properties of the food (that is, the weight or temperature), but to the internal reactions that occur during digestion, and the physical effects.

Table 13: Tastes and their Qualities

Taste *Rasa*	**Sweet** *Madhura*	**Sour** *Amla*	**Salty** *Lavaṇa*	**Pungent** *Kaṭu*	**Bitter** *Tikta*	**Astringent** *Kaṣāya*
Elements *Mahābhūtas*	earth/*pṛthvī* water/*jala*	earth/*pṛthvī* fire/*agni*	water/*jala* fire/*agni*	fire/*agni* air/*vāyu*	air/*vāyu* space/*ākāśa*	air/*vāyu* earth/*pṛthvī*
Qualities *Guṇas*	Cold Heavy Moist	Hot Light Moist	Hot Heavy Moist	Hot Light Dry	Cold Light Dry	Cold Heavy Dry

Hot/*Uṣṇa* and Cold/*Śīta*

Hot and cold foods produce either a heating (*vidāhī*) or cooling (*avidāhī*) effect in the body. A cooling effect is produced by bitter, astringent, and sweet *rasas*, and a heating effect is produced by pungent, sour and salty *rasas*. Heating foods increase metabolism, produce acidity and burning sensations during digestion, and promote perspiration. Cooling foods are opposite to these, are soothing and digested more slowly.

Heavy/*Guru* and Light/*Laghu*

Heavy foods are denser in terms of the nutrition and energy provided, but take longer to digest. Fried food, cakes, yogurt and cheese are heavy. Sweet, salty and astringent *rasas* are all heavy. Sweet and salty tastes are especially aggravating for *kapha* as they share the common element of water/*jala*, and are also heavy in nature like earth/*pṛthvī*, promoting solidity and lethargy. Light/*laghu* tastes (bitter, pungent, sour) stimulate digestion but do not promote tissue growth. Soup, salads and fruits are light.

Dry/*rūkśa* and moist/*snigdha*

Pungent, bitter and astringent tastes are *rūkśa* (having a drying effect) and if taken in excess, cause weakening and dehydration of body tissues. Sweet, sour and salty tastes (*snigdha*) have a strengthening effect on the body. *Snigdha* foods generally contain a lot of moisture in the form of fats or oils, so one should be very careful about the quantity consumed. Such foods are necessary for strength, energy and lubrication, but if eaten excessively can cause weight gain or production of *āma*.

Potency—*Vīrya*

Vīrya refers to the strength and effectiveness of a particular herb or plant. When considering herbs, the potency (*vīrya*) or digestive result (*vipāka*) is usually paramount to taste/*rasa*. The *vīrya* of herbs are classified according to hot/cold, heavy/light, moist/dry or dull/sharp. However, hot and cold are the most commonly used classifications when considering *vīrya*, and herbs are generally considered heating (*uṣṇa vīrya*) or cooling (*śīta vīrya*).

The potency/*vīrya* of herbs is linked to their *rasa*, which is determined by the elements present. Those herbs with a heating *vīrya* have the element of fire/*agni* in their *rasa* and aggravate *pitta* (sour, salty and pungent). The herbs that have no fire/*agni* present have a cooling *vīrya* that alleviates *pitta* (sweet, bitter, astringent). Herbs with a drying *vīrya* have air/*vāyu* present, aggravating *vāta* (bitter, astringent, pungent). Those herbs with a moist *vīrya* have the element of water/*jala* (sweet, salty) or earth/*pṛthvī* (sour), increasing *kapha*.

The seasonal dominance of different elements affects the *vīrya* of herbs and foods grown at that time of year. For example, air/*vāyu* dominates in dry seasons, so many of the foods and herbs grown then are dry and have a *rasa* that shares the air element (bitter, astringent or pungent). Such foods are more potent during the hot, dry period as they are dry in nature and receive their nourishment from the heat.

When the sun is less powerful and there is abundant rain, herbs with water/*jala* and/or earth/*pṛthvī* elements are more potent due to the moisture and soil richness. Vegetation with sweet, salty or sour *rasa* thrives when conditions are damp and wet. These have a moist *guṇa* and *vīrya*, and their growth is enhanced by the conditions of compatible seasons. Their potency is at its peak during the cooler, wetter months.

This knowledge is beneficial for choosing the right time to pick herbs for medicinal use. Herbs should be picked when rich in taste and highly potent. So herbs of a pungent taste (such as ginger or garlic) should be picked in the late winter season when they possess the highest potency and thus the strongest medicinal properties.

Similarly, fruits and vegetables are best eaten when ripe and in season. Herbs should also be stored to maximize their *vīrya*/potency. Exposing them to the light, air, humidity or heat can destroy medicinal properties and weaken *vīrya*.

Table 14: Tastes and Potency/*Vīrya*

Taste *Rasa*	**Sweet** *Madhura*	**Sour** *Amla*	**Salty** *Lavaṇa*	**Pungent** *Kaṭu*	**Bitter** *Tikta*	**Astringent** *Kaṣāya*
Elements *Mahābhūtas*	earth/*pṛthvī* water/*jala*	earth/*pṛthvī* fire/*agni*	water/*jala* fire/*agni*	fire/*agni* air/*vāyu*	air/*vāyu* space/*ākāśa*	air/*vāyu* earth/*pṛthvī*
Vīrya (see note)	3. Cooling 1. Moist	2. Heating 3. Moist	3. Heating 2. Moist	1. Heating 1. Drying	1. Cooling 2. Drying	2. Cooling 3. Drying
Aggravates	*Kapha*	*Kapha* *Pitta*	*Kapha* *Pitta*	*Vāta* *Pitta*	*Vāta*	*Vāta*
Alleviates	*Vāta* *Pitta*	*Vāta*	*Vāta*	*Kapha*	*Kapha* *Pitta*	*Kapha* *Pitta*

Note: 1 = most 2 = medium 3 = least

Digestive Effect—*Vipāka*

The *rasa* of foods or herbs, as perceived in the mouth, changes when it is assimilated into the body. This change in taste takes place during digestive processes in the gastro-intestinal tract and in the cells during formation of the *dhātus*. The taste that occurs during the digestive process or as a consequence of metabolic action is called *vipāka*. *Vipāka* is literally translated as "the final taste following digestion". Knowledge of *vipāka* allows us to anticipate the ultimate internal effect that a particular substance will have on the *tridoṣa*.

There are three types *vipāka*:

- **sweet**/*madhura* is found in foods or herbs with a sweet or salty *rasa* (water/*jala* element).
- **pungent**/*kaṭu* in those foods with pungent, bitter and astringent *rasa* (air/*vāyu* element).
- **sour**/*amla* in foods with a sour *rasa* (no water/*jala* or air/*vāyu*).

The *vipāka* becomes significant in the long-term consumption of specific foods or herbs. It serves to aggravate the *doṣa* that shares its main element. So sweet *vipāka* aggravates *kapha*, pungent *vipāka* increases *vāta* and sour *vipāka* influences *pitta*. The excessive use of herbs or foods with a particular *vipāka* produces symptoms similar to the characteristics of the related *doṣa*. These are listed in table 15.

Table 15: Tastes and *Vipāka*

Taste: *Rasa*	**Sweet** *Madhura*	**Salty** *Lavaṇa*	**Sour** *Amla*	**Pungent** *Kaṭu*	**Bitter** *Tikta*	**Astringent** *Kaṣāya*
Elements *Mahābhūtas*	earth/*pṛthvī* water/*jala*	fire/*agni* water/*jala*	earth/*pṛthvī* fire/*agni*	fire/*agni* air/*vāyu*	space/*ākāśa* air/*vāyu*	earth/*pṛthvī* air/*vāyu*
Vipāka	sweet *madhura*		sour *amla*		pungent *kaṭu*	
Influences	*kapha*		*pitta*		*vāta*	
Generates	saliva, mucus, fatty tissue		acid, bile	gas, dryness, dehydration, emaciation		

Unique Impact—*Prabhāva*

The therapeutic benefit of herbs may be determined by any one (or combination) of the factors already discussed. That is, by the taste (*rasa*), qualities (*guṇas*), potency (*vīrya*) or the consequence of their digestion (*vipāka*). However, there are some herbs whose medicinal value is determined only on the basis of the special action produced (*prabhāva*).

This factor is operating in cases where two herbs have a similar *rasa, guṇa, vīrya* and *vipāka* but produce different internal actions. This unique and hidden action is called *prabhāva*. An example is with the herbs *dantī mūla* and *citraka mūla*. They have same *rasa, guṇa, vīrya* and *vipāka*, but *dantī mūla* acts as a laxative and *citraka mūla* does not. This difference is explained by their *prabhāva*.

CHAPTER 8

Diet

The information about *rasa* allows quite specific dietary choices to be made, in terms of individual food items and your *doṣa*. However, Āyurveda also provides more general guidelines on nutrition and eating habits, with the aim of encouraging thorough digestion and maximum absorption of nutrients.

Dietary Guidelines

Food eaten according to the dietary guidelines provides energy and good health. The same food eaten in contradiction to these principles can cause discomfort or ill health. The most significant dietary guidelines are:

Appropriate Quantities

The amount of food eaten at any one meal is crucial for proper nutrition and also complete digestion. Eating too much or too little is equally hazardous to health. The proper amount of food is essential to maintain good health and attain longevity. According to *Caraka Saṁhitā*, the stomach is divided into three equal parts. When eating, one part of the stomach should be filled with solid foods (vegetables, rice, grains, breads), the second part should be filled with liquids (juices, soups, water) and the third part of the stomach should be left empty for the movement of air and the *tridoṣa*.

If you are unsure, a simple rule is that it is better to stop when you feel you still have some capacity, as eating less than your maximum ability is always preferable to eating more. Consistently under-eating can produce a gradual disturbance to the *vāta doṣa*, but over-eating produces an immediate disturbance to all three *doṣas*.

Overeating causes obesity and related disorders such as diabetes, heart disease and hypertension, strain on internal systems and organs and *āma* production. A person eating much less food than required eventually loses strength and has less energy and vitality. Functions of mind such as concentration, memory and intelligence become impaired, and *ojas* and sensory power are diminished.

People often complain that after meals they feel discomfort, lethargy and heaviness. This is due to either eating an improper quantity of food, or improper types and combinations of foods. *Caraka Saṁhitā* lists the symptoms of eating improperly as:

- Feeling of heaviness in the stomach;
- Disturbance or change in the heart-beat;
- Pain in the back or stomach;
- Discomfort in walking, breathing, talking or laughing;
- Laziness or drowsiness;
- Dissatisfaction of any of the senses.

Jaṭharāgni Power

The strength of the digestive fire/*jaṭharāgni* needs to be considered when determining the appropriate quantity and nature of food to consume. The basic rule is that whatever one eats should be completely digested, thus avoiding *āma* production. Heavy foods (greasy, oily and fried foods, sweets, dairy products) are harder to digest and therefore should be consumed less frequently than lighter foods.

When *jaṭharāgni* is weak (*mandāgni*), such as during convalescence or old age, consuming smaller quantities and eating light foods assists digestion. Soups and broths, steamed vegetables, juices and fresh fruits are light and more easily digested by a weak *jaṭharāgni*.

You should eat only when the digestive fire is ready. That is, when all food previously eaten has been digested and you are hungry. Consuming food before the previous meal has been digested creates *āma*. It remains undigested, as the *jaṭharāgni* cannot process additional food prior to processing the food already in the stomach. The additional food eaten cannot be converted to either *āhāra rasa* or *malas*. Instead, it becomes toxic (see chapter 5).

The digestive power corresponds with the movement of the sun. It increases until midday when the sun is at its peak, and then gradually decreases. *Jaṭharāgni* is therefore strongest in the middle of the day. Lunch should be the main meal, when food can be easily digested and absorbed. Breakfast and dinner should be lighter as *jaṭharāgni* is weaker.

Sāttvic Food

Regular use of *sāttvic* foods helps prevent disease and maintain good physical, mental and spiritual health. According to Āyurveda, eating *sāttvic* food and practicing a *sāttvic* lifestyle are the best preventive medicines.

Sāttvic food is fresh, pure and vegetarian. This includes fresh fruits and vegetables, grains, whole grain breads, nuts, seeds and salads. Foods that have a naturally sweet taste are *sāttvic*. This does not include refined sugar products, but refers to anything that has a sweet taste without any additives, such as grains (rice, wheat and barley), breads, honey and fruits. Milk, herbal teas, pure fruit or vegetable juices and water are also included in this group. Organically grown foods are preferred, as fertilizers, pesticides, chemicals and preservatives are *tāmasic*.

Mushrooms, onions, garlic and the excessive use of spices should be avoided, as they are *rājasic* and *tāmasic*. Alcohol, products containing caffeine (coffee, chocolate, tea, cola) and meat should be moderated or eliminated from the diet. Chapter 4 has further details on *sāttvic* food and the role of food on the mind.

Vegetarianism

Authentic Āyurvedic dietary advice is based on a purely vegetarian diet. There have been some misconceptions about vegetarian food, and the role of vegetarianism in Āyurveda. Some authors have included meat in their dietary guidelines, or proposed that people with a *vāta* constitution need the proteins that animal foods provide. Others claim that Āyurveda is based on vegetarianism for religious reasons, rather than any biological or health grounds.

- ***Caraka's* advice**

It is true that eating meat was included in the original Āyurvedic texts. The ancient authors of Āyurveda considered different groups of people in their dietary advice (*sāttvic, rājasic* and *tāmasic*). *Caraka* mentions that meat is nouṛṣing when prepared and eaten under certain circumstances. However, this was under vastly different conditions to those of meat production and consumption in modern times. Meat formed a small proportion of the overall diet, was obtained using traditional hunting methods, and the animal lived in its native environment.

Caraka provides the guidelines for eating both vegetable and animal products. The characteristics of animals not to be eaten are described. *Caraka* does not recommend meat be eaten routinely, which is how it has sometimes been interpreted. Rather, *Caraka* states that meat is nutritious when used for treating certain diseases, those weak or convalescing, and states of dehydration or emaciation.

Furthermore, in those cases, meat is "unwholesome" if it comes from an animal that was raised in a habitat that is not its natural environment, or in an area to which it is not native. If it has eaten food that does not form part of its natural diet, or that does not come from its native environment, it is also toxic. If the animal has died a natural death, has been killed by other animals or with poisonous means, is very thin, fat, old or young, eating its meat is detrimental to health (*Caraka Sūtra Sthāna* 37:311).

It is clear that meat, as it is prepared today, does not meet these guidelines for healthy eating. Animals are farmed intensively in artificial and often unclean conditions. They are injected with antibiotics and growth hormones such as estrogen, or fed fodder that is enriched with substances to improve meat quality or increase quantity. For economic reasons (to increase profits in comparison to costs) they are forced to eat food they would never consume in their natural environments.

The methods used to slaughter them are usually brutal, where the animal is in a state of fear and pain. The meat begins to decompose from the time of death of the animal. It is then usually processed, frozen, canned, preserved or smoked. Such preparation compounds the *tāmasic* qualities already present. It may be days, weeks or even months before the meat is eaten. Consumption of these animal products promotes a *tāmasic* mind *guṇa* that is fearful, apathetic, dull and so on (see chapter 4 for more details on *tāmasic guṇa*).

- **Physical considerations**

Biologically, humans are structured for eating plant foods. Our teeth and jaws are not suitable for a carnivorous diet. Academics from the University of Arkansas and the John Hopkins School of Medicine have spent years analyzing the design of human teeth. They investigated links to the diets of primates and wear patterns on the teeth of fossilized remains of our ancestors. They have concluded that teeth with moderately sharp cusps, like ours, were only used for cutting through foods like fruits, nuts, shoots, leaves and flowers.

Carnivores have biological features that differ from herbivores. Their intestines are short and digestive acids very strong. The length of the human intestine is three to four times that of a typical carnivore, and digestive acids weaker. Meat therefore takes a long time to process, sometimes exceeding several days. In that time, a significant amount of toxicity/*āma* is produced. This internal accumulation is a form of self-poisoning. For example, uric acid is produced from eating meat, and can create kidney stones, gout, gallstones and rheumatism. Eating meat has also been linked to strokes, heart attacks, obesity, cancers and many other ailments.

Dr. Jenson, a leading American nutritionist, expresses this concept clearly when he states "Animal proteins putrefy very quickly in the intestinal tract, and that is why we should be careful with meats...meat is one of the most putrefactive foods...Fermentation takes place in an underactive bowel and favors the multiplication of undesirāble toxic bacteria, while the friendly acidophilus bacteria may be almost destroyed...toxic protein byproducts may find their way into the bloodstream, where they cause a great deal of trouble." (1998:56)

- **Nutritional considerations**

The value of meat in a human diet is usually linked to its protein content. It is a widespread fallacy that this protein is vital for human sustenance and cannot be obtained from any other source. Proteins required for physical strength and health are found in a wide variety of foods. The protein value of plant foods is often equal to, or even greater than meat or animal products. For example, a comparison of the protein value of 100g of the following foods is:

• egg yolk	13.7	• soya beans	43.2
• fish	21.5	• chickpeas	24.6
• lamb	18.5	• peanuts	26.7

The daily requirement for protein is markedly less than many people assume. In modern times, the problem with Western diets is usually excess consumption of protein rather than a deficiency. Many components of protein used by the human body (amino acids) are actually manufactured internally. Of the twenty-two amino acids that protein provides, the human body produces thirteen without any input from dietary sources. The remainder can be obtained from plant foods.

Some people assume that vegetarian diets lack the B group of vitamins. This vitamin group is essential in the diet, and a deficiency can lead to fatigue, poor concentration or memory and insomnia. Sufficient intake of vitamin B, including B12, can be obtained from milk, cheese, and whole grains. A balanced and varied vegetarian diet easily provides all the vitamins required and prevents the need for any supplements.

Many people who have adopted a vegetarian diet in the West eat fish, seafood and eggs. These items are excluded from an Āyurvedic vegetarian diet. The consumption of anything that is the product of fertilization (formed from reproduction between two animals) is considered *tāmasic*. Any item that was once a living being, or consists of the material to form a living being, like eggs, is not included in the diet.

- **Health and vegetarianism**

Animal protein in the form of flesh is not essential for human growth and development. A human can develop normally from birth, obtain complete nourishment and experience total health, with a purely vegetarian diet.

In fact, various studies have demonstrated vegetarians have longer life spans, lower incidences of particular cancers and higher bone densities than non-vegetarians. Dr Campbell, of Cornell University, has found that adopting a plant-based diet can prevent the majority of all cardiovascular diseases, cancers and degenerative illnesses.

A balanced intake of vegetables, grains, nuts, legumes and seeds provides sufficient iron, protein, calcium, protein, and all the required vitamins and minerals for health, vitality and energy.

There is a huge range of tasty and satisfying vegetarian recipes that are easy to prepare and *sāttvic* in nature. Vegetarian food does not mean bland, tasteless or raw vegetables and salads!

Although Āyurveda is associated with particular spiritual and ethical principles, such as not killing living beings, the vegetarian facet of the diet is also related to a literal interpretation of *Caraka's* principles for healthy eating. A plant based diet minimizes the consumption and internal production of toxins and takes human physiology into account, which differs from that of meat-eating animals. If meat is still a preferred food item despite all of these considerations, intake should be moderated and organically raised animals favored.

Those pursuing spiritual growth adopt a purely vegetarian diet due to its *sāttvic* quality. Meditating, *yoga* and other *sāttvic* lifestyle principles are less effective if meat, or any other *tāmasic* or *rājasic* foods form part of the diet. When adopting a *sāttvic* lifestyle, a consistent approach is more favorable to achieve positive outcomes. Therefore, discipline in choosing a *sāttvic* diet is just as important as other *sāttvic* lifestyle considerations like meditation, regular sleeping habits and ethical behavior.

Other Considerations

Caraka's guidelines for eating include:

- Food is best eaten hot and freshly prepared.
- Food should be tasty and easy to digest.
- Food should be consumed in proper quantities.
- Eat when you are hungry.
- Foods should complement, not contradict each other.
- Eating in a pleasant environment is preferable.
- Eating should be paced properly (not too fast or slow).
- While eating, distractions should be minimized.
- Food should be eaten according to constitution.

Food items

A good representation of *rasas* in the diet provides nutrition to all *dhātus*. Heavy items should be minimized. Old or stale foods, fast foods and processed or packaged foods should be avoided or eaten infrequently.

Regular consumption of certain foods is not recommended. These include dried, preserved or pickled vegetables and fruits; yogurt, cheese and any dairy product that contains additives or preservatives; fried foods and refined sugar products; and foods that are frozen or chilled like ice creams, cold drinks and frozen vegetables.

Order of eating food items

According to Āyurveda, foods that increase *kapha* should be eaten first. These are heavy, oily, fried or sweet foods. Sweet foods (*madhura rasa*) include grains, legumes and breads. These foods, usually solid or semi-solid in nature, should fill one third of the capacity of the stomach.

Foods that increase *pitta* should be eaten next, and another third of the stomach can be filled with them. Foods that are salty, sour and acidic, and liquids are included in this group. The final third of the stomach is reserved for air itself (*vāta*). The meal should end with a sweet dish to satisfy the senses.

Timing

Food should be freshy prepared and served hot. Eating at intervals of at least four to five hours allows complete digestion. Snacks should be avoided, but fruits and fruit juices can be consumed between meals without disturbing or overburdening the digestive process.

Sufficient time should be given to chewing, to ensure the thorough mixing of saliva (and the digestive enzymes within in it) with the food, which assists *jaṭharāgni*. *Kapha* foods especially should be chewed thoroughly, as they are heavy in nature and more difficult to digest.

Regular meals and fasting

It is best to eat meals regularly, around every five hours. Skipping meals aggravates *pitta*, and consistently under-eating aggravates *vāta*. Fasting occasionally enhances digestive power/*jaṭharāgni*, but excessive fasting can be detrimental. Frequent hunger weakens *dhātus* and destroys *ojas*. Crash diets, and other extreme forms of controlling food intake, are harmful for both the body and mind.

Fasting one day per fortnight maintains the strength of the digestive system and cleanses the intestine. On days of fasting, foods such as fruits and light vegetable soup can be eaten. Drinks can include juices, herbal tea and water with lemon juice.

Combination of different foods

Foods eaten should have complementary rather than contradictory natures. The food should also complement the person's constitution, lifestyle, climate, digestive fire and energy requirements. For example, heating and cooling foods should not be mixed, and heavy, cold foods should not be eaten in a cold, damp environment. Fruits should be eaten separately from meals. Drinking should be avoided within one hour before or after meals. However, buttermilk after lunch assists digestion and alleviates all three *doṣas*.

Cleanliness

Hygiene is an important consideration for health, and it is important to maintain cleanliness while preparing, cooking and eating food. There are four aspects of cleanliness in relation to food: the cook, the place of cooking, the place of eating, and the person eating the food.

The cook should be physically clean, and have pure and positive thoughts while cooking. Cooking should be done with love and devotion, as the consciousness of the person cooking influences the nature of the food prepared. The place of eating should also be clean, and before starting to eat a person should wash their hands.

Eating-place and attitude

Eating in a peaceful atmosphere, free from distractions and noise, is conducive to digestion. While eating, one should focus on the food rather than socializing, watching television or reading. Eating while standing, moving or driving a car is not recommended, and it is preferable to eat in a sitting position.

Eating while experiencing negative emotions (distress, anxiety, anger, depression, greed) can aggravate particular *doṣas*; being calm and relaxed is beneficial. The food should be appreciated, valued and welcomed into the body, rather than criticized or disliked.

Constitution

Your constitution (*doṣa*) is a factor to take into account when choosing food. You should mainly eat food with a taste/*rasa* that does not aggravate your *doṣa*. Spices can also be chosen according to your constitution. The *guṇas* of food should be considered prior to a meal. As mentioned, the heaviness, lightness, heating and cooling effects help determine the suitability of a meal.

Quality

Caraka provides guidance on how to select good quality food. Fruits and vegetables that are dehydrated, old, out of season or insect damaged are not of a nutritious quality. They should not have been exposed to the weather, such as the wind, sun or rain. When shopping, choose fruits and vegetables that are ripe (indicated by color), pleasant smelling, firm, and free of bruises or blemishes.

Organic fruits and vegetables are more nutritious than foods that have been sprayed with pesticides and grown with chemicals. Always wash vegetables and fruits thoroughly before use. Genetically modified foods, or those containing preservatives, additives, artificial colors and flavors are lower in quality and nutritional value.

Dear Dr Chauhan

...During the last two years I have suffered from insomnia and had a lot of stress in my life. I had wrong eating habits because I used to often overeat, eat a lot of sweets and the combination of food was improper. I work in an office and sit at a desk for most of the day, with very little movement. I am prone to constipation and usually can evacuate only after eating a lot. During the last few months I have also been affected by strong headaches.

Since I received your information, I have been trying to follow some recommendations. I have changed my diet, and follow the advice on daily routines like massage with sesame oil etc. The result is amazing. Now I fall asleep very quickly, and I don't want to sleep during the day. I have more energy and I am more peaceful. My headaches are gone, and the problem with constipation has also lessened. Thank you so much for your help.

Ms MD Sweden

Chapter 9

Complete Health

Sama doṣa samāgniśca samadhātu malakriya prasannātmêndriya manā swastha ityabhidhīyate

Health is defined as the balanced functioning of doṣas, tissues, metabolism, enzymes, wastes and a contented state of senses, mind and soul. (Suśruta Saṁhitā Sūtra 15:48)

HEALTH often seems to be in a precarious state—difficult to obtain, and then complicated to maintain. It becomes clear why, when the definition of health according to Āyurveda is considered. A state of complete health is when all three *doṣas*, seven tissues/*dhātus*, thirteen types of metabolic activity/*agnis*, three wastes/*malas* and ten senses/*indriya* are all operating effectively and in balance. Apart from those purely physical considerations, the mind and the soul need to be balanced and contented as well. In modern times, this may seem like an optimistic or even impossible goal to achieve.

Āyurveda is the only medical science to have defined "health". In the Āyurvedic sense, health is not merely being free of physical pain or the symptoms of disease. The mind is a very important consideration in the overall assessment of well-being. A person can only be said to be healthy when the mind is clear, calm and contented (balanced), complementing a balanced body.

In many cases, people may not have any physical problem or symptoms of illness, but they are very unhappy or agitated at the psychological level. According to Āyurveda, these people are not healthy. Thousands of people are in this category. They may be disturbed, depressed, irritable and anxious. Or they may suffer from insomnia due to stress, or feel generally unfulfilled and aimless. These types of conditions mainly originate in an unbalanced mind.

Unfortunately, most of our attempts to become happy and peaceful relate purely to the physical body and to materialistic ends. We strive to achieve physical perfection or to obtain items thought to bring security and pleasure, such as a high-income career, car, house, designer clothing or jewelry. We rarely pay attention to our mind and soul, even though they are largely responsible for our health. Our lifestyle and diet, which we think provide happiness and pleasure, may not really be healthy for our mind and soul.

That is why, even after achieving material comfort and obtaining good physical health, we are often still not contented. Fruitlessly, we strive even harder to achieve more physical comforts, and are confused when this does not create a sense of satisfaction. We struggle to obtain transitory physical pleasures, mistaking this for genuine and lasting happiness. In the process, we over-stimulate and disturb our senses, creating physical and psychological imbalances.

This situation is like keeping a beautiful bird inside an intricate, precious cage. Rather than feeding the bird (soul) and listening to it sing, all of your energy is devoted to polishing and maintaining the cage (body). You are so busy looking after the cage (body), that you forget the bird (soul) is inside and don't even notice when it begins to waste away from neglect.

Why do we persist in following lifestyles or diets that make us unhappy or physically sick? It is because we assume that if we nurture the physical, the rest takes care of itself. However, despite our best efforts, time and resources spent meeting all of our physical needs and desires, we are unable to achieve lasting contentment and peace. We have not learnt how to tend to the needs of our mind and soul, so have ignored our spiritual and psychological health. Overlooking the mind and soul means that the majority of our genuine needs are ignored.

Physical perfection, measured by muscle size, weight or strength, or momentary physical satisfaction of the senses, is not the means to achieve health and happiness. Complete health and genuine contentment are obtainable with Āyurvedic principles. Āyurveda considers the individual an integrated soul, mind and body and the health advice encompasses all these factors. It describes diet and hygiene, as well as lifestyle, conduct and attitude that can bring total health.

Āyurveda teaches us how to live in both society and the natural universe without disturbing the natural balance, and how to live in harmony with each other and the Earth. This inclusive approach automatically achieves peak physical fitness, normal weight and peace of mind. Spiritual growth, mental balance and the maintenance of physical well being are complementary and equal aims of this science.

Today, many people feel uncomfortable when the word "spiritual" is mentioned or discussed. Spirituality simply means, "relating to the soul." As anything relating to the body is the "physical", and anything relating to the mind is "psychological", whatever relates to the spirit (or soul) is "spiritual". It is essential to understand both the needs of the mind and soul when attempting to obtain complete health, as they are equal partners with the body in determining our welfare.

An understanding of these aspects can bring happiness and peace. Material things may give temporary happiness to the body, but they do not meet the needs of the soul. That may be one of the reasons why there is so much suffering and anguish today, despite the wealth available for material goods and physical pleasure. Diet (the physical) is only one factor in maintaining health. Spirituality and mental harmony are equally important.

Spirituality

Āyurveda is a science that teaches us how to live in a natural balance. This natural balance is not only limited to proper internal functioning of our body but also means a balanced relationship with the Earth and with our fellow human beings. Harmonious relationships with our family, friends, colleagues and community are one aspect. Everything on Earth is included in this equation, all the animals and creatures, plants, the climate and seasons, as well as God—the creator of this universe. Harmonious existence incorporates all these factors, and cannot be disregarded in the quest for health.

Orthodox Western medicine initially questioned and doubted the role of the mind and spirituality (the soul) in health. However, many clinical studies have now demonstrated the link between the body-mind-soul components of a person. Modern medical scientific research has confirmed that religion and spirituality are a significant factor in well-being, with a positive link to health and longevity.

Studies by the National Institute of Healthcare Research in America suggest it may even be better for your health to go to church than to go to the gym! Forty-two separate studies into the role of religion and health established that regularly attending a place of worship is linked to a longer life, one of the most definitive measures of health. This extensive clinical research is a clear indication that spirituality is linked to mortality.

These studies, which considered 126 000 people, demonstrated that the survival chances after surgery of those who engaged in some form of religious worship was significantly higher than those who did not. People with a religious faith were less likely to be obese or diabetic. The research also found that those who never attended church had almost twice the risk of death in the nine-year follow-up period, than those who attended a place of worship regularly. This correlated to a difference in life expectancy of almost seven years.

Another study conducted by the University of Texas confirmed that the rate and length of survival after open-heart surgery was linked to religious belief and the comfort and support that this provides. Those with a religious faith were three times more likely to survive. Studies by Stanford University researchers and University of Pennsylvania psychologists have also found that people who have faith in God have higher immunity and are naturally resistant to stress. These studies are only a few among many that have reached such conclusions.

Religious belief brings meaning and purpose to life, and offers support in times of anxiety and stress that no medication or therapy can supply. Further studies are only corroborating initial research conducted. Prayer or religious worship is now a verified facet of good health. Religious rites, including prayer and mantra, are not meaningless rituals but can have a profound, positive impact on the mind and body.

While this is a fairly recent area of investigation for modern science, Āyurveda has acknowledged it for thousands of years. Āyurveda recognizes the supreme omnipresence of God, and encourages each person to develop a relationship with that Divine being, for the benefit of the soul (spirit). Consequential physical benefits only reflect the integration between the soul, mind and body.

Āyurveda incorporates the concepts of spiritual growth through meditation, yoga and personal ethical values. It does not attempt to impose a specific religion on anybody, and advocates values common to all religions. Āyurveda seeks only to inform us that we are a part of a larger, divine system. How an individual chooses to acknowledge God is a matter of personal choice: the most important thing is the recognition, not the method used.

Lifestyle

The lifestyle regime proposed in Āyurveda encompasses spiritual and psychological aspects. The guidelines are based on living according to *sāttvic* principles, including adopting personal ethics and a code of morality such as speaking the truth, serving humanity, not exploiting others, respecting elders and devotion to spiritual growth. Exercise (*yoga*), meditation and controlling negative emotions (greed, envy, anger and violence) further enhance the mind and body.

Diet, adequate sleep and exercise, cleansing therapies, and regulated sexual activity are the main factors of complete health. The lifestyle routine is based on balance in all things. Eating, sleeping and sex are undertaken within natural limits; and working, socializing, exercising and relaxation are engaged in with a balanced attitude. No one activity should be engaged in excessively, and one area of life should not be sacrificed for another. Moderation is the key to health and happiness.

> ***Yuktāhāra vihārasya yukta-ceṣṭasya karmasu***
> ***yukta-svapnāvabodhasya yogo bhavati duḥkha-hā***
>
> *One who is regulated in eating, sleeping, working and recreation can end the material pains of physical existence and experience the state of bliss. (Bhagavad Gita 6:17)*

Maintaining balance and routine throughout life can make older age more comfortable, productive and enjoyable. Studies in Southern California in the 1970s considered the factors that contributed to longevity and good health in old age. People who had balanced lifestyles and regular routines, such as eating three meals a day, going to bed early and so on, lived over a decade longer than those who did not. In contrast, those who took large quantities of vitamins did not live any longer than the average (Chopra 1991:192). Features of a balanced life are discussed throughout the rest of the chapter.

The *Tri-upastambha*

The *tridoṣa* are the three main pillars on which the health of an individual depends, and the three pillars supporting them are the *tri-upastambha* (supplementary pillars). The *tri-upastambha* are food (*āhāra*), sleep (*nidrā*) and regulated, ethical sexual activity (*brahmacarya*). Food was discussed in the previous two chapters, so sleep/*nidrā* and sex/*brahmacarya* are considered here.

Sleep—*nidrā*

Human beings spend almost a third of their lives sleeping. Sleep is the natural method to restore lost vitality and is considered "the diet of the mind". During sleep, the body is rejuvenated and strength restored. The *srotas, dhātus* and *ojas* are actively rebuilt and repaired.

Sleep occurs when *kapha* blocks the *srotas*, causing the body to become tired. The senses are unable to connect effectively with their objects. This is most noticeable with the eyes losing their ability to focus and the eyelids becoming heavy. The mind disconnects from the physical realm and the sleeping state commences. If the mind is still active during the sleeping state, vivid dreams are experienced.

For a healthy mind and energetic body it is necessary to have regulated and sound sleeping habits. Staying up late aggravates *vāta* and causes many *vāta*-related disorders. Without sufficient sleep, the senses are not rested and their functions become impaired. The mind is also not given the opportunity to relax and regain energy. Concentration may be poor, and lethargy or confusion may be experienced.

Āyurveda advises going to bed early, around 11pm at the latest, and rising early or before sunrise. This is usually around 6am depending on season. This routine helps to maintain the balance of *doṣas* in the body. Our internal "body clock" (circadian rhythm), operates most effectively when harmonized with the external environment. For example, rising in the early morning and sleeping at least six hours at night is healthy.

When our internal rhythm is disturbed and in conflict with the environment, which can occur when we change time zones, travel long distances, work night shifts or have insomnia, it can have physical impacts. These include constipation, headaches, appetite problems, poor concentration, *vāta* aggravation and nervous system disorders. (see chapter 12 for methods to alleviate insomnia.)

Six to eight hours of sleep is usually sufficient for a healthy adult. Sick people, children, old people, laborers, those who have traveled extensively or those lacking in physical strength can sleep for longer periods, depending upon their condition. This assists in stabilizing *doṣas* and *dhātus*.

Sleeping excessively can be as detrimental to health as not sleeping enough. Sleeping during the daytime should be avoided as it aggravates *kapha*, unless you are in one of the categories mentioned above. Resting for half an hour after lunch is beneficial, as is resting in the afternoon during summer when the days are longer, hotter and drier. If you rest during the day, dozing in a sitting position (in an armchair) prevents aggravation of *kapha*.

Sex—*brahmacarya*

Āyurvedic values and sexual activity has often been a source of confusion. When referring to *brahmacarya*, the word "celibacy" is usually used. Strictly speaking, celibacy is not an accurate interpretation of this concept. Regulated or controlled sexual activity is a more precise explanation, although not a literal interpretation.

The concept of complete abstinence from sex (celibacy) is related to the spiritual aspects of Āyurveda. *Brahma* actually means "study of spirit" and *carya* is "routine". So *brahmacarya* is the routine to be followed when studying to achieve spiritual enlightenment. Being distracted by sex, or lacking the ability to control sexual desire, hampers this form of spiritual study. Celibacy is for those who have dedicated their lives to spiritual enlightenment and have renounced physical pleasure.

A whole branch of Ayurveda is related to reproduction, including formulae for a range of aphrodisiacs (*vājīkaraṇa*). The main aim of this specialized field is to create healthy children, within a harmonious family structure. The important role of sex between a husband and wife, as an expression of their love and affection, is acknowledged. According to Āyurveda, people who are emotionally committed and monogamous may engage in physical intimacy for reproductive purposes.

Āyurveda recognizes that sex is an instinctive urge and natural activity of human beings. However, sexual activity, like any other area of life (such as eating and sleeping), should be governed by ethical and moral considerations and not engaged in excessively. Like eating and sleeping, sex should not be performed indiscriminately only because it is a pleasurable activity.

The *tri-upastambha* have specific biological functions for the body (nutrition, restoration and reproduction). Sensory gratification is of secondary importance. If any of these activities are engaged with the primary objective of satisfying the senses, disorders and disease can be generated. Just as if we eat too much we become obese, or if we sleep too much we become physically weak and mentally dull, engaging in excessive sexual activity has associated physical consequences.

The concept of *brahmacarya* is therefore based on several health factors. It prevents people from contracting sexually transmitted diseases, which have many detrimental physical repercussions. Psychological disturbance is also minimized, as stress, anxiety and confusion are more easily generated in physical relationships with no long-term emotional commitment. An unwanted or unplanned pregnancy, or even the risk of one, can be especially stressful.

Brahmacarya preserves *ojas*, which is essential for immunity and longevity (the health value of *ojas* is discussed in chapter 6). *Ojas* is directly connected to the reproductive fluids/*śukra dhātu*.

If an excessive amount of *śukra dhātu* is lost from the body, the quality and quantity of the *ojas* produced will be affected. To make up for the *śukra* deficiency, nutrition from *majjā dhātu* will be absorbed which in turn will take nutrition from the *asthi dhātu* and so on. Therefore, the quality of all the body tissues is negatively affected.

Preserving the *śukra dhātu* is considered essential for the mental, physical and spiritual health of an individual. A deficiency of *śukra dhātu* is the cause of many physical disorders. A person who has lower than normal quantities of this vital tissue also suffers from mental confusion and emotional problems such as stress, anxiety, fear and anger. In addition, the *doṣas* (particularly *vāta)*, are aggravaṭed by excessive sexual activity and symptoms of increased vāta may be experienced.

For these reasons *brahmacarya*, or regulated and ethical sexual activity, is considered equally important as the other two features of the *upastambha* in maintaining health. Without the support of the *upastambha* the *tridoṣa* becomes weak. This results in the onset of many chronic and incurable diseases. A person with a disciplined and controlled sexual life has a good memory and intellect, determination and strong immunity.

Following *brahmacarya* can actually enhance sexual activity. Self-discipline and control in this respect can make physical intimacy more pleasurable. It increases satisfaction, as well as the quality of *śukra dhātu*. Waiting until you are in a committed and monogamous relationship allows sex to be a genuine expression of caring and love. A lack of emotional closeness, rapport and trust can lead to inhibitions and tension, making sexual activity unpleasant. *Brahmacarya* aims for positive sexual expression as one aspect of a sincere and supportive relationship.

Other Basic Factors

Exercise

Maintaining a balance of the *tridoṣa* and following the guidelines for eating, sleeping and sexual activity keeps a person in good physical condition. However, in modern life, there is usually a high presence of *rajas* (passion) and it may not always be possible to strictly follow all the methods advocated for ensuring health.

When in the *rājasic* or *tāmasic* modes, people have a tendency to become attracted to certain foods and practices which are not really positive for their health. This includes overeating, irregular meals or sleeping, alcohol, caffeinated drinks and processed snack foods. All of these habits lead to the formation of toxins or *āma*.

Regular exercise can clean out these toxins before they accumulate and cause harm to the body, by increasing perspiration and respiration. Exercise improves the circulation system, immunity is increased, muscles are strengthened and relaxed, and the elimination of *malas* is assisted. It stimulates the *jaṭharāgni* (digestive fire), which increases appetite. This can be positive, if the diet is healthy and balanced. However, it can also encourage the habit of overeating, which is harmful if the exercise is discontinued but the quantity of food eaten remains excessive.

Exercise should be gentle and pleasant, and not strain or over-exert the body. It is best to choose a form of exercise appropriate to your constitution. *Kapha* types have high endurance and strength so they can exercise more than *vāta* types, who are weaker in endurance, muscle and joint strength. Those with a *pitta doṣa* may enjoy exercise which involves a challenge. Walking in pleasant surroundings, swimming, stretching or rhythmic and regular activity is beneficial for all *doṣas*.

Āyurveda advises *yoga* as the most suitable form of exercise. *Yoga āsanas*/physical postures are considered the best form of exercise for the body, as they involve all muscle groups and are not strenuous. *Yoga* postures improve muscle tone and strength as well as flexibility, functioning of internal systems and mental clarity. The nervous and endocrine systems are balanced, which directly affects the functioning of organs and other systems within the body. After practicing *yoga* postures, you feel refreshed and relaxed instead of tired and sore.

In addition to physical postures, *yoga* also teaches different types of *prāṇāyama* (breathing exercises), *mudrā* (gestures) and *kriyās* (activities). These facets of *yoga* consider the mental and spiritual aspects of health. *Yoga* postures are an easy form of exercise to learn, and instruction is widely available. It is usually advised that *yoga* is learnt from a qualified instructor, as this ensures that the subtleties of the *āsanas* are clearly understood and applied.

The physical aspect of *yoga* is only one part of an eightfold system. The ultimate purpose of *yoga* is to achieve self-realization and to have a peaceful mind under all circumstances. Each level is a further step towards that goal. The physical postures/*āsanas* aim to free the body of physical ailments and increase strength and immunity, in order to enable spiritual development. Along with the *āsanas*, certain lifestyle regulations are recommended which assist in achieving stability of mind and sound health. The eight parts of the *yoga* system are:

- *Yama* moral and ethical rules of conduct
- *Niyama* self-control and disciplined routine
- *Āsana* physical postures
- *Prāṇāyama* breathing techniques
- *Pratyāhār* withdrawal of senses and focus on inner mind
- *Dhāraṇā* concentration
- *Dhyāna* meditation
- *Samādhi* identification with pure consciousness

Natural urges

There are particular automatic reflexes undertaken by the body to regulate internal systems. These "natural urges" are involuntary mechanisms of the body. There are thirteen natural urges: hunger, thirst, urination, defecation, ejaculation (or the sexual urge), breaking wind, burping, vomiting, sneezing, yawning, crying, sleeping and breathing (especially heavily after exercise).

All these urges and activities have an important role in regulation of the body, such as removing wastes, gas or irritations, or providing nourishment and sustenance. Suppressing any of these urges can create disturbances inside the body. For example, withholding the urge to sneeze can create headaches, itching and irritation of the nose and impairment of the sense of smell.

Suppressing the urge to eat, drink, sleep or eliminate wastes can severely harm your health. The consequences of not expressing natural urges depends upon which urge is suppressed, but can include emaciation, dehydration, heart disease, fainting, convulsions, fever, nausea, cramps and pain in various organs.

In modern times, the expression of these urges is sometimes considered offensive or a sign of lack of self-control. People often suppress the need to sneeze, burp, yawn or cry, for example, in order to appear polite or "civilized". In certain circumstances and contexts this is understandable, but if it is possible, the urges should be attended to in private. Occasional suppression when the situation demands it is acceptable, but consistent and regular suppression should be avoided.

Other urges need to be suppressed in order to maintain health and mental balance. Negative human emotions and actions (mental, physical or verbal) should not be expressed. Vindictive deeds, stealing, greed, anger, fear, jealousy, envy, conceit, attachment or possessiveness, lust, violence, aggression, and adultery are among these. Gossiping, harsh or critical speech and lying should also be avoided.

Understanding, controlling and avoiding these negative emotions and urges is better for physical and mental health (both your own and others') than expressing them. Preventing the development of negative psychological urges through adopting a *sāttvic* attitude and lifestyle is one aim of Āyurvedic health.

Hygiene

Personal hygiene is an important precautionary measure. A clean body plays a significant role in keeping disease away, and therefore serves as a protective mechanism. Washing before eating and before sleeping, and when arising in the morning is one aspect of this. Different methods of keeping the body healthy through personal hygiene have been described in the form of detailed daily and seasonal regimens. These are considered in the next section.

Daily and Seasonal Routines

Systematic routines have been developed in Āyurveda for personal hygiene and *doṣa* balance. These vary according to day, night and season. The daily sequences may initially appear time consuming, complicated, or even meaningless, but they have been designed for specific purposes. These include hygienic factors, *tridoṣa* harmony, internal balance and reducing stress on your body and mind.

Once the daily and nightly routines have been followed a couple of times, they become a natural part of life and easy to adhere to. The steps are described in detail for information, and to explain the reasoning behind them. The complete routine has been included, but some steps are optional may be omitted depending upon personal preference. The routines are not "rules" but practical guidelines for living on a daily basis.

Daily Routine—*Dinacaryā*

Waking

One should wake up in the *brahma muhūrta*, which is the two-hour period before sunrise. This is a favorable time for commencing the day, and gives peace of mind. After waking fully, sit quietly in bed for a minute or two and think about your daily activities. This allows you to gather your thoughts and plan your day. At this stage of the day, there is a greater ability to concentrate, and motivation and determination is at its height. It is especially beneficial to think about or meditate on some good habits or positive changes that you wish to make.

Washing the face

After getting up, one should go to the sink (wash basin) and wash the face with tepid (room temperature) water. The eyes, nose and mouth should be cleaned with water. In extremely cold conditions, or if the person is suffering from a cough, cold or sore throat, it is beneficial to use warm water for washing the face.

Fill the mouth with water and hold it for 30 seconds. With the water still in the mouth, sprinkle water on your open eyes. Spit the water out, close the eyes and massage the eyelids gently with your palms for about one minute. Be gentle and do not apply too much pressure. Look into the mirror to ensure the face, eyes, nose and neck are clean and there are no abnormal signs such as swelling, lumps, insect bites, cuts or bruises.

Evacuation of bowels

Next, drink a glass of water. In winter the water should be warm. Avoid drinking tea or coffee as they contain caffeine, which increases heat (*pitta*) and causes constipation. Going to the toilet to empty the bowels is important in the morning. If you have no urge, drink another glass of water and briefly walk around your room (50 or 100 steps). The water and movement helps in the downward motion of stool and gases, and can stimulate evacuation.

Many people have "habitual constipation". They are in the habit of going to the toilet to empty the bowels either after breakfast or at some other time the day. Early morning is the best time to do this, as the waste material/*mala* (feces) should not stay in the colon for too long. The *mala* are toxic and if not evacuated in a timely fashion, start to form gases that aggravate the *apāna vāta*. This causes problems like constipation, hemorrhoids, and blockage of channels/*srotas*. Not evacuating stool in the morning may cause headache, laziness, nausea, lack of appetite, formation of wind, pain in the legs and indigestion.

In Asian and Eastern countries, after evacuation the anus is always washed. There is usually a tap near the toilet for this purpose. It is not the custom in most Western countries to do this, but it is very beneficial for maintaining a proper energy and elemental balance. The rectal plexus, which is also a seat of one of the six energy *cakras*, is activated when defecating. Cleaning it with water brings it back to the normal state.

The use of toilet paper can increase the activation (aggravation) due to the dry friction. If you have an aversion to using water for this purpose, or there are no facilities near the toilet to do so, there are many varieties of moist or wet cleansing tissues that may be substituted. After going to the toilet, wash your hands with soap.

Cleaning the teeth and tongue

In ancient Āyurvedic texts, the use of herbal sticks for oral hygeine purposes is mentioned. Small sticks from various trees, about ten inches long and the thickness of a finger, were used. The stick was crushed by chewing one end of it, to make a brush for cleaning the teeth without hurting the gums. Pungent, astringent or bitter tasting herbs or trees were used to make these sticks, such as *neem, karañja*, and *karvīra*.

These trees have anti-bacterial effects in the oral cavity. The juice secreted from these plants prevents dental diseases and strengthens the gums. In modern times, it is not usually possible to go out and bring home a branch of a tree for brushing your teeth! However, Āyurvedic tooth powders or pastes are often available in health food shops, which include the parts of certain trees and herbs that are good for oral hygiene.

After brushing the teeth, the tongue is also cleaned. Toxins are often deposited on the tongue in the form of mucus. Āyurvedic science at a more advanced level includes an analysis of the condition, color and location of these mucus deposits to identify corresponding organs that may be imbalanced or diseased. This is a very accurate diagnostic tool for practitioners.

A specially designed metal tongue scraper is used to clean the tongue. In ancient times, gold, silver or copper was used. Today, metals and plastic are used because they are cheaper and lighter. These are commonly available in India and Asia, and may be available in health food outlets in the West. The tongue scraper should not have sharp edges and should be curved or flexible.

The tongue should be scraped gently three or four times to ensure that the entire area of the tongue is cleaned, including the back. This removes the mucus, which improves taste and breath. If you cannot find a tongue scraper, a toothbrush can be used. Use the index and middle finger to cleanse the deeper end of the tongue.

Chewing cleansing herbs

After cleaning the teeth and tongue you can chew a clove or fresh betel leaf. Chewing herbs keeps the mouth fresh, free from odors and also helps in perception of tastes. Other herbs that can be chewed are *kaṭukā, pūga, sūkśmailā* and leaves of *jātī*. After eating, herbs may also be chewed for the same purpose. Commonly available herbs in the West that refresh the breath include mint and parsley.

Gargling

After chewing herbs, gargle two or three times with warm water in winter, or room temperature water in summer. This removes any remaining particles of food or herbs and rinses the mouth. Sesame oil can also be used to gargle, in moderation. This keeps the jaws and gums strong, which assists in the proper chewing of food.

Exercise

Simple exercise may be undertaken for 15 or 20 minutes. Yoga postures, brisk walking and muscle stretching are very beneficial to strengthen and co-ordinate the body parts and relax the muscles. It also relaxes the mind and is therefore important, as our mind is usually under great stress with modern lifestyles. Some simple breathing exercises (*prāṇāyama*) are very good to maintain a proper function of life air (*prāṇa*). These activities enhance physical and mental efficiency and productivity. If there is only enough time for brief activity, the yoga routine of "salute to the sun" (*sūrya namaskāra*) should be undertaken. This is partly illustrated below, and described fully in appendix 3 (p. 229).

Oil massage—*abhyanga*

Following exercise, massage with oil (*abhyanga*) is undertaken. In the daily routine, one can apply sesame oil or mustard oil. During summer, coconut oil may be used. Olive oil can be substituted if none of these oils are available.

First apply oil to the head and massage gently for a few minutes. Head massage prevents headache, graying of hair, baldness, insomnia, diseases related to the nervous system and impairment of sense organs. Put one or two drops of oil in each ear and use the fingertip to apply oil in the inner portion of nose. Do not put oil in the eyes. Once the head is finished, apply oil on other parts of the body and rub gently.

If it is not possible for you to do it this every day due to a busy schedule, twice a week or every three days is recommended. Spend at least 5-10 minutes for *abhyanga* and then relax for 5 minutes. On weekends you can spend a longer period of time massaging (about 20-30 minutes), with 15 minutes relaxation. The oil massage prevents muscle stiffness, dry skin and skin disorders, and gives strength to the body, balances the *doṣas*, nourishes the *dhātus* and increases *ojas*.

Taking a bath

The next activity in the daily routine is taking a bath or shower. Water of normal temperature (not extremely hot or cold), natural soaps and shampoos are suitable. Warm water can be used in winter. Clean every part of the body thoroughly. Essential oils or aromas may be used according to choice.

After the shower, rub the body with a towel. This opens the pores of the skin, removes the oil and old skin and increases blood circulation. It is preferable to take a shower in the morning rather than at night, as it refreshes you after sleep. However, in summer or depending upon the days' activities, a shower in the evening in addition to the morning shower can be revitalizing.

Meditation ॐ

Wear clean clothes after showering. The clothes should be comfortable, not very tight fitting and suitable for the weather. Before eating breakfast, meditating for 5-10 minutes helps clear the mind and relieve tension. This is very positive for mental and spiritual health. Sit in a relaxed position in a quiet and peaceful place. Breathe deeply and methodically. Clear the mind of thoughts and concentrate on the word *aum* or a *mantra*.

A *mantra* is a word or sequence of words that is repeated. It has spiritual energy and calms the mind, elevates consciousness and produces harmony. A *mantra* is usually unique to you and received from a bona fide spiritual teacher. If you do not have one, the word *aum* is spiritually powerful and may be used instead. The symbol for *aum* is ॐ, and focusing on this symbol can also enhance clarity and peace of mind.

Other considerations

Āyurveda advises that a person should cut their nails, hair or beard regularly. The use of fragrances, ornaments (such as jewelry) and proper footwear is also mentioned. Apply *añjana* or *kājala* (a black paste or ointment of collyrium) to the eyes and eye lashes daily or weekly. The use of collyrium makes the eyes healthy by cleansing and protecting them.

Eating was considered in the previous chapter, so it is sufficient to mention here that regular meals should be eaten during the day. If hungry between meals, snacks like nuts, fresh or dried fruits are suitable. The natural urges should always be attended to promptly.

Work

Relax whenever possible between the long working sessions. Even sitting back on a chair, closing the eyes and relaxing the mind for 2-3 minutes can make a big difference to your peace of mind and ability to concentrate. If possible, lie down or sit comfortably on a relaxing chair after lunch. Close your eyes and focus on your breathing for about five minutes. Deep, abdominal breathing is relaxing and rejuvenating.

Try to maintain a co-operative, cordial and positive atmosphere in your work place, and avoid stress and anxiety. Don't drink too much tea, coffee or cola drinks, or eat salty, processed snacks. This helps prevent over stimulation of the nervous and digestive systems. Walking around briefly or stretching occasionally, if sitting for long periods, can prevent muscle soreness and stiffness, fatigue and eyestrain. Do not work for long periods without taking breaks.

Nightly Routine—*Rātricaryā*

When you return home in the evening, try to relax for at least five minutes. If you have a family, talking or playing with family members will ease the pressure and stress experienced during the day. If you feel tired, take a shower and have a gentle head massage (with or without oil). After the shower wear comfortable clothing.

Try to eat dinner early, if possible before sunset and no later than two hours before bed. The evening meal should consist of food that is light and easily digested. Avoid deep fried, cold foods, dairy products and sweets. Rice and yogurt should be also avoided. The ideal meal consists of salads, boiled or steamed vegetables, vegetable soups and breads.

If reading or writing during the night, adequate light and a chair that supports the back are required. Do not read, write, use computers or watch television for too long. Over indulgence in sex should be avoided. Going to bed early is good, especially if you have a busy or important day coming up the following day. Try to go to sleep by 10 pm or 11 pm at the latest. Brushing the teeth and washing prior to going to bed is hygienic.

Seasonal Routines—*Ṛtucaryā*

The seasons have a natural effect on the *tridoṣa*. According to *Caraka Saṁhitā*, the strength of a person is enhanced when suitable diets and routines are adopted according to each season. To attain this level of health, one must have knowledge of the qualities of the seasons and their influence on the *tridoṣa*. The *doṣas* accumulate during seasons that share their elements or qualities. Once the *doṣa* has accumulated beyond a certain limit, it becomes aggravated and symptoms of this may be manifested. Seasons opposite in nature to a *doṣa* pacify it.

For example, *vāta* is aggravated when conditions are dry, windy and cool, such as during autumn. In winter, when it is wet and cold, *kapha* accumulates. When it is hot, *pitta* is increased. Aggravated *doṣas* are alleviated by diets and lifestyles that opposite in nature to the prevailing conditions. So, when it is hot and *pitta* is aggravated, cooling foods and drinks are beneficial. And when it is cold and *vāta* or *kapha* are aggravated, heating foods are more appropriate. Seasonal routines to alleviate *doṣas* when they are naturally aggravated are explained below.

Winter

In winter there is natural accumulation of *kapha* due to the cold and wet environment, so efforts should be made to keep warm and dry. *Vāta* may also become aggravated due to the cooler weather. Warm baths and sauna (*svedana*), sunbaths and living in an insulated or heated house are beneficial. Heavy, warm, dry clothes should be worn. In winter, massage should consist of mainly dry rubbing. If there is aggravation of *vāta*, warm oil may be used.

Avoiding cold or frozen foods and drinks, and light foods, is recommended. Warm drinks and foods that have a heating effect are preferable. During winter the digestive power/*jaṭharāgni* is stronger. As the external atmosphere is so cold, the body retains heat inside and attempts to preserve it. Therefore, the internal digestive fire becomes stronger and is able to metabolize oils, fats and dairy products (yogurt, milk, cheese). Heavier foods can form a larger part of the diet, because they are easier to digest with a strong *jaṭharāgni*.

Spring

As the heat of the sun increases in spring, accumulated *kapha* starts to break up and disperse throughout the body. This weakens the digestive fire/*jaṭharāgni* and causes many *kapha* related disorders. Coughs, sinus problems and hay fever are common during spring.

The heavy and heating diet adopted in winter should be replaced with foods more suitable for warmer weather. Lighter foods that are cooler in nature should be substituted. Sleeping during the day should be avoided as it aggravates *kapha*. Regular physical exercise, gargling with warm water (or herbal decoctions) and drinking warm water are beneficial for preventing disease and alleviating symptoms of aggravated *kapha*.

Summer

During summer, the sun is at its strongest and the heat increases *pitta*. Staying in a cool room or shady place during the day is recommended. Excessive exposure to the heat and sun may cause sunburn, heat or sunstroke. Aromas or essential oils that give a cooling effect like sandal or rose may be used. One should wear light colored clothes, and clothes should be loose and comfortable.

The diet should mainly consist of cooling, sweet foods and drinks. Cucumber, watermelon, fruits, fruit juices (not acidic or citrus varieties), grains, wheat, rice, and milk are ideal. Lots of water (6 to 8 glasses) should be consumed. Sour, pungent and salty foods should be avoided. Hot, spicy, and acidic foods such as chilies, onions, garlic and spices should be also be excluded from the diet or used in small quantities. Tea, coffee, alcohol and smoking should be avoided.

Autumn

In early autumn *pitta* is aggravated, and as the conditions become cooler *vāta* is increased. There is a lot of heat in the blood, causing skin irritations like rashes, inflammations, dryness and itching. Massage is good for the skin, and fluid intake should be maintained at 6–8 glasses to a day to cleanse the internal systems. Clothing that provides protection from the wind should be worn.

The digestive fire/*jaṭharāgni* is not very strong, so heavy foods should be minimized in the early part of the season. Sweet, light foods are recommended. As it becomes colder and wetter, foods can become heavier and more heating in nature. Try to avoid sour, acidic foods, as they will increase *pitta*. Eat those vegetables and fruits that are in season, and rice, barley and wheat.

Dear Dr Partap

Thanks for your health advice. What I found to help me the most is simply sticking to a regular routine of waking, sleeping, eating, exercise, meditating, etc. Keeping a routine helps me a lot for some reason. I guess it's because I have a lot of vāta in my constitution. Also, thanks for all the stress reduction suggestions. I already use sandalwood incense and essential oil and meditate. These help me a lot. Keep up the great work, and keep those suggestions coming. Life seems to dish out an amazing number of daily challenges that always keep one on their toes, so the less stress, the better!

Mr PM USA

Chapter 10

Disease

Dharmārtha-kāma-mokśāṇām ārogyam mīlam uttamam rogāstasyapahartārah śreyaso jīvitasya ca

Health is the supreme basis for achieving the goals of religion, economic development, sense pleasure and liberation. And disease destroys health, well being and one's very life. (Caraka Sūtra Sthāna 1:15)

OCCASIONALLY we can fall sick even though we may have a healthy lifestyle, eat the right foods and avoid those things we know cause illness. Sometimes there is no warning, but typically we experience symptoms that intensify until we are mildly incapacitated or even bedridden. Being sick is not a pleasant experience, which is why the Āyurvedic guidelines for healthy living are based on preventing sickness and disease.

Āyurveda offers treatments that can heal and cure disease. Detailed diagnostic and remedial techniques identify the cause of illness and determine appropriate treatments. The diagnostic techniques are non-invasive, and are based on observation and comprehensive questioning about aspects of physical functioning such as sleep, appetite, location and severity of pain and elimination of wastes. Once the symptoms have been assessed, herbal remedies or detoxification therapies (*panca karma*) are prescribed to bring the body back into balance.

The primary aim of Āyurveda is to increase strength, energy and longevity. Therefore, the treatment of disease (*vikṛti*) is a significant part of the discipline. Āyurvedic doctors require many years of theoretical and practical training. The preparation of herbal remedies is a complex science involving plants, herbs and minerals. The formulae may even include gems, crystals and metals that have been crushed into fine powders and processed for internal use. Alchemy (*Vedic chemistry*) is one aspect of Āyurveda that is extremely technical and may involve heating, burning and processing metals hundreds of times for internal administration.

The remedies produced are very powerful, with strong healing properties. The *śāstrīya* method of pharmaceutical preparation is a strict technique of processing the materials used in remedies, which ensures that potency and effectiveness are maximized. The remedies come in many forms, including powders, tablets, pastes, decoctions and infusions. Each has various uses in the treatment of disease.

The *panca karma* therapies (discussed in the following chapter) also require extensive training to administer, and have a special role in the treatment of disease. This chapter focuses on the causes of disease, diagnosis and disease manifestation. These concepts cover the core principles of disease treatment in Āyurveda, which are:

- Locating the root cause;
- Identifying the development of the disease; and
- Providing a permanent cure.

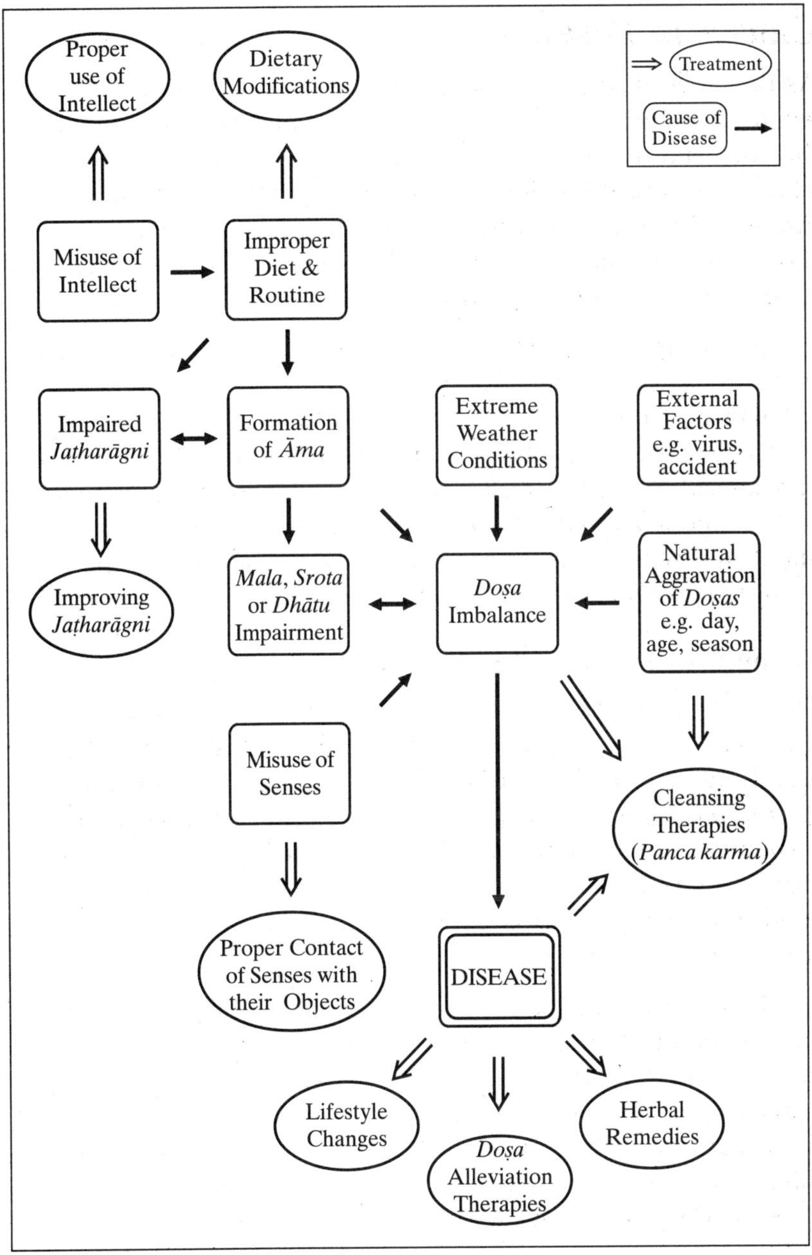

Figure 6 Causes of Disease

Causes of Disease

As discussed in the previous chapter, one is in a state of health when all the physical systems and functions are balanced, and the soul and mind are peaceful and stable. The body enjoys a situation where it has high immunity, strength and resistance to disease. When a component of our body or internal systems (*doṣas, dhātus, malas, indriyas, jaṭharāgni*) is in an unbalanced state, the environment for disease is established.

It may appear unclear what the root cause of a disease is, as there are so many components of the body that can become unbalanced. However, according to Āyurveda, the root cause of disease is always an imbalance of *tridoṣa*. Once *tridoṣa* becomes unbalanced, it triggers an imbalance in other body components, such as the *jaṭharāgni, dhātus, ojas* or *indriyas* and then disease manifests. Without an imbalance in *tridoṣa* the disease process cannot commence.

Three Causative Factors

There are a variety of factors that may cause disease. However, these can all be categorized according to three main causes identified by *Caraka*. These are the improper use of intellect (*prajñāparādha*), improper contact of the senses with their respective objects (*asātmêndriyārtha saṁyoga*) and seasonal variations (*kāla* or *pariṇāma*). These factors can all lead to conditions where disease can be generated, as they create an imbalance in the *tridoṣa*.

These three causes relate to mental, physical and environmental factors. As long as these factors are balanced, the *doṣas* are balanced and disease cannot be generated. Disease is manifested when the causal factors become unbalanced, which can occur due to three reasons: an excessive (*atiyoga*), deficient (*hīnayoga* or *ayoga*) or incorrect (*mithyāyoga*) action or situation. These concepts are clarified in the following pages.

Misuse of intellect—*prajñāparādha*

Prajñā means "wisdom" or "intelligence", and *aparādha* means "offence". So the literal meaning of *prajñāparādha* is "an offence against wisdom". That is, doing things without discriminating as to whether it is favorable or harmful for the body or mind. These actions may be verbal, mental or physical. The actions generated by *prajñāparādha* aggravate the *tridoṣa* and stimulate the *rajas* and *tamas guṇas*, allowing diseases to become established.

Excessive/*atiyoga* forms of this include talking too much, or excessive thinking, reading, mental work or physical activity. A deficiency (*hīna-yoga*) of these actions is not undertaking these activities sufficiently, like not speaking at all or very little, and not working or engaging in any intellectual or physical activity.

Incorrect (*mithyā-yoga*) forms include gossip, lying, inciting violence and irrelevant, illogical or harsh speech. Actions that are motivated by greed, anger, material attachment, envy, ego fear, grief or delusion also are *mithyā-yoga.* The physical form of this includes the suppression of natural urges or performing unnatural activity such as smoking cigarettes, driving recklessly or participating in dangerous sports.

In brief, all actions that impact on the body-mind in a negative way are *mithyā-yoga*. The person has not considered the detrimental health consequences of such activities. Or, the person is aware of the potential dangers, but ignores these and proceeds to engage in those activities anyway. Examples include smoking cigarettes despite health warnings on the packet, or continuing to drink alcohol excessively even though negative effects may have been experienced many times before.

Misuse of senses—*asātmêndriyārtha saṁyoga*

Asātmaya means "improper", *indriya* means "sense organs", *artha* is "the objects of the senses" and *saṁyoga* means "to combine" or "to link". *Asātmêndriyārtha saṁyoga* refers to improper contact of the senses with their objects, and results in an over stimulation or deficiency of sensory activity. This harms the body-mind, which requires moderation and harmony internally and externally for healthy functioning. Table 16 provides examples of the misuse of senses.

Table 16: Misuse of Senses

	Excessive *Atiyoga*	Deficient *Hīna-yoga*	Incorrect *Mithyā-yoga*
Eyes—sight	Looking at bright lights (the sun or fire), staring for a long time at a television or computer	Staying in dimly lit rooms or indoors, not using eyes, sleeping a lot during the day	Reading or looking from uncomfortable distances (too far away or too close), unpleasant view
Ears—hearing	Noise pollution, very loud noise, constant noise	Not hearing or listening, straining to hear low noises/inaudible sounds	Listening to unpleasant, negative, destructive or irritating noises
Nose—smell	Odors that are strong, or extreme, or cause allergies or itching	Not using sense of smell, or minimal use	Odors that are poisonous or noxious, foul, that induce illness, pollution
Tongue—taste	Eating when not hungry, eating a lot, tasting too many things	Not eating, avoiding tasting anything, tasting only a small variety of foods	Eating contradictory food items, or opposing to season, constitution etc, eating *tāmasic* food
Skin—touch	Touching something too hot or cold, rough or excessive massage or scrubbing	No skin contact, or very minimal skin contact	Alternating hot and cold sensations (sauna then cold shower), touching infectious or dirty items

Seasonal variations—*pariṇāma* or *kāla*

The external environment can trigger disease by unbalancing the body through unnatural or extreme variations in temperature, rainfall or wind. Excessive or *atiyoga* of *pariṇāma* is extraordinary or unexpected climatic conditions, such as excessive heat in summer or cold in winter. Deficient/*hīna-yoga* seasonal conditions include very mild temperatures in summer or winter. The normal temperature variations are not experienced. Incorrect/*mithyā-yoga pariṇāma* occurs when conditions are opposite to the normal season, such as being cold in summer or warm in winter.

Pariṇāma or *kāla* also refers more generally to the effects of time, and the natural physical transformations that occur over time. For example, seasonal influences on the *doṣas*, and the disorders associated with specific phases of life and aging are all in this category.

Role of *Doṣas*

Although the *doṣas, dhātus* and *malas* are all factors in good health, the *tridoṣa* is the central factor. If the *tridoṣa* is balanced, *jaṭharāgni* operates effectively and the body will be in balance. If the *doṣas* become aggravated, *jaṭharāgni* may become impaired and produce *āma*, which disturbs the *dhātus, srotas* and *malas*. In this way, the *doṣas* are directly or indirectly responsible for any imbalance manifested in the body.

The other bodily constituents are not independent disease causing factors, even though they may appear to be. They may contribute to a *doṣa* becoming unbalanced, but disease will not manifest until the *doṣa* is aggravated. That is why maintaining balanced *doṣas* is considered a primary goal of health, and a thorough knowledge of all *doṣas* and their divisions is required when prescribing appropriate treatments.

Despite particular symptoms, it is not always a clear exactly which *doṣa* is aggravated. Identifying the aggravated *doṣa* is not always a matter of simply considering physical symptoms. Sometimes the physical symptoms may even be misleading. Without a thorough examination, an incorrect treatment may be recommended and the condition can be aggravated rather than alleviated.

For example, a cold/*pratiśyāya* is not always caused by aggravated *kapha* just because the symptoms include a runny nose and mucus congestion. There are a variety of *pratiśyāya*, one of which is caused by aggravation of *pitta*. If a proper examination is not performed, it may seem that heating (anti-*kapha*) remedies are the appropriate treatment. However, as the root cause is *pitta* related, the patient will not respond to this treatment, and will become worse as heating remedies increase *pitta*.

Masked symptoms may further complicate identification of the aggravated *doṣa*. This is because as well as the three states or conditions of *doṣas* mentioned in chapter 3, there is another state known as the covered state (*doṣa avaraṇa*). This is very common, and relates to the *vāta doṣa*.

Covered state

The covered state is a potential condition of the *vāta doṣa*. In this state, the functions of the *vāta doṣa* are obscured by another *doṣa*, or an increased *dhātu* or *mala*. This aggravates *vāta* because its circulation is blocked. Sometimes, even one type of *vāta* (*prāṇa, udāna, samāna,* etc.) may block the circulation of another *vāta* division. Although treatment is relatively straightforward once the aggravated *doṣa* has been identified, the process can sometimes be confused by this factor.

Failure to consider the covered state will create difficulties in the treatment process. Without knowledge of this state, the root cause of disease may not be identified. As the causative factor is not *vāta*, the correct treatment involves removing the blockage that has led to the *vāta* disturbance. Alleviating *vāta* in these situations will not provide a complete cure, as this is only a symptom and not the cause of the disorder. Therefore, treatment must involve alleviating *vāta* in addition to the covering factor.

When *vāta* is covered by another *doṣa, dhātu* or *mala*, it displays symptoms similar to the responsible *doṣa, dhātu* or *mala*. For example, if *vāta* is covered by *kapha*, the symptoms will be similar to *kapha* disorders such as a feeling of heaviness, laziness, cold, cough and congestion. If an excess of muscle tissue (*māṁsa dhātu*) covers *vāta* the symptoms may include boils, acne, edema and swelling in addition to increased *vāta* symptoms.

The importance of *vāta*

Of the three *doṣas, vāta* is the most important for health. The body can only function normally when *vāta* provides assistance. *Vāta* is responsible for all movement in the body, and governs the transportation of all fluids and wastes. Even the movement of food through the digestive tract, which is responsible for the formation of *doṣas, dhātus* and *malas*, requires *vāta*. It is also responsible for the functioning of body components and the other *doṣas*. Therefore, it is essential that *vāta doṣa* functions properly.

Vāta aggravation causes eighty different types of disease. *Pitta* disorders create forty physical illnesses, and *kapha* aggravation twenty. An imbalance of *vāta* is therefore by far the most serious, due to the number and severity of physical complications that can arise.

Modern lifestyles are particularly *vāta* aggravating, as activity, traveling, late nights, and irregular or erratic lifestyle routines are common. For these reasons, assessing *vāta doṣa* is important when considering the state of health. The aggravation of *vāta* should always be considered even if symptoms of *vāta* disturbance are not apparent, due to its physical significance and the potential of a covered state operating.

Doṣa aggravation

The aggravation (increase) of a *doṣa* may be indicated by changes in diet and activity. There may be an aversion to the types of foods or activities that led to the *doṣa* aggravation, and a preference for foods and activities that have opposite qualities. For example, if there is an aggravation of *kapha*, one symptom may be an aversion to sweet, heavy foods such as fried or greasy food and dairy products. Instead, light foods may be preferred. If *pitta* is aggravated, there may be an aversion to hot, spicy, sour and salty foods and a desire for cold drinks or food.

Other symptoms vary according to the *doṣa* and are linked to the parts of the body it governs. If there is aggravation of *vāta*, symptoms include pain in the abdomen, wind and gas formation. Symptoms of increased *pitta* are burning sensations in the stomach, skin irritations and blood disorders. *Kapha* aggravation may be indicated by heaviness, laziness or lethargy, or mucus in the chest, throat and nose. The symptoms may appear individually or in clusters.

Once an increased *doṣa* is observed, efforts should be made to decrease it. This is mainly achieved by following a diet and routine that are opposite in nature to the aggravated *doṣa*. That is, eating foods and engaging in activities that have opposite qualities to that of the increased *doṣa*. (Specific methods to achieve this are discussed in chapter 3.) This is a mild treatment method, but care should still be taken not to disturb the other *doṣas* while trying to alleviate the increased *doṣa*.

Balancing, or alleviating, the appropriate *doṣa* can sometimes be achieved by increasing another *doṣa*. For example, in the state of increased *kapha*, increasing *pitta* may balance it. However, this method of treatment always carries the risk of aggravating *pitta*. For this reason, the preferred method of treatment is always to use methods to alleviate the increased *doṣa* directly, rather than indirectly through increasing an opposing *doṣa*.

Tendency to Disease

The tendency to particular diseases is related to the dominant *doṣa*. Depending upon the dominant *doṣa*, there will be a susceptibility to the disorders linked to it. As each *doṣa* has specific locations in the body, these sites are particularly prone to disease (chapter 3; see also appendix 1).

For example, people with a predominantly *kapha doṣa* will be prone to disorders of the upper body, or those involving mucus, phlegm, congestion and fluid retention. Asthma, bronchitis, respiratory or sinus disorders, allergies of the eyes and nose are some examples. They are also more prone to becoming overweight (solidity, heaviness) than other *doṣas*.

People with a dominant *pitta doṣa* are prone to disorders of the middle body, including digestive disorders or stomach ulcers, and those related to an excess of heat in the body such as fever and skin problems (redness, itching, boils, acne, freckling). *Vāta* types are susceptible to disorders of the lower body, and those related to an excess of air (dryness); constipation and colon problems, rough or dry skin, dehydration and joint impairments.

This is because the dominant *doṣa* can easily become disturbed, due to its disproportionate presence. In addition, people are attracted to foods and activities that reflect their own elemental composition, so there is a tendency to prefer those items that aggravate their *doṣa*. If these habits and preferences are not moderated, there is a danger that the dominant *doṣa* will become unbalanced.

It is usually more difficult to treat conditions that are related to your *doṣa* (for example, treating *kapha* disorders in a *kapha* type person), as these conditions have become established in a favorable environment, which encourages and supports their development.

Identification of Disease

Methods to identify disease include examining the patient and using specific diagnostic tools.

Patient Examination

The Āyurvedic doctor (*Vaidya*) makes a careful diagnosis after scrutinizing a range of factors, some of which the patient may not even consider relevant. In addition to gathering information from specific questions about symptoms, lifestyle, diet and medical history, the physician systematically observes other features that may provide clues to the cause and duration of the illness.

For example, a doctor uses the senses (sight, hearing, touch, smell) to assess physical condition and severity of symptoms. The doctor can see the shape and location of any symptoms, or the color, texture and state of skin, eyes, hair, nails and tongue. The overall constitution and strength of the patient can also be quickly observed, such as physical build, age and robustness.

Sounds of the body, such as respiratory or digestive noises, tone of voice, and noises made from joint movements provide further details. Touch determines the *guṇas* (qualities) of the body and nature of symptoms displayed (for example, dry, moist, hard, soft, rough, hot, cold). The pulse is also assessed through touching the wrist. Smell or odor of tissues and wastes (such as perspiration) may be abnormal or indicative of particular internal complications.

The entire demeanor of the patient during the consultation provides the doctor with additional information. Emotional state and nature, strength and vitality, intelligence, and character can all be ascertained from attire, posture, body language, breathing patterns and even gait and bearing. These features give the doctor information about the patient without them even being aware of it. The Āyurvedic doctor can usually undertake a thorough examination without the patient removing a single item of clothing or undergoing any tests.

The primary goal of the examination is to locate the unbalanced *doṣa/s* that caused the illness or disease. The methods used by the *Vaidya* (observation, touch and questioning) are all aimed at identifying the *doṣa* disturbance. For example, a person with hot, flushed skin and symptoms such as burning sensations, fever, digestive disorders or urinary infections has a disturbance of *pitta*. Dry, cracked, rough skin that is cold indicates an imbalance of *vāta*. Fluid retention, swelling, moist skin and dull, watery eyes and symptoms such as chest congestion are *kapha* related.

One of the significant methods of investigating *doṣa* aggravation is by checking the pulse. In recent years, some Āyurvedic doctors have promoted pulse diagnosis as the only method of examination. However, patient examination is quite complex and involves a range of considerations in addition to the pulse. Establishing the state of health just by checking the pulse might appear mystical or fascinating, but in order to confirm the diagnosis, many other factors must be taken into account.

There are eight types of assessment (*parīkśā*) that a doctor uses to arrive at a diagnosis and determine an appropriate treatment regime. These are examinations of:

Pulse—*nāḍī*	quality, regularity, strength, speed.
Urine—*mūtra*	color, consistency, frequency, patterns of oil on the surface.
Stool—*purīṣa*	whether it floats, color, smell, presence of blood or mucus.
Tongue—*jivhā*	color, shape, type and location of mucus and abnormalities.
Eyes—*netra*	color, shape, vision, dryness, tremors, puffiness, eyelashes.
Sound—*śabda*	from intestines, heart, lungs, joints, voice.
Touch—*sparśa*	skin temperature, swellings, tenderness.
Appearance—*ākṛti*	weight, height, color of skin, nails, hair.

Diagnostic Methods

Āyurveda uses five types of evaluative tools, known as the *panca nidāna,* to diagnose disease. *Panca* means five, and *nidāna* is "diagnostic methods." These are the cause (*nidāna*), preliminary signs (*pūrva rūpa*), symptoms (*rūpa*), exploratory methods (*upaśaya*) and disease development (*samprāpti*).

The *panca nidāna* refines a diagnosis in cases where one *nidāna* may create a number of different diseases. For example, the aggravation of *vāta* causes eighty different types of diseases. It is not usually only sufficient to know the cause/*nidāna* of the disease is that *vāta* is aggravated. For a permanent cure, the particular disease out of the eighty potential diseases that are caused by *vāta* needs to be identified.

Diagnosing which of the *vāta* divisions are involved, which *srotas* or *dhātus* are affected and the location of the accumulated *vāta* (*dūṣya*) requires additional diagnostic tools (the *panca nidāna*). Simply implementing an anti-*vāta* therapy may not permanently eradicate all *vāta* related disorders, if the affected *srotas, dhātus* and *dūṣya* have been overlooked.

As well as those considerations, the entire disease process, starting from the cause/*nidāna*, to the symptoms and manifestation of the specific disease, requires assessment. Even the preliminary signs (*pūrvarūpa*) or the symptoms (*rūpa*) may be similar in some diseases. The diagnostic methods become crucial in these cases.

For example, Āyurveda recognises five different types of cough, with similar major symptoms. However, the same remedy will not be effective in treating each of those five forms of cough. The treatment of a cough caused by aggravation of *pitta* is different from that caused by the aggravation of *kapha*.

To determine the appropriate treatment, understanding the development of the disease (*samprāpti*) is necessary. The knowledge of *panca nidāna* is therefore valuable in diagnosis of diseases that appear similar according to their *nidāna, pūrvarūpa* and *rūpa*. Prescribing the right treatment to permanently cure the disease is assisted by a thorough application of these diagnostic techniques.

Description of *Panca Nidāna*

Causative factor—*nidāna*

Nidāna is the disease-causing factor. Diet, life style or external factors like environmental variations (excessive heat, cold or rain), injuries or any other factors that disturbs the *tridoṣa* are considered *nidāna*. Depending on their origin, nature and specific qualities, they are classified into many different types. The main *nidāna* have been discussed in the section on causes of disease and are illustrated in diagram at the start of the chapter.

Preliminary indications—*pūrva rūpa*

Pūrva rūpa are preliminary signs of disease. These symptoms appear before the actual onset of any illness, and are warning signs that disease may soon manifest. Each disease has specific *pūrva rūpas*. If there is any confusion about a specific diagnosis on the basis of *nidāna*, then *pūrva rūpas* need to be considered.

For example, in the case of epilepsy, the *pūrva rūpas* include dimness of vision, particular odors or tastes becoming prominent and a throbbing pain all over the body.

Symptoms—*rūpa*

Rūpa, or the symptoms of a disease, indicate the actual onset of the manifestation process. When *rūpa* appear, the disease becomes more pronounced with obvious and clearly defined symptoms. The *rūpa* can be considered the advanced form of the warning signs (*pūrva rūpa*). The severity and number of *rūpas* present provide the doctor with indications of physical impacts, the possibility of cure and the length of time healing may take.

A metaphoric example of these concepts is a fire. First there is smoke, which can be considered *pūrva rūpa*. When the fire starts to ignite, flames and heat are produced. These are the *rūpa*, the more specific, definite characteristics of a fire. They can give an indication of the size and intensity of the fire. The fire itself may be considered the disease, and the log of wood may be compared to the body.

Exploratory treatment—*upaśaya*

There are certain diseases which have identical *nidāna, pūrva rūpa* and *rūpa*. For example, fever may be a symptom of typhoid, malaria or pneumonia. In ancient times, when scientific testing techniques did not exist, a specific diagnosis was aided by *upaśaya*. This involves investigating and eliminating potential diagnoses through diet, herbal remedies or physical therapies.

For example, in the case of fever mentioned, the doctor might try prescribing quinine to see if the symptoms are alleviated. If that reduces the severity of symptoms, it confirms that the patient has malaria. If quinine makes no difference, malaria can be eliminated as one of the potential diseases. Similarly, dietary changes may be recommended by a doctor to confirm an opinion about a suspected diagnosis. *Upaśaya* is used still today in Western medicine, to determine the cause of an allergy or food intolerance, for example.

Development of the disease—*samprāpti*

Samyaka means "proper" and *prāpti* is "to get." *Samprāpti* is to get the proper knowledge about the pathway of disease manifestation. This provides complete knowledge of the disease progression, starting from the cause, the *doṣa/s* involved and the location where aggravated *doṣa/s* have accumulated (*dūṣya*). All the bodily changes that occur from the time of exposure to the *nidāna*, to the actual onset of disease and its manifestation are placed under the category.

Benefits of *Panca Nidāna*

In addition to identifying the nature, location and treatment of disease, *panca nidāna* also helps in the prevention of disease, as it provides an understanding of causes/*nidāna*. Avoiding or taking certain precautions prevents exposure to the specific factors that generate disease. For example, water often contains bacteria that cause a variety of diseases. Destroying the bacteria by chlorinating, filtering or boiling the water can prevent those diseases.

If we know that certain foods or particular activities aggravate a *doṣa* we can avoid those *nidāna* and prevent disease manifestation. In addition, avoiding the specific *nidāna* will supplement treatment undertaken to cure the disease. Remedies or treatments will not be effective if you continue with the diet or factor that has generated the disease.

Similarly, if we have knowledge about the preliminary signs and symptoms of a particular disease (*pūrva rūpa* and *rūpa*), steps to combat the disease can be implemented at that stage, before the disease has actually manifested. Therefore, the establishment of disease, and subsequent damage to the body can be prevented with an understanding of *panca nidāna*.

This knowledge also helps in determining the specific treatment according to the stage of the disease process. Once the disease has actually manifested, investigating the severity of symptoms (*rūpa*) helps in determining the appropriate treatment. In the same way, the exploratory treatments (*upaśaya*) and disease pathway (*samprāpti*) allows a thorough understanding about specific aspects of the disease, and permits us to refine treatment regimes in order to ensure the cure is permanent.

The Six Stages of Disease Manifestation

The disturbance of *doṣas* may cause immediate symptoms, or they may manifest over time. For example, in the case of an accident or external injury, the *tridoṣa* equilibrium is severely disturbed and symptoms (such as pain, bruising or swelling) may appear immediately. In other conditions, the *doṣas* gradually express their disturbed state by progressively displaying symptoms. For example, diabetes has initial symptoms of increased thirst and urination, and then emaciation, eye disorders and even coma can occur.

A chronic disease usually does not just appear instantaneously. The process of development is over a period of time, and involves a variety of stages. The disease can be treated at each stage of manifestation, preventing further development. *Ṣaḍa* means "six", *kriyā* means "an action" and *kāla* is "time". *Ṣaḍavidha kriyākāla* therefore can be literally translated as "six time periods of treatment", to prevent further development of a disease.

The treatment phases are related to the stage of disease manifestation. The stages are sequential, and the disease can only progress when the previous stage has reached a critical level. At each stage, dietary modifications, lifestyle routines or herbal medicines can alleviate symptoms and prevent further development. Āyurveda is the only medical system that advises on methods of treating a disease before it has fully manifested. Treatment can commence when symptoms of *doṣa* disturbance are observed, before a disease has actually developed.

Table 17: Disease Manifestation and Treatment

Stage of disease manifestation	Treatment
1. **Accumulation** of doṣas/incubation *Sancaya*	Stop and prevent further accumulation of *doṣas* • Diet and lifestyle modifications
2. **Aggravation** of *doṣas* *Prakopa*	Alleviation of *doṣas* • Diet, *pūrva karma, panca karma*
3. **Spreading** of *doṣas* *Prasara*	Prevent further dispersal • As above
4. **Relocation** of *doṣas* *Sthāna saṁśraya*	Transference and elimination from the body • *Panca karma* plus herbal remedies
5. **Manifestation** of disease *Vyakta*	Dependent upon nature of disease • Remedies and therapies specific to disorder
6. **Chronic stage** of disease *Bheda*	Medication and therapies • As above

Accumulation—*Sancaya*

Sancaya means "collection" or "accumulation". As a result of exposure to causative factors (*nidāna*), the *doṣa/s* begin accumulating in the specific parts of the body they govern. As previously mentioned, *vāta* is predominant in the lower part of the body (below the navel), *pitta* is mainly located in the middle portion of the body (between the navel and the chest) and *kapha* is situated in the upper body (chest, throat and head).

The *sancaya* of the *doṣas* takes place in their respective locations, when the *doṣa* is increased. For example, if a person increases *kapha* with diet and lifestyle choices (eating sweet, greasy, fried or cold foods, sleeping during the daytime and not exercising) then *kapha* will start to accumulate in the lungs, throat and head. Similarly, if a person is eating food that increases *vāta*, over a period of time *vāta* will accumulate in its natural locations of the colon, rectum and bladder.

The accumulation of a *doṣa* is not sufficient in itself to cause serious problems. However, if it is ignored until it has accumulated in large quantities, an aggravation (*prakopa*) will eventuate and the second stage of the disease process will commence. It is always preferable to stop the process in the initial stage of accumulation, when the disease is 'incubating'. Treatment involves a *doṣa* alleviating diet and routine.

Aggravation—*Prakopa*

In this stage the *doṣa/s* remain in their respective locations, and the symptoms are similar to those that appear in the accumulation stage. These are related to the places of the body that the *doṣa* governs. For example, *vāta* may cause throbbing pain in the abdomen; *pitta* aggravation can result in acidic burping, skin irritations and excessive thirst and *kapha* may cause nausea, dyspepsia and diminished appetite.

As the *doṣas* are still present in their respective physical locations, the symptoms are mainly confined to those areas. The only differences between the accumulation and aggravation stages are that the symptoms become more severe, and the *doṣas* are ready to move to other physical locations.

The treatment for *prakopa* is also a *doṣa* alleviating diet. Elimination therapies include enema in the case of aggravated *vāta*, laxatives in *pitta* disorder, and supervised induced vomiting in *kapha* cases. These physical therapies are very beneficial and provide immediate relief, as the accumulated *doṣas* are eliminated from the areas in which they have gathered.

Spreading—*Prasara*

If the *doṣas* are not treated in the *prakopa* stage, and the person continues to follow the diet or lifestyle that caused the initial accumulation and aggravation, the *doṣas* start to spread to other parts of the body. This dispersal of *doṣas* is termed *prasara*, an "overflow" of *doṣas*.

As already explained, *vāta* is responsible for the movements of fluids, *doṣas, dhātus, malas* and so on. In rare situations, the *doṣas* move independently. They may spread alone or in combination with other *doṣas*. Frequently, they combine with *rakta* (blood) and spread through its circulation network.

Depending on the various combinations, fifteen types of *prasara* or overflow are described in Āyurveda. They are all the possible combinations of *vāta, pitta, kapha,* and *rakta*.

Doṣas may spread upwards, downwards or diagonally. They may move towards different organs, limbs or joints and produce disease in that area. While mobile, the *doṣas* display characteristic symptoms. *Vāta* produces abdominal distension, and pain in the intestines and colon. *Pitta* produces heat and burning sensations all over the body. *Kapha* produces heaviness, fatigue, and vomiting.

In this stage, treatment involves stopping their spread and transferring them back to the place of the original accumulation. This is a slightly more difficult treatment in comparison to the first two stages. As the *doṣas* are still mobile, treatment should involve directing the *doṣas* towards their respective location where they can be eliminated or alleviated. The *pūrva karma* treatments like massage (*snehana*) and heating therapy (*svedana*) stimulate the *doṣas* to move to their natural locations.

Relocation—*Sthāna Saṁśraya*

If the spread of the *doṣas* is not stopped, they move throughout the whole body via the *srotas* and establish themselves in places that are weak. This relocation of *doṣas* in places other than their normal sites is called *sthāna saṁśraya*. The places or organs with strong immunity may be able to resist the aggravated *doṣas*, but weaker areas allow them to stabilize. The aggravated *doṣas* merge or mix with the *dhātus* of the place where they locate themselves.

Symptoms vary according to the place (organ or system) where the *doṣas* have relocated. For example if *doṣa/s* stabilize in the abdomen, they will cause diarrhea, dysentery, constipation, indigestion and so on. If they stabilize in the bladder, they will cause obstructed urination or other urinary disorders. This is the stage when the warning signs/*pūrva rūpa* of the disease appear.

The process of disease manifestation can still be halted, as the actual symptoms/*rūpa* of the disease have not yet appeared. However, treatment becomes more difficult with the advancement of the disease process. The line of treatment can involve moving them back to the place of accumulation and then eliminating them. Alternatively, treatment at this stage can involve balancing the *doṣas* in the place of relocation.

For example, if *vāta* has transferred to the natural site of *pitta*, it should be treated like *pitta*. The use of laxatives will help to eliminate *vāta* in this case, although laxatives are mainly used to eliminate *pitta*. Similarly, if *pitta* goes to the site of *kapha*, it should be treated like *kapha* and if *kapha* goes to the site of *vāta*, it should be treated like *vāta*.

The specific treatment varies according to the *doṣa*. Depending on the *pūrva rūpa* displayed, the doṣa involved is identified and diet or herbs are used to balance it. A treatment opposing to the causative factor also helps to stop further manifestation of the disease.

For example, symptoms like a burning sensation when passing urine, and dark yellow discoloration of urine indicate relocation of *pitta* in the urinary system. The treatment will be *pitta* alleviating, which includes taking cooling drinks and foods. Avoiding the causative factor means not consuming foods or drinks that increase *pitta* (tea, coffee, chilies, pickles and salty or sour tastes). Taking diuretic herbs like *gokśuru* will help to eliminate the increased *pitta*.

Manifestation—*Vyakta*

The definition of *vyakta* is "expressed" or "presented". The symptoms of disease become obvious and clearly expressed in this stage. The symptoms/*rūpas* can be observed, and the disease identified. The treatment in this stage varies according to the disease, and particular Āyurvedic medicines may be used.

This is the stage at which the disease is usually noticed by most patients, and diagnosed in modern medical systems. Modern medicine arrives at a diagnosis and treatment after confirming all of the symptoms of a particular disease. Āyurveda describes various treatments, diets and remedies prior to this point in the disease process, which can stop the disease from fully manifesting.

Chronic Stage—*Bheda*

If the disease is not treated despite manifestation at the *vyakta* stage, it will enter into a chronic stage that may not be easy to treat or could even become incurable. The literal meaning of *bheda* is "differentiation". In the fifth stage, the general form of the disease can be diagnosed based on symptoms displayed. But in the sixth stage, special features appear. On the basis of these special features the disease can be further differentiated into a specific type. For example, in the *vyakta* stage, diabetes may be diagnosed. But in the *bheda* stage, the particular form of diabetes can be determined.

In this stage, along with the specific symptoms, various complications also appear. The *dhātus* or *srotas* may be severely impaired in function or formation. These complications may lead to irreversible damage. It is easier to treat disease in its initial stages, in the same way that it is easier to remove a weed in its germinating stage or when it is a seedling. If it is not removed then, the roots will spread and it will become more difficult to dislodge.

Classification of Disease

Disease can be classified in a number of ways. As disease is generated by an imbalance in *tridoṣa*, common classification systems are based on either the type of *doṣa* aggravation or the cause of the *doṣa* aggravation.

According to the type of *doṣa* aggravation, disease may be divided into two groups. The *nānātmaja* category includes those diseases caused by an aggravation of only one *doṣa*. A disease caused by an aggravation of more than one *doṣa* is classified as *sāmānyaja*.

The *tridoṣa* need a causative factor to become disturbed in the first place. *Caraka* lists the following three categories of disease, depending upon whether the initial imbalance of *doṣas* was caused by an internal, external or psychological factor:

- **Endogenous** or internal (*Nija* or *Śārīra Roga*): The *doṣa/s* are unbalanced by internally aggravating factors such as improper diet, life style and irregular routines for exercise, sleeping, and daily life. The misuse of the intellect and senses can come within this category.
- **Exogenous** or external (*Āgantuka Roga*): The *doṣa/s* are unbalanced by an external factor, like bacteria, injury, accidents, fire, poisons, animals, pollution and environmental factors. Unnatural seasonal variations are included in the exogenous category.
- **Psychological** (*Mānas Roga*): An imbalance of *doṣa/s* due to an excess of *rajas* and/or *tamas guṇas* can cause some diseases. Disorders like depression, anxiety, stress and negative emotional states like anger, greed, envy, are among these. Psychosomatic disorders, or the physical conditions generated from anxiety and stress are also in the *mānas roga* category. The misuse of the intellect and senses can create excess *rajas* or *tamas*.

Suśruta mentions a fourth category of disease, the "natural" disorders or *svābhāvika roga*. The imbalance of *doṣa/s* in this category is caused by naturally occurring physical factors. This includes the symptoms experienced when thirsty, hungry, tired or old. Although these are natural processes of life, one can suffer from severe physical consequences as a result of hunger, thirst or old age. Conditions relating to any of these factors are classified in the *svābhāvika roga* category of disease.

CHAPTER 11

Therapies

ĀYURVEDA employs a variety of therapies to treat disorders and prevent disease. The primary aim of these therapies (*cikitsā*) is to rebalance the *doṣas, dhātus, malas* and mind *guṇas*. The therapies also eliminate toxins/*āma* from the body, and increase both the quantity and quality of *ojas*. Additionally, these processes soothe the senses and enhance general physical and mental well-being.

As the aims of Āyurveda are to maintain health and cure disease, therapies are not limited only to those who are sick or suffering from an imbalance/*vikṛti*. Most other health sciences only treat physical disorders and illness. Āyurveda is unique in the field of medicine as it also offers treatment for healthy people. Therapies that cleanse and rejuvenate the body enhance an existing state of health and increase the lifespan.

Aim of Therapy

Although retaining the balance of *doṣas* is the main aim of therapy/*cikitsā*, an Āyurvedic doctor provides additional treatments to increase physical and mental strength. These therapies also improve the functioning of the digestive and elimination systems. When treating disease, the aim of *cikitsā* is not only to alleviate symptoms; it is also to remove the root cause of imbalance. The aims of therapy include:

- Treating and removing the root cause of imbalance;
- Increasing the power of digestion/*jaṭharāgni*;
- Maintaining proper elimination of wastes/*malas*;
- Enhancing immunity/*ojas*;
- Developing a spiritual/*sāttvic* temperament.

Types of Therapies

The definition of "therapy" as any method of balancing the *doṣas* embraces many activities. A *doṣa* balancing diet and routine is one form of therapy. Treatments also include methods to increase the weight and strength of weak patients, or reduce obesity in others. Exercise, meditation, internal cleansing, use of gems, herbal pastes and compresses, sweating, massage and herbal medications are other therapies used in Āyurveda.

Therapies may be broadly classified as those for healthy people and those for the sick. The treatments for healthy people enhance *ojas* and longevity. These are mainly rejuvenation therapies (*rasāyana*) and aphrodisiacs (*vājīkaraṇa*). Internal cleansing may also be used to maintain health, but is more often prescribed to treat a specific condition.

Wastes and toxins are produced internally as a result of metabolic activities and the digestive process. An accumulation of these wastes disturbs the *doṣas*. There is also a natural aggravation of *doṣas* according to season. To maintain good health and treat disease, the toxins and excess *doṣas* should either be balanced inside the body (*śamana*) or removed from the body (*śodhana*), through the use of herbal medicines or detoxification therapies.

Śamana therapy involves using different types of herbal medicines or diets to decrease aggravated *doṣas* (chapter 3). Externally, medicated oils, massage, herbal pastes or hot/cold compresses can be applied for the same purpose. *Śodhana* eliminates increased *doṣas* from the body. The three main therapies discussed in this chapter are internal detoxification (*śodhana*), rejuvenation (*rasāyana*) and treatment for addictions (*madātya*).

Internal Cleansing—*Śodhana*

To remove excess *doṣas* or impurities, *panca karma* treatments are used. The elimination process/*śodhana* involves three distinct parts: preparation (*pūrva karma*), cleansing and elimination therapies (*panca karma*), followed by post therapy care (*pascāta karma*). This entire process is usually referred to simply as *panca karma*, the most significant aspect of *śodhana*.

Śodhana is carried out under the guidance of an expert physician, using highly specialized techniques. The *panca karma* therapist works closely with the doctor to treat the patient according to the diagnosis. The complete process can take either 53 or 129 days, during which time the patient must stay under the supervision of the doctor to ensure that the proper diet and lifestyle is maintained.

It is preferable that the location be pleasant, relaxing, peaceful and free from pollution and noise. The place of treatment needs to be well equipped with all facilities, drugs, herbs and remedies that may be required in case of any complications. An Āyurvedic specialist usually avoids risks by taking extreme care when prescribing and administering therapies. A thorough knowledge of the constitution, strength and diet of the patient, as well as the disorder, is also necessary.

The *āma* produced by modern lifestyles has led to the establishment of many *śodhana* clinics in India, which provide internal detoxification. Often, these *panca karma* centers do not offer therapies based strictly on traditional methods and processes that take months to complete, but versions of them that take only a few days or weeks to undergo. The three stages of the internal cleansing process are described in the following pages.

1. Preliminary treatment—*pūrva karma*

Preliminary treatments (*pūrva karma*) prepare the body for *panca karma* therapy. Consisting of oil treatment and heating (sweating) therapies, they stimulate toxins in the body and encourage them to accumulate in specific locations. This assists in their elimination when *panca karma* is undertaken.

- **Oil treatment—*snehana***

Snehana is advised for those patients who wish to undergo heating therapy (*svedana*), any form of *panca karma* and those suffering from *vāta* related disorders. Medicated oils may be taken orally, to mobilize toxins internally. Vegetable oils (mustard, sesame, olive, castor, coconut, *neem*) are mainly used, although animal oils in the form of cow or buffalo *ghī* are also effective.

External *snehana* primarily involves oil massage. Specially chosen herbal oils are applied to the body, according to the physical condition of the patient. This treatment is not only relaxing, but improves circulation and the metabolism, assisting impurities in the body to gather and be released. Massage opens and cleans the pores of the skin, which are sometimes blocked with toxins/ *āma*.

Massage also enhances good health and longevity by softening and lubricating the skin, preventing dryness, wrinkles and skin disorders. It reduces swelling, regulates the digestive system and prevents *vāta* diseases associated with old age such as pain, swollen joints, gout and loose muscles. It is also beneficial in cases of insomnia, depression, anxiety, stress and nervous system disorders.

- **Heating therapy—*svedana***

Heating therapy (*svedana*) consists of using techniques to encourage sweating, such as applying steam or warm compresses to the body. The perspiration carries toxins out of the body, and the heat generated disperses the *doṣas*, and opens the channels, pores and cell membranes. *Caraka Saṁhitā* has divided *svedana* or sudation into two main categories: thermal *svedana* (thirteen types) and non-thermal *svedana* (ten types).

Thermal *svedana* involves direct exposure to heat. The thirteen forms differ according to the herbs used, method of applying the heat, part of the body heat is applied to and intensity of the heat. Some of the methods are quite elaborate and require the construction of special rooms or cottages that have herbs on the walls and other features, or particular types of fires. Techniques include steaming, baths, herbal poultices or compresses and herbal vapors. Warm oil, water, milk or herbal decoctions may also be poured onto specific parts of the body.

Non-thermal *svedana* are activities that produce or increase heat in the body, causing sweating. Forms of non-thermal *svedana* include exercise, wearing heavy clothing, hunger, drinking alcohol, fear, anger, heating herbs and exposure to the sun.

2. Cleansing therapies—*panca karma*

Panca karma involves purifying therapies to enhance metabolic processes. It is used in chronic disease treatment, as well as reducing seasonal imbalance of *doṣas*. *Panca* means "five" and *karma* means "action"; *panca karma* entails five techniques:

- *Vamana* emetics
- *Virecana* laxatives
- *Basti* medicated enema
- *Nasya* nasal administrations, and
- *Rakta mokśaṇa* blood-letting.

Panca karma treatments are not necessarily sequential. One treatment, or a combination of them, may be used depending upon the condition experienced. *Panca karma* can eliminate excess *doṣas* from the body, as well as *āma*. Although *snehana* and *svedana* also eliminate *doṣas*, wastes and *āma* from the body, they cannot completely remove all of this toxic material.

The treatments are undertaken according to specific guidelines, and administered and supervised by trained therapists. The patient is always prepared beforehand, with a particular diet for at least 24 hours prior to treatment. The therapy is carefully administered according to the patient's condition, as well as the season, time of day and characteristics of the disorder. Particular procedures also follow the treatments. The therapies are always administered in a clinic or *panca karma* centre.

- **Emesis—*vamana***

In this treatment, supervised induced vomiting (emesis) removes excess *doṣas* from the stomach. *Vamana* is the preferred therapy to eliminate excess or aggravated *kapha*, as this accumulates in the upper part of the body (stomach, chest, throat and lungs). For this reason, *vamana* is usually done in spring, when there is a natural aggravation of *kapha*. It may also be done at other times depending upon the symptoms of the patient.

Three hundred and fifty-five herbal preparations for instigating *vamana* in humans are described in the ancient texts. The dose and type of the herb prescribed is crucial. The physician chooses a preparation to suit the condition, age, strength and constitution of the patient. *Madanaphala* is the most effective herb for *vamana*, as it is powerful yet is least likely to cause any complications.

Vamana is specifically recommended for those suffering from chronic nasal allergies, acute fever, tuberculosis, infections of the respiratory tract, asthma, goiter, diabetes, weak digestion, cholera and poisoning. In addition people suffering from nausea, loss of appetite, epilepsy, diarrhea, inflammatory diseases, anemia and stomatitis may benefit from this treatment.

- **Purgation—*virecana***

Virecana is the elimination of *doṣas* by purgation. In this process herbs that are laxative in effect are given to the patient orally. The special action (*prabhāva*) of the herbs activates the *apāna vāta* located in the colon, anus and small intestine. This results in purgation, or elimination of wastes from this area of the body. It is the usual method to elimiate excess *pitta*.

Two hundred and forty-five preparations of herbal remedies are described for inducing *virecana*, with *Trivṛta* the preferred herb. The chosen herb is usually powdered and given in the form a paste with water. The dose differs according to the season, time of day, constitution, strength, disease and age of the patient.

Virecana is beneficial for those suffering from *pitta* disorders like chronic fever, diabetes, cholera, peptic or duodenal ulcer, dysuria, worm infestation, herpes, anemia, headache, backache, burning sensation in the eyes or mouth and heart diseases. *Virecana* is also recommended for skin diseases, moles, warts, pigmentation, psoriasis and skin allergies, asthma, chest infections, jaundice, epilepsy, gout, diseases of the uterus, cataracts, and edema.

- **Medicated enema—*basti***

Basti is mainly used for elimination of *vāta* from the colon, and is the preferred form of treatment for *vāta*-related disorders. As the majority of diseases are caused by *vāta* aggravation, this is the most important of all the *panca karma* therapies. The method is very similar to a standard enema, but is specialized according to the disease being treated. With enemas, warm water is generally used, whereas in *basti* treatment various herbal decoctions and medicated oils are used.

Basti means "bladder", as the original instrument used for this type of elimination was the bladder of a buffalo, pig or goat. The urinary bladder was removed after the animal died naturally, and then it was dried under the sun and lubricated with oil. The *basti* performed the function of an enema pot, to hold the decoction of the herbs or medicated oils. Small or large sized bladders were used depending on the age, strength and constitution of the patient. Rubber bags or metal pots of various sizes are now used instead of the bladders of animals.

The *basti* is either an *anuvāsana*, in which the liquid used is oily, or a *nirūha*, which uses herbal decoctions. In addition to the *basti* administered through the rectum, another form of *basti* (*uttara basti*) is administered through the urinary tract. *Basti* is used to treat many disorders including constipation, headaches, infertility, convulsions, paralysis and gout.

- **Nasal administrations—*nasya***

The elimination therapies described above (*vamana, virecana, basti*) cannot eliminate accumulated impurities or *doṣas* from the head, which is the specific role of *nasya*. The herbs that eliminate *doṣas* from this area are administered in a fine powder or medicated oil form through the nostrils. *Vāgabhaṭṭa* states that "*Nāsā hi śiro dwāram*" or "The nose is the door to head." *Naysa* is also known as *śiro-virecana*. *Śiras* means "head" and *virecana* is "elimination".

In general *nasya* therapy is useful for the diseases that manifest above the neck and *vāta*-related disorders. *Nasya* is specifically recommended for those suffering from headaches and migraine, toothache, dislocation of the jaw, stiffness of neck and jaw, rhinitis, facial paralysis, tetanus, thyroid enlargement, hoarse voice, difficulty in speaking or stuttering, cataracts, disorders of the eyes and neck, shoulders, mouth, nose, throat or head.

- **Blood letting—*rakta mokśaṇa***

This type of elimination therapy is mainly used for *pitta* disorders or those requiring surgical treatment. It is also called *rakta visrāvaṇa*. *Rakta* means "blood" and *visrāvaṇa* or *mokśaṇa* means "to let flow". In this type of treatment, the therapist makes an incision on particular blood vessels and allows impure blood to flow out. Impure blood is dark in color, thick and stains cloth. Pure blood is bright red in color, medium in consistency, and can be removed from cloth by washing it with water.

Depending upon the disease, the incision of particular blood vessels is required. The size of the incision also varies according to the disease. Certain blood vessels (known as *avedhya sirā*) should never be cut. There are almost one hundred of delicate and important blood vessels, which mainly supply the vital organs of the body. Death or disability can result from damage to any of them.

There are two types of *rakta mokśaṇa*. The first method involves using an instrument to make an incision; the other uses natural methods. Natural methods include using leeches (*jalokā*), cupping with a horn (*śṛnga*) and cupping with a gourd (*alābū*). It is effective for all types of abscess, skin diseases, edema, diseases of the ear lobe, tumors, herpes, boils, breast cancer, fissures, and diseases of the teeth and lips. It is also beneficial for people whose blood has become impure due to poisoning.

3. Post-therapy treatment—*pascāta karma*

After *panca karma* treatment, *pascāta karma* (or post-operative treatment) is administered. This ensures that the patient is gradually returned to his or her normal diet and lifestyle, and that the benefits of the *panca karma* treatment are retained. As *panca karma* treatment can weaken the patient's organs and internal systems, a normal diet and routine should not be returned to immediately. *Pascāta karma* involves *saṁsarjana* to restore the digestive fire, and *śamana* to balance any remaining toxins in the body.

- ***Saṁsarjana karma***, where the patient is advised to have a special diet that is light and easily digested. This includes thin gruel (*peyā*), boiled rice (*vilepī*) and vegetable soup (*yūṣa*), either with or without fats and salt. Combinations of these foods are eaten over seven days, and then, according to constitution and season, the normal diet is returned to.

- ***Śamana karma*** is the use of herbs to balance any toxins that may be left in the body.

Rejuvenation Therapy—*Rasāyana*

Once the body has been cleaned of toxins and wastes with *panca karma*, it can be rejuvenated with *rasāyanas. Rasāyana* therapy not only helps prevent and cure disease, but also enhances youthfulness, beauty and longevity. *Rasāyana* is described as "*Yajjarā vyādhi nāśanam tad rasāyanam*" meaning "That which destroys old age and disease is called *rasāyana*." *Caraka Saṁhitā* states that any treatment that increases *ojas* in a healthy person is a *rasāyana*. Any herb, food, diet or activity that restores vitality, enhances youthfulness and cures disease can therefore be considered a *rasāyana*.

Caraka Saṁhitā describes at least sixty-three combinations of rejuvenating herbs. However, a *rasāyana* is not necessarily a formulated medicine or a compound of herbs, but can be an activity (like exercise, yoga, meditation or prayer) or diet (like fruits, milk or *ghī*). If taken in the proper way, a *rasāyana* prevents premature aging and keeps one young and active, physically and mentally.

Aim of *rasāyana*

Rasāyana therapy aims to maintain enzymes and metabolism in peak condition, and to enhance the generation of new cells and tissues in the body. *Rasāyanas* prevent and alleviate conditions associated with old age, and increase *ojas*. *Caraka* considers that *rasāyanas* improve memory, intellect and positive health, and restores youthfulness. They also enhance complexion and skin tone, quality of voice and the strength of sensory and motor organs.

Scientific and medical advances, combined with health education and awareness, have led to increased life spans. The proportion of elderly people in the population has increased dramatically. Elderly people can maintain independent, healthy and active lives if they take *rasāyanas* that provide *ojas*, strength, immunity, vitality and determination. *Rasāyanas* ensure that complete health is maintained for the entire duration of life.

The ultimate aim of *rasāyanas* is to increase longevity in order to serve humanity. Āyurveda is based on the ideal of alleviating suffering in society. This branch, or the science of rejuvenation, was developed to enable people of good character and conduct to maintain strength and increase energy in order to be of advantage to their community. So the goal of *rasāyana* is broader than just improving the individual: it aims to improve the health of the individual for a social benefit.

Operation of *rasāyanas*

As mentioned above, the main function of *rasāyana* is to increase *ojas* and enhance metabolic activity. Internally, catabolic (destructive) and anabolic (constructive) activities occur continuously. Anabolic activities produce *ojas* and new cell and tissue growth, while catabolic activities decrease *ojas* and destroy cells and tissues.

When a person is young, the quantity of *ojas* produced is greater than that destroyed. Therefore, a young person is usually strong, active and balanced in all mental and physical functions. When the number of cells destroyed exceeds the number of cells produced, the person becomes weaker and ages. In old age, the formation of new cells and *ojas* slows down considerably, resulting in diminished vitality. This process can be countered by consuming *rasāyanas*, which sustain and increase the *ojas* in the body.

Rasāyana therapy operates most effectively when it is combined with a *sāttvic* lifestyle. *Rājasic* or *tāmasic* factors like drugs, alcohol, irregular daily routines, excessive sexual activity and eating foods that are not *sāttvic* reduce the quality and quantity of *ojas*, even when one is young. Negative emotions like greed, envy, ego, anxiety, stress and anger also diminish *ojas* and therefore lower immunity and weaken the body.

Suitability

You do not need to wait until old age to take *rasāyanas*. The sooner one starts, the greater the benefit. Before starting the therapy, physical and mental health should be considered. Physically, the body of the individual should be clean from any wastes, and *panca karma* is usually undertaken for this purpose. To obtain the maximum result from *rasāyanas*, all the channels/ *srotas* should be clean and there should be no toxins/*āma* present.

The digestive fire/*jaṭharāgni* should be functioning normally. This is important because if the *jaṭharāgni* is weak, the *rasa dhātu* formed will not be of a high quality. This will affect the formation the other *dhātus* and ultimately the *ojas*.

As Āyurveda deals with the mind/*manas,* in addition to the body/*śarīra*, the therapies also encompass both of these components. Therefore, one who wishes to take *rasāyanas* should also purify the mind prior to therapy. The patient should think, speak and work in a way that is conducive to the healthy development of society. Āyurveda emphasizes good conduct, which in itself has a beneficial impact on the body-mind.

Psychologically, one is suitable for taking *rasāyanas* if honest, compassionate, spiritual, intelligent, fair spoken, clean and free from anger and other negative emotions like greed and jealousy. The person needs to abstain from alcohol, have self-control, regulated sexual habits, and be moderate and balanced in lifestyle. Meditation and a *sāttvic* diet and lifestyle complement *rasāyana* therapy. A *sāttvic* diet and lifestyle are considered *rasāyanas* in themselves, because they encourage the formation of high quality *dhātus*, which ultimately leads to an increase in the quality and quantity of *ojas*.

A person who does not undergo physical and psychological purification will not be able to obtain the full advantage of *rasāyana* therapy. Those wishing to undertake *rasāyana* therapy should follow a disciplined lifestyle incorporating the points mentioned above. During the period of *rasāyana* therapy, excessive traveling, talking and activity should be avoided.

Classification of *rasāyanas*

Rejuvenation therapy is classified according to the method of its administration or the result produced.

- **Method of administration**

1. *Kuṭīpraveśika*: is administered under the instructions of a doctor, while the patient remains within the confines of a particular environment. *Kuṭī* means "cottage" and *praveśa* is "to enter". Arrangements may include the construction of a special type of cottage, which faces either east or north and is pleasantly furnished, with sufficient ventilation and lighting. The surrounding environment should be clean, natural and peaceful, and the atmosphere *sāttvic*.
2. *Vātātapika*: particular herbal remedies are prescribed by a doctor and taken without interrupting the normal daily routine. *Vāta* means "air" and *ātapa* is "heat" or "sun". So this form of *rasāyana* is administered while a person remains exposed to the air and heat. The *vātātapika* method is good for people who are engaged in a busy daily life, because use of this *rasāyana* does not interfere with the normal lifestyle.
3. *Ācāra*: no herbal remedies are used, and a particular routine is adopted. *Ācāra* means "discipline" or "routine". So, *ācāra rasāyana* involves showing discipline in lifestyle through following particular routines. This includes guidelines on diet, sleeping and sexual activity (the *tri-upastambha*) that encourage physical and psychological renewal.

- **Aim or result**

1. *Ajāsṛka*: is administered for the general maintenance of health. This type of rejuvenation therapy is used to attain a good state of health and well-being, and to improve the overall quality of life. It may not necessarily include special herbal formulae, but perhaps lifestyle, dietary or exercise considerations that benefit health. This includes a *sāttvic* diet, adequate sleep and regulated sexual activity.

2. *Naimittika*: if the *rasāyana* is to cure a particular condition or disorder it is classified as *naimittika*. The purpose of the *rasāyana* in this instance is to counteract a specific factor that is causing a disorder in the body. Some examples of *naimittika rasāyanas* are *dhātrī* for *pitta* disorders, *mandūkparṇī* to strengthen the nervous system, *brāhmī* to improve memory and *triphalā* to eliminate toxins.
3. *Kāmya*: fulfills a specific physical purpose and is aimed at maintaining the activities of a particular organ, or enhancing the activity of an internal system. The purpose is not to treat a specific disorder (*naimittic rasāyana*), or enhance general health (*ajāsṛka rasāyana*) but to strengthen and revitalize certain tissues or systems. *Kāmya rasāyana* may treat the life air (*prāṇa*), memory and intellect (*medhya*), lifespan (*āyus*) or vision (*cakśu*).

Commonly used *rasāyanas*

- ***Harītakī***

Harītakī is a tree native to India. The fruits have five out of the six tastes/*rasas* (excluding salty), are heating (*uṣṇa vīrya*), light and easily digested. This strengthens digestion/*jaṭharāgni* and cures many diseases. It also enhances the senses and increases intellect, eliminates toxins and prevents disease. *Harītakī* can be taken regularly in a powdered form. The dose is about one teaspoon of powder, once or twice daily. It is usually taken with water or milk but, depending on the disorder or condition of the person, it may be taken with other substances.

- ***Āmalā* or *Āmalakī***

Another potent *rasāyana* is *āmalā*, which is also known as *āmalakī*. It contains five tastes/*rasas* (except salty) and is cooling in nature (*śīta vīrya*). This is the richest natural source of vitamin C. It is a very good *rasāyana* for people with a *pitta* constitution or suffering from *pitta*-related disorders. *Āmalā* increases the power of digestion/*jaṭharāgni*, helps in formation of high quality tissues/*dhātus*, gives strength to the senses/*indriyas* and increases *ojas*. The dose is usually one teaspoon in powdered form, taken twice a day with water or milk.

- ***Triphalā***

Tri means "three" and *phala* is "fruits". *Triphalā* is a combination of the fruits of three herbs (*harītakī, āmalā* and *vibhītaka*) and is good for internal cleansing. There are various methods of consuming *triphalā*. *Caraka Saṁhitā* recommends taking *harītakī* powder in the morning, *vibhītaka* powder before meals and *āmalā* powder after meals. This dosage needs to be continued for at least one year in order to get the full rejuvenating effect. Another method is to make a paste of *triphalā* powder with water in an iron pot, and take some every morning with water and honey.

- ***Śilājīta***

Śilājīta is a black-colored, sticky mineral from mountainous regions. It is purified and processed before being used as a rasāyana. It has very good rejuvenating effects and is also used as an aphrodisiac. *Śilājīta* is prescribed for diabetes, diseases of kidney and urinary tract infections. The dosage is less than a quarter of a teaspoon, taken with milk once or twice daily.

- *Brāhmi, śankhapuṣpī, yaṣṭīmadhu, gudūci* and *pippalī* also have rejuvenating effects. *Brāhmi* and *śankhapuṣpī* are specifically used for improving memory and intellect (*medhya rasāyana*).
- Licorice, saffron, *ghī*, honey and milk are other commonly available *rasāyanas*.
- A *rasāyana* you can make at home involves soaking four almonds and seven raisins in water overnight. In the morning, remove the skin from the almonds and eat with the raisins and a cup of warm milk.

Addictions—*Madātya*

Drug abuse and addiction are widespread problems. Millions of people battle addictions to nicotine, alcohol and illicit drugs. Initially, a person may start to take a drug socially or as an artificial way to relax. Becoming addicted is not the intention of recreational drug use, but addiction can occur when drug use becomes frequent. Eventually it can become a habit, which is not only costly but also destructive.

Āyurveda considers addiction under the topic of *madātya*, which means "intoxication". *Madātya* is the state or symptoms that arise due to continuous use or a high dose of substances that are intoxicating (*madkāri*). Although *madātya* describes intoxication of any kind, alcohol (*madya*) was the original reference. All the main texts of Āyurveda, including *Caraka Saṁhitā*, *Suśruta Saṁhitā* and *Aṣṭānga Hṛdaya*, describe *madātya*.

According to modern medicine, there are four stages involved in the process of addiction or drug dependence. These are acute intoxication, symptoms of withdrawal, drug dependence and finally drug abuse. The state of *madātya* is comparable to the third and fourth of these stages.

There are four types of *madātya* depending upon which doṣa has become aggravated:

- ***Vāta* aggravation**: creates symptoms like headache, difficulty in breathing, insomnia, vivid dreams, hallucinations, anxiety, constipation, shaking or tremors and erratic moods and thoughts.
- ***Pitta* aggravation**: if the drugs disturb *pitta* it may cause burning in the stomach and digestive problems, excessive sweating and thirst, diarrhea, fever, giddiness and eye redness. Aggression and violence can also be triggered.
- ***Kapha* aggravation**: when *kapha doṣa* is disturbed by drug use, the symptoms include excessive sleep, lethargy, heaviness in the body, nausea and vomiting.

- ***Tridoṣa* aggravation**: a combination of the above symptoms indicates that all three *doṣas* are aggravated.

In addition to these specific symptoms of particular *doṣa* aggravation, common symptoms of intoxication or drug abuse/ *madātya* are restlessness, piercing pain in the heart, sweating, diarrhea, thirst, fever with chills, loss of appetite, abdominal discomfort, dizziness and disturbed sleep.

These symptoms are experienced with a variety of drugs like heroin, opium, cannabis, cocaine, alcohol, barbiturates and nicotine. This indicates that *madātya* mentioned in ancient Āyurvedic texts and the effects of modern narcotics are very similar. Therefore, the treatment for *madātya* can be effectively used for a variety of drug addictions, not just alcohol.

Treatments

The treatment in all cases involves remedies to balance the *doṣas*, depending upon the *doṣa/s* involved. When treating a person suffering from a drug addiction, the initial step is to locate the main *doṣa/s* aggravated and prescribe alleviating treatment. Herbal remedies may be used to treat withdrawal symptoms, remove accumulated impurities and encourage the regeneration of tissues and cells. Some commonly available herbal treatments for *madātya* are:

- **Lemon**: The juice of half a lemon can be mixed in one glass of water and taken several times a day;
- **Ginger**: A pinch of powdered ginger is taken twice a day with water. Or, boil some ginger in one cup of water until it has reduced to half a cup. Add half a cup of milk, two cardamom seeds and one teaspoon of honey. Drink daily.
- **Cumin**: A dose of half a teaspoon twice a day is recommended;
- **Grapes**: Drink a glass of grape juice twice a day. One teaspoon of raisins soaked in water for at least for four hours can be eaten in the morning and evening; or
- **Apples**: Drink a glass of apple juice two or three times a day. Cooked apples may also be eaten.

People who are influenced by drugs often lose their sense of discrimination and can become confused or erratic. This occurs due a deterioration of intelligence/*medhā*. As mentioned in the section on *rasāyanas*, there is a particular group of herbal compounds that promote intelligence. These *rasāyanas*, known as *medhya rasāyanas*, can improve memory, concentration and comprehension.

Some of the *medhya rasāyanas* mentioned in *Caraka Saṁhitā* are *mandūkparṇī, brāhmī, yaṣṭīmadhu, gudūci* and *śankhapuṣpī*. These herbs can be used individually in powdered form. The dose of powder of each is half a teaspoon twice per day with milk, honey or water. These herbs are also used to prepare a number of formulae, which may include other ingredients such as minerals and processed metallic ashes.

Psychotherapy or counseling is another form of treatment for people who are dependent on drugs. This can help determine the root cause of the addiction. Treatment that heals the mind is known as *sattvāvjaya* therapy. The basic goal of this type of treatment is to increase *sattva guṇa*. Meditation, yoga and establishing a daily routine that minimizes stress and anxiety assist treatment and promote a *sāttvic guṇa*.

A study was conducted in the United States in 1972 to assess drug abuse and meditation. This research considered nearly 2000 people who meditated and their patterns of drug use. The results indicated that the longer the person had meditated, the less drug dependence was exhibited. After eighteen months to two years of meditation, most of the people in this group no longer used drugs in any form. A similar study carried out in 1974 found that after one to three months of meditation, about 50% of the group had stopped using cannabis. The results increased in proportion to the length of time that meditation was undertaken (Chopra 1991:162-163).

Caraka Saṁhitā mentions some activities that provide serenity and uplift the mind and soul, classified as "activities that make you happy" (*harṣaṇī kriyā*). These include walking or sitting in beautiful gardens or near lakes, flowers, associating with good friends, wearing neat and clean clothes, listening to soft music and other forms of quiet and gentle relaxation and entertainment. All these activities pacify the excited and disturbed *doṣas* or *guṇas* that have been influenced by the drug abuse.

A complete treatment for addictions may therefore involve several different treatments over several weeks or even months. Initially, *panca karma* cleans the body of accumulated toxins. Herbal remedies then treat the addiction and its physical or psychological effects. Dietary modifications to increase *sāttvic* foods and encourage the formation of *ojas* are implemented. Psychological counseling, and activities such as meditation and *yoga* assist the mind to become balanced and clear. With support and discipline, an addiction can be controlled and eradicated.

Schedule for drug withdrawal

Caraka Saṁhitā advises a graduated schedule for withdrawing from drugs. On the first day, one quarter of the intake of the drug is given up. This is replaced with a positive habit, such as exercise, *yoga*, meditation or dietary changes. On the second day, drug intake is reduced by half the normal consumption, and the positive habit correspondingly increased. This is continued on the third day. On the fourth day, three quarters of the drug intake is relinquished, and the positive habit is increased again. This is maintained on the fifth and sixth days. On the seventh day, the drug is given up totally and the positive habit fully adopted.

So, for example, if you smoke thirty cigarettes a day, on the first day you would reduce intake by around seven cigarettes. On that day, you could begin meditating for five minutes. On the second and third days, you only smoke fifteen cigarettes and meditate for ten minutes. On the fourth, fifth and sixth days, the number of cigarettes smoked would be around eight, and meditation could be increased to fifteen minutes; and on the seventh day, no cigarettes are smoked and meditation is increased to around twenty minutes.

The actual duration for this program can be increased according to the individual. Regardless of the schedule adopted, a slow and steady process is more likely to eradicate drug use and minimize physical and psychological side effects. Sudden cessation of a drug of dependence can be traumatic and may lead to relapses, which can be disheartening and lower faith in the ability to quit. Setting realistic goals and working towards that daily can build confidence and gradually restore health. An example of a schedule for quitting drugs is:

- Set goals for reducing drug consumption (daily, or every few days).
- Begin reducing drug intake according to the goals set.
- Undertake a one-day fast to cleanse the body.
- Establish a regular daily routine for eating, sleeping and exercise.
- Assess which *doṣa* is imbalanced from the symptoms experienced.
- Modify diet to alleviate aggravated *doṣa/s* (chapter 3).
- Increase intake of water and *sāttvic* foods (chapters 4 & 8).
- Use some of the home remedies mentioned (such as lemon or ginger) daily.
- Self-massage daily, or have a massage and/or sauna weekly.
- Begin practicing meditation and deep breathing (*prāṇāyama*).
- Enjoy other forms of gentle relaxation or exercise (*yoga*, walking).
- Use relaxing aromatherapy oils like lavender or sandalwood.
- Talk to a counselor or close friend to maintain commitment.
- Avoid the company of those who use drugs.
- If available, take *rasāyanas*.

CHAPTER 12

Home Remedies

An elementary knowledge of simple home remedies can treat many ailments. The time-tested home remedies for particular conditions are often more effective than antibiotics, codeine or "painkillers". The use of home remedies has benefits in addition to restoring health and vitality. You do not have to endure side effects, and you also save a lot of money! Of course, for chronic health conditions it is recommended that you seek medical advice, and only take home remedies as an adjunct to any treatment prescribed. But for many conditions, home remedies can offer relief and effective treatment.

Although prescribed medicines may offer immediate relief through suppressing or temporarily alleviating symptoms, curing some conditions permanently proves more difficult. Obesity, anxiety and depression, headache, constipation, indigestion, skin diseases, arthritis, menstrual pain, fatigue and asthma are widespread, chronic conditions that are often unable to be suuceesfully treated with conventional medicine. These disorders are all treated effectively and cheaply using Āyurvedic herbal home remedies, as described later in this chapter.

Home remedies can have amazing results. In some countries it is difficult to obtain traditional Āyurvedic formulae, as mentioned in the ancient texts. But Āyurveda is not limited to these herbal compounds. The basic principles of Āyurveda can be applied in any part of the world, through using herbs and foods that are commonly available and prepared in your own kitchen.

As patients from all over the world visit my online Āyurvedic Clinic for consultation and advice, I have had the opportunity to explore the use of home remedies. Hundreds of people have been offered information about treatments that can be prepared in their home using herbs and foods available in their region. Many positive and wonderful results from the use of these remedies have been reported. It is remarkable that even without any physical contact or direct consultation with the patient, home remedies have proven to be very beneficial.

Dear Dr Chauhan

Thank you so much for writing back to me. I have followed the advice on nutrition you gave me. I am now sleeping all night long without interruption, my tension headaches mysteriously vanished and I have indigestion much less frequently. The neem has worked wonders. My eczema is now all cleared up, although it took some time for this to happen.

I am Roman Catholic and there is a part in the mass where you take the hand of the person next to you and wish them peace. I did not go to mass for almost a year because of the eczema on my hands. People looked at me as though they were afraid they might catch it. Now that my hands have cleared up, I have been able to return to church and this has meant a great deal to me.

Ms PL Canada

Another patient to benefit from a simple home remedy was Maria, a two-year old girl from Mexico. Maria had been suffering from acute diarrhea for about a week. Doctors diagnosed an infection of the colon and rectum, prescribed strong antibiotics and recommended chicken soup. After taking the prescribed medicines, her symptoms became even worse. She started passing blood with the stool.

At this point, her worried father contacted me. I advised a simple diet as a remedy for the sick girl, including pomegranate juice, banana and boiled rice with split mung beans (*mūnga dāla*). The preparation of rice and *mūnga dāla* is known as "*khicaḍī*", and a recipe for this is in appendix 5. After three days of the diet, her father wrote to me—

> *Dr. Chauhan,*
>
> *I hope you are doing well...Thank you for your help, our daughter Maria is much better now. She is able to eat rice, bananas and carrots. The khicaḍī worked very well and we stopped feeding her chicken. Modern medicine, although technically advanced, still lacks the insight and wisdom that ancient medicine has to offer.*
>
> *Mr BD Mexico*

This chapter discusses the preparation of home remedies, and specific treatments for some common conditions that prove difficult to treat with conventional medicine. If required, more specific and potent herbal remedies are available from an Āyurvedic physician.

What is a Home Remedy?

Anything that is easily available in or around your home, and has a medicinal use, is known as a home remedy. When used for medical purposes, herbs, vegetables, fruits, spices, grains and oils are considered home remedies. Different exercises, massaging techniques, colors, aromas, gems and cleansing therapies can also be used as home remedies. "Home remedies" is not a separate branch or section of Āyurveda. Any formula or herb that is easy to prepare and easily available, may be classified in this category.

Herbs can be taken in the form of a juice, paste, powder, infusion or decoction according to the requirement. In certain cases, the herbs can be mixed or cooked with *ghī* or oil. A large variety of different remedies can be prepared from a few common herbs and spices. Spices like clove, cinnamon, black pepper, cumin, fennel, rock salt, turmeric and coriander are useful home remedies. Ginger, honey, licorice, garlic, onion, basil and mint also have a multitude of medicinal uses. Some herbs and spices and their uses are described in appendix 4.

Preparation of Home Remedies

Home remedies are prepared in the same way and with the same purpose as other Āyurvedic medicines. While preparing a home remedy, the main aim is to obtain the maximum therapeutic benefit while making it palatable. The manufacturing process in Āyurveda is very specific and plays an important role in the healing process. For this reason, efforts should be made to follow instructions carefully. Some common methods of preparing home remedies are:

- **Juice**: If the herbs are available in a fresh form, it is possible to consume the juice. This may be taken from the leaves, flowers or stems of the herb. The parts of the herb used are crushed or ground in a mortar and pestle, to make a paste. This paste is put in a piece of cloth and squeezed to take out the juice. Dose: one to two tablespoons.
- **Powder**: Dried herbs are used for powders. The herbs are usually dried in a cool, shady and well-ventilated place, although some herbs are dried in direct sunlight. The herbs are then ground into a fine powder and stored in a dry, airtight bottle. The powder may be taken with water, or if specified, with milk or honey. Dose: half to one teaspoon.
- **Decoction**: A decoction is prepared by boiling the herb in water (ratio: 1 part herbs to 16 parts water). The herbs are broken into pieces and soaked in water overnight. This mixture is then boiled until it reduces to one quarter the volume, filtered and stored in a glass bottle. The dose is one to two tablespoons.
- **Infusion**: Herbs are soaked in water to make an infusion (ratio: 1 part herbs to 8 parts water). Hot infusions result from adding herbs to hot water, or gently heating but not boiling

the mixture. This is strained and taken internally. Herbal teas are forms of hot infusions. Cold infusions are made from soaking the herb overnight. Honey can be added. Dose: half to one cup.

- **Paste**: A paste can be made from either fresh or dried herbs. The flowers, roots, stems, leaves or bark are ground and mixed with water. Pastes are mainly used for external application, in cases of cuts, burns and swellings. The paste should be thick enough to be applied in a layer to the skin.
- **Tablets**: The herbs are first dried separately and then mixed in powder form, in a fixed proportion. Water or herbal juice is added to this powder to make a paste, from which tablets of a specific size or weight are made. Tablets remain potent for a longer time than juices, powders, pastes or decoctions.
- **Medicated *ghī* and oil**: These are cooked with herbal juices, decoctions or pastes. The *ghī* should be heated with the herbal mixture at a moderate, controlled temperature. High temperatures can easily burn the *ghī* or oil, destroying its effectiveness. Medicated *ghī* and oils are used internally (dose: half to one tablespoon) and externally for massage.

Home Remedies for Common Problems

Simple home remedies can be very effective in relieving symptoms, and preventing further development of a disorder. However, once a disease has fully manifested and reached the final stage of development, specific treatments are required. Home remedies may also support treatments prescribed by a doctor. In some cases, even a proper diet can be a home remedy as it reduces the severity of symptoms experienced and avoids unintended aggravation of the condition.

Following the dietary and lifestyle guidelines already mentioned usually prevents and alleviates symptoms of common ailments. Many ailments are caused by ignoring the principles of nutrition and diet, or balanced lifestyle considerations.

Adopting a *sāttvic* diet (chapters 4 and 8), minimizing the formation of *āma* (chapter 5), keeping regular routines and not suppressing the natural urges (chapter 9) are all common factors in maintaining and restoring health. Exercise and minimizing stress through meditation, *yoga* and breathing exercises (*prāṇāyama*) also promote healthy living. Some specific remedies for commonly experienced problems are detailed below.

Anxiety and Depression

Imbalance of *triguṇas* causes a dull, unhappy and depressed state of mind. Anxiety and depression can result from negative emotional states like worry, tension, sadness, anger or greed. Financial concerns, family problems or unsatisfying life events can also contribute to this state of mind. In this situation, *sattva* is decreased and *rajas* and *tamas* are increased. Imbalance of the *doṣas*, inadequate digestion or diet and the formation of *āma* are physical factors in the development of anxiety or depression.

Dear Partap

When I was about 19, I had a sudden onset of anxiety attacks and became very despondant. It got so bad I could hardly function. It was a stressful time of my life, with a lot of family problems as well as pressure about my career. I am 33 now but it has never really gone away completely. I sometimes get the sensation of smothering, with a vice-like pressure on my head. I feel emotionally, spiritually and mentally dead! My body, mind and spirit have really taken a beating and I just want to rebuild strength in all departments. Where should I start?

Mr MA Chile

Diet

Heavy foods that are difficult to digest should be avoided (fried, spicy, salty foods). Processed foods, or those containing preservatives, artificial flavors and colors should be minimized. White flour and its products (cakes, pastries, pizza and white breads), smoking, tea, coffee, alcohol, cola and carbonated drinks should be excluded.

Drink 3 or 4 glasses of water immediately after waking. It is beneficial if this water is stored in a copper pot overnight. Fresh fruits and vegetables or their juices, sprouts, nuts, dried fruits, honey, milk, *ghī*, fresh butter and buttermilk are beneficial. Drink warm milk before bed.

Herbs

- Soak 7 almonds in a glass container overnight. In the morning, remove the almond skins and grind the almonds together with 4 black peppercorns, 1 tbsp of rose petals and 1 tbsp of anise seeds. Add 1 cup of milk and simmer it on a low heat for 5 minutes. For sweetness, 1 tsp of honey can be added. Drink this mixture once per day. The paste can also be eaten with a cup of warm milk. Take daily for 40 days.
- Take a tsp of honey with a pinch of cinnamon before bed.

Exercise

An early morning or evening walk can be beneficial. Creative activities and regular meditation are also useful. Lying down, relaxing the body and concentrating on breathing can relieve tension.

Other

Bowels should be emptied daily. Castor oil may assist if constipation is a problem (1 tbsp before bed). The natural urges should not be suppressed. Massage with sesame oil twice weekly can be positive for both the body and mind. Or, massage oil made from ½ cup of almond oil and 10 drops of jasmine and/or lavender oil can reduce tension. Sandalwood incense and soft music are also relaxing. Loneliness and idleness should be avoided.

Medicines

Bṛhada vātacintāmaṇi rasa, Brāhmī ghṛta, Āmalakī rasāyana.

Arthritis

Arthritis is a disorder characterized by inflammation and pain in the joints. In Āyurveda, it is known as *āmavāta*. A weak digestive fire/*jaṭharāgni* disturbs the digestive process and toxins/*āma* are produced. The *āma* is mixed with the *rasa* and *rakta dhātu*, causing blockage of channels/*srotas*. *Vāta* is aggravated and becomes mobile, combining with *āma* and accumulating in the joints. The pain and deterioration of joint mobility is a symptom of aggravated *vāta*, with the stiffness symptomatic of *āma*. *Vāta* increases naturally in old age.

> *Dear Dr Chauhan*
>
> *I am a 47 years of age, a house-wife with three children. I have felt severe pains in almost all of my joints for a long time. This is especially in the joints in my hands and legs. I was diagnosed with rheumatoid arthritis and treated with painkillers, which caused internal bleeding. Later on, I was prescribed steroids. I feel very weak even though the pain in my joints has lessened. I'd like to know whether the symptoms of arthritis can be treated with diet, as it has not improved much despite all the medication I have taken. Yours sincerely*
>
> *Mrs MC India*

Diet

Avoid fried, greasy, excessively spiced, cold, chilled and sour foods. Vegetables like peas, cauliflower, cabbage, broccoli, radishes, potato, beans and anything else that promotes gas, indigestion or constipation should be avoided. This includes blackberries, starchy foods, cheese, chocolate and coffee. White flour and sugar products should also be avoided. Dairy products and bananas can block channels/*srotas*, so are best excluded. Foods high in acids, like rhubarb, plums, cranberries and citrus fruits should also be minimised, as these create joint irritation.

Light and easily digested foods such as steamed or boiled vegetables, or vegetable broth are recommended. Vegetables like squash, zucchini, eggplant and spinach are good. Seasonal fruits may be taken in moderate quantity. Wholemeal bread and cereals can also be eaten occasionally. Garlic, ginger, cumin, fennel, coriander, cardamom and cinnamon can be used in food preparation.

Herbs

- Take 10 garlic cloves and 1 tsp each of dry ginger powder, black pepper, long pepper, asafoetida, cumin, turmeric and fenugreek. Mix the crushed cloves with all the powdered herbs to make a paste. Take 1 tsp of the paste and fry it in ½ tsp of *ghī*. Take it twice a day.
- A mixture of equal quantities of powdered fenugreek seeds, turmeric and ginger can be made. Take 1 tsp in the morning and the evening, with warm water or milk.
- Camphor, wintergreen or cinnamon oils may be applied externally.
- A paste can be made from mixing an equal proportion of finely chopped fresh red chilies and ginger with ½ cup of sesame oil. Rub the paste onto the affected area. If skin becomes irritated, discontinue use.
- A variation of herbal oil for massaging the joints can be made from ½ cup of mustard oil and 4–5 cloves of crushed garlic. Heat the oil over a low heat in a pan with the garlic and 1 tsp of cumin seeds. When the seeds become red, remove from heat. Filter, and while it is warm, massage on affected joints.

Exercise

Light, gentle exercise is beneficial. The joints should not be kept completely immobilized, but energetic or excessive activity is not recommended.

Other

The body should always be kept warm. Warm baths are relaxing and relieve joint pain. Cold and windy weather should be avoided. Joints should not be restricted or bandaged tightly. Constipation and indigestion should be avoided as they produce toxins/*āma* and further irritate the joints. Water kept in a copper vessel for at least 12 hrs should be taken in the morning on an empty stomach. This cures and prevents joint stiffness.

Medicines

Āmavātāri rasa, various types of gugglu, Ajamodādi powder.

Asthma

Asthma is called *tamaka śvāsa*. It is increasing in modern times due to pollution and stress. Asthma usually originates from afflictions of the stomach and gastrointestinal tract, which is why preliminary symptoms may include indigestion, constipation or diarrhea. Deposits of *āma* (mucus) in the lungs and respiratory tract create obstruction in breathing and cause wheezing, coughing or sneezing. Asthma may be triggered by allergies to pollen, dust, smoke, dog and cat hair.

Hello Dr. Chauhan

My ten-year old son has just been diagnosed with asthma. When he has trouble breathing, he becomes really distressed. He is also scared about experiencing the symptoms, because he becomes so uncomfortable and it interferes with his activities. What recommendations do you make to prevent these asthma attacks so that it is no so traumatic for him?
Kindly yours

Ms RT United Kingdom

Diet

Eating at least 2 hours before going to bed is recommended. Eat less than the full capacity of the stomach, and eat slowly. Drinking warm water or herbal teas throughout the day can be beneficial. Heavy foods including dairy products, fried foods, cold foods, rice, beans and legumes should be avoided. The use of spices, pickles and chillies in cooking should also be minimized. Honey, nuts and seeds can be taken in a moderate amount.

Herbs

- Mix an equal quantity of honey and ginger juice, add a pinch of black pepper. Take this mixture at least three times a day.
- Boil 3–4 cloves of garlic in a cup of milk and drink daily.
- Drinking ginger tea mixed with crushed garlic cloves can also alleviate asthma.
- Mix 1 tsp of turmeric powder with a glass of milk and drink 2 or 3 times per day on an empty stomach.
- To help prevent mucus, boil 1 cup of milk with 1 tsp of fennel powder, 2 cardamom seeds and 1 tsp of turmeric powder. Drink it while warm.

Exercise

Avoid excessive or physically demanding exercise. *Yoga* can be beneficial. Breathing exercises (*prāṇāyama*) can also be helpful. Breathe deeply and rhythmically to strengthen the respiration system.

Other

Inhaling steam from boiling water mixed with caraway seeds can provide relief. Massaging the chest with mustard oil mixed with a few drops of camphor oil assists in loosening the phlegm and easing breathing. Avoid exposure to cold air and wind. Bathing or showering in cold water is not recommended.

Medicines

Śwāsakāsacintāmaṇī rasa, Śwāskuṭhāra rasa, Apāmārga kśāra.

Coughs, Colds and Flu

Congestion and irritation of the respiratory tract are usually caused by aggravation of *kapha*, although *pitta* and *vāta* can also be the cause. *Kapha doṣa* is increased by foods, environment and life style that are similar in nature to *kapha* (damp, cold, heavy, solid). If food is not digested properly, it will transform into toxins/*āma*. This also serves to increase *kapha*, especially if it is deposited in the sites governed by *kapha* like the chest and upper body (head, neck, lungs and stomach).

Diet

Any foods that increase *kapha* should be avoided. This includes dairy products, sugar products, bananas, refrigerated or frozen food and heavy foods (oily, greasy and fried foods). Steamed vegetables, vegetable soup, wholegrain breads, fruits that are not juicy (especially apple and papaya) are to be included in the diet. Honey is good to take, either in herbal teas or mixed with the herbal remedies mentioned below. Spices are fine to use while cooking, if desired. Overeating should be avoided.

Herbs

- Mix equal quantities (around 1 tsp each) of ginger powder, turmeric and black pepper. Take about ½ tsp of this mixture twice a day with warm water, or mixed with honey.
- Mix about ½ tbsp each of ginger, black pepper, cardamom, clove, cinnamon and turmeric powders. 3 tsp of raw sugar can be added. Mix ½ to 1 tsp with honey and take twice daily.
- Mix ½ tsp fresh ginger juice with ½ tsp of honey and take three times a day. Or a warm infusion of ginger with honey is also beneficial.
- Take 1 tbsp of crushed licorice root and boil with 2 cups of water. Reduce to half. Drink while warm. This can be consumed 2 or 3 times per day.
- Mix ½ tsp of turmeric powder and ½ tsp of ginger powder in 1 cup of water and simmer on a medium heat for 5 minutes. Honey can be added. Drink it warm.
- A garlic decoction made from 4 cloves of crushed garlic and 1 cup of water can offer relief. Boil until it has reduced to half the volume. Add a pinch of salt and drink warm. This can be taken 2–3 times daily.

Exercise

Breathing exercises (*prāṇāyama*) may be useful to cleanse the respiratory tract and increase immunity. Sit in a relaxed posture. Breathe with a natural rhythm through the nostrils. Breathe in to the count of 8, hold the breath for the same period of time then exhale to the count of 8. The length of time can be increased gradually.

Other

A massage oil to relieve congestion is made from crushing 4 garlic cloves and adding to ¼ cup of mustard oil. This is heated until the garlic starts to blacken. While the oil is still warm, gently massage onto the chest, back and neck. This is especially beneficial for children.

Inhale the steam from hot water containing a few drops of lemon or eucalyptus oil. Fasting for one day, with water and lemon juice, can expel toxins. The body should be kept warm, especially the head, chest and feet. Sleeping during the day is not recommended, as this only serves to further increase *kapha*.

Medicines

Mulethī powder, Sitopalādi cūrṇa, Samśarkarā, Lakśmīvilāsa rasa.

> *Dear Dr. Chauhan*
>
> *I used to dread winter because I knew it would always involve spending at least three or four days sick in bed with the flu. This is the first year where I have managed to avoid a runny nose, stuffy head and congested chest. As soon as symptoms of the flu started to appear, I tried the ginger and honey tea and your tips on diet. It made a big difference and I'll remember some of the remedies to tell my friends.*
>
> *Ms JB Finland*

Fatigue, Exhaustion and Weakness

The body is made up of seven vital tissues/*dhātus*, with *ojas* (the essence of these *dhātus)*. The *dhātus* and *ojas*, which are produced from the food we eat, provide strength, energy and vitality to body. (The formation and function of *dhātus* and *ojas* are covered in chapter 6.) If the mechanism of the formation of *dhātus* is disturbed, toxins/*āma* are produced instead of healthy *dhātus*. Deterioration of vital tissues occurs and weakness, fatigue and exhaustion result.

Dear Dr Chauhan

I wonder if you might be able to give me some ideas about what to do regarding a problem I have suffered from for nearly a decade. I am 69 years old, and although medical people tell me I'm remarkably fit for my age, I spend most of my days fighting off the urge to go back to bed. I have lots to do and many interests, but the urge to sleep is so powerful that I just can't concentrate. So I think, "Well, I'll just have a nap and then maybe I'll be able to get things done." Then, when I wake up again, nothing has changed and I'm still sleepy and unable to concentrate!

Two doctors have prescribed sleeping pills. But what I really need is some help in escaping the urge to go back to sleep within two hours of waking up. What can you advise?

Mr CP United States

Diet

Heavy foods and processed, fast foods, and foods that contain a lot of preservatives and chemicals should be avoided. Food should be taken according to digestive power. Green leafy vegetables (especially spinach, celery, parsley), carrots, asparagus, pumpkin, fresh fruits, fresh milk, fruit juices and vegetable soups are good. Nuts, raisins, pumpkin seeds and grains should be eaten, as well as fruits such as apricots, cherries, raspberries, oranges, pears, figs, dates and prunes.

Herbs

- The almond and milk mixture described under "anxiety and depression" can be useful for fatigue as well, particularly mental fatigue.
- Take a total of 5 tbsp of a mixture of finely chopped dried dates, almonds, pistachio nuts and quince seeds daily. This can be eaten with milk.
- Wash around 1 tbsp of black raisins in warm water and boil them in 1 cup of milk. Eat the raisins, and drink the milk. The quantity of raisins can be gradually increased to 3 tbsp.
- Put 2–3 dates to soak in water in the morning. That evening, boil them in 1 cup of milk until the milk has reduced by half. Cool, add 1 tsp honey. Eat the dates and drink the milk. This can be taken one hour before going to bed.

Exercise

Regular exercise improves energy levels and increases the circulation of blood and oxygen. Sedentary lifestyles and sleeping during the day should be avoided.

Other

Rub the body vigorously with a towel after showering to improve the circulation of blood. Massage twice a week with sesame oil is also beneficial. Inhaling peppermint oil (from a handkerchief or your hand) can reduce fatigue.

Medicines

Kārśyahara loha, Candraprabhā vaṭi, Aśwangandhādi cūrṇa

Headache

There are eleven different types of headache in Āyurveda. Migraine is the most severe, and is called "*ardhāvabhedaka*" which literally means "cutting and throbbing pain in the head". The cause of headache is aggravation of *vāta* and *kapha*. Mental strain or over-work, irregular eating habits, indigestion and dry foods aggravate *vāta*. The *vāta* is obstructed in the head region by *kapha* and causes headache. Throbbing pain is a symptom of aggravated *vāta*. As the pain intensifies, *vāta* disturbs *pitta* and vomiting may occur. Headache may also be a symptom of other disorders.

Diet

Fried, spicy, cold and dry foods should be avoided. Pickled and smoked foods, avocados, pineapple, bananas, citrus fruits, plums, peas, raspberries, chocolate, yogurt, cheese and alcohol should be excluded from the diet, or intake minimized.

Milk and sweet foods should be taken regularly. Coconut water is also good. Light foods which do not aggravate the *doṣas* like simple cooked vegetables without oil, vegetable juices and soup, fruits like apples, pears, mangoes, grapes and fruit juices can be consumed. Rice, salad and buttermilk are good. Nuts can be eaten in small amounts.

Herbs

- Medicated oil made with cloves or menthol, and massaged onto the head can be soothing.
- Put 2-3 drops of sesame or mustard oil into each nostril and inhale.
- Drink 1 tsp of honey mixed in a glass of water each morning on an empty stomach.

Exercise

Regular meditation and *yoga* are recommended.

Other

The *panca karma* therapy of *vamana* (supervised vomiting) may offer relief. Purification procedures like *basti, śīrodhārā* and *nasya* are good for headaches. Regular bowel movements should be maintained. The natural urges should not be suppressed. Resting in a quiet, dark room for the duration of the headache is recommended. Skipping meals or dieting excessively can trigger headaches, so meals are best regulated and fasting avoided. You should also try to reduce anxiety, anger, worry and stress. Massage daily is recommended.

Medicines

Godantī bhasma, Pathyadi kwātha, Śaḍabindū taila, Pravāla piṣṭi.

> *Dear Dr Chauhan*
>
> *Thank you for your advice on treating headaches. The diet and oil massages have helped me tremendously. I am becoming completely headache free for many days at a time. I used to take strong painkillers often, but have only had to take them on a few occasions since following your advice. I am very, very grateful. I have adjusted my diet and have been using an oil massage made of coconut, grapefruit, orange, and lavender oils. I am so happy to be free of the pain that had plagued me for years, without using drugs.*
>
> *Ms CL USA*

Indigestion and Constipation

Indigestion is caused by weakness of the digestive fire/*jaṭharāgni* and is known as *ajīrṇa*. Improper eating habits like not eating regularly, excessive fasting, overeating, eating incompatible foods, eating food which is excessively hot, cold or dry and drinking a lot of water during or after meals can contribute to *ajīrṇa*. Mental stress, suppressing natural urges and irregular sleeping habits can also affect *jaṭharāgni*. If digestion is weakened and unbalanced, the *doṣas* become aggravated and *āma* is produced. Constipation, hyperacidity, flatulence and lack of appetite are all symptoms of *ajīrṇa*. (The digestive process is discussed in chapter 5.)

Diet

Drink 2 glasses of water in the morning, gradually increasing the volume up to 6 glasses. Drink buttermilk after meals (recipe in appendix 5).

Heavy and spicy foods, or those that promote gas, should be avoided. Steamed or boiled vegetables, fresh fruits and vegetables soups should be increased in the diet. Turnips, sprouts, prunes, apples, pears, grapes and berries are good. Food should always be freshly prepared and be chewed thoroughly. Meals should be taken regularly, around every 4 to 5 hours.

Herbs

- Peel and chop a medium piece of ginger. Put in a glass container and add 1 tbsp of cumin seeds. Cover the ginger with lemon juice, add a pinch of salt and mix. Place the container in direct sunlight for 2 days in summer and 4 days in winter. Take ½ tsp before meals.
- Wash 3 or 4 dried figs and 15 raisins in hot water, and then soak overnight in a cup. In the morning, eat the fruit and drink the water they were soaked in. This mixture should also be taken in the evening.
- Soak 1 tsp of fenugreek seeds in 1 cup of water overnight (or for at least four hours). Boil it to reduce to around ¾ of a cup, filter and drink warm. This can be taken once or twice a day.
- Add 2 tbsp fresh lemon juice to 1 cup of water and drink two or three times a day.

Exercise

Light physical exercise (walking, *yoga,* swimming) is good. Relaxation, and tension relieving activities help prevent unnecessary stress that can upset the digestive process. Meditation and breathing exercises are good for reducing stress.

Other

Regularity in lifestyle is beneficial; that is, eating, sleeping and exercising according to a set daily routine. A one-day fast can be useful.

Medicines

Śivākśāra pācana, Avipattikara cūrṇa, Śankha vaṭī, Triphalā.

> *Dear Partap*
>
> *According to your suggestions for constipation, I made some changes in my daily routine. I'm drinking the juice of half a lemon in water twice a day, after lunch and dinner. At night I take 2 tablets of triphalā. In the morning I drink 4-5 glasses of water and go for walk. This is working perfectly. This has changed two things. My appetite has improved and I feel hungry more often. I no longer suffer from dull pain and gas formation. At present, I feel perfectly OK. I can't believe how simple it was to fix something that had been bothering me for years!*
>
> *Mr KC United Arab Emirates*

Insomnia

Sleep is a periodic state of rest, which is essential for physical and mental rejuvenation. Insomnia (sleeplessness) deprives a person of vital rest and interferes with activities during the day. Insomnia is common in elderly persons due to natural aggravation of *vāta*. Common causes for insomnia are anxiety, overwork, worry and over-excitement. Constipation, overeating at night or going to bed without eating, drinking tea, coffee or taking drugs and suppressed emotions may also contribute. Sleeping patterns become irregular, leading to lapses in memory and lack of concentration. Lack of co-ordination, confusion, irritability and emotional instability can result.

Diet

A balanced diet, which includes green leafy vegetables, berries, tomatoes, corn, citrus fruits, mangoes, pineapple, melons and dairy products, is preferred. Whole grains and almonds, peanuts and other nuts or sesame seeds should be included. Foods that increase *vāta* (dry, gas forming etc) should be strictly avoided. Alcohol, smoking and anything containing caffeine (coffee, tea, cola or chocolate) should be eliminated.

Herbs

- Mint tea before bed is relaxing. Take around 10 crushed fresh mint leaves, or ½ tsp of dried mint and boil it with 1 cup of water. Add 2 tsp of honey and drink it warm.
- Chamomile tea is also benefical to drink in the evening.
- Eat an apple and drink a glass of warm milk before bed.
- Sprinkle 1 tsp cumin seeds on a ripe banana; eat before bed.
- Add 1 tsp of *ghī* to warm milk and drink before bed.

Exercise

A *yoga āsana* called "dead body posture" (*śavāsana*) is calming. Lay on the back in a relaxed position. Systematically concentrate on releasing tension from every part of the body starting from the feet and finishing with the head. Eyes should be closed and the mind focused on breathing. This can be done for 5–10 minutes. Other useful *āsanas* are *śīrṣāsana, sarvāngāsana* and *uttānāpādāsana*. A *yoga* book or teacher can explain these positions.

Other

Massaging the head or feet with or without oil assists in inducing sleep. If oil is preferred, almond, *āmalā* or *brāhmī* oil can be used for the head, and mustard oil for the feet. A few drops of lavender oil can be added. Or, put a few drops of lavender oil on your pillow, or a sachet of dried lavender under it. Putting 2 drops of warm mustard oil in each ear and putting cotton balls in them before bed is also beneficial. Taking a warm shower in the evening to relax the muscles is good. Sufficient sunlight during the day should be obtained.

Prāṇāyama is useful. One method is to lie on the left side, inhale deeply expanding the abdomen completely. Hold the breath for as long as comfortable and then breathe out slowly. Repeat 8-10 times.

Medicines

Śankhapuṣpyādi cūrṇa, Brāhmī vaṭi, Sarpagandhā-ghana vaṭi.

Menopause

Menopause occurs due to hormonal changes in the female body, and results in an imbalance of the *tridoṣas*. Joint pain, deterioration of bones, hypertension, insomnia, anxiety, and diminished or excessive libido can result due to aggravated *vāta*. Hot flushes, disturbed digestion, and the growth of unwanted body hair are symptoms of aggravated *pitta*. Depression and obesity are caused by aggravated *kapha*.

> *Dear Dr Partap*
>
> *I've read that Āyurveda can treat menopause with herbs. What herbs are good to take during this phase of my life? It is popular in the West to prescribe estrogen replacement therapy, but I don't don't want to take that. Any suggestions would be helpful. Thanks*
>
> *Ms DR Canada*

Diet

Fruit/vegetable juices, and vegetable soup are beneficial. The diet should mainly include vegetables, fruits, seeds, nuts and grains. Vitamin E is very important and can be obtained from sprouts of seeds and beans (including chickpeas and mung beans), wheat germ, cold pressed vegetable oils, butter and milk, whole grains and dark green vegetables. Calcium intake should also be sufficient. Dairy products, especially warm milk and *panīra* cheese (recipe in appendix 5) are good sources of calcium. Sesame and sunflower seeds, nuts and dried fruits are additional sources. Soy products (beans, flour, milk etc) should be included regularly.

Herbs

- Around ¼ cup of beet juice can be taken three times a day.
- Boil 1 tsp of carrot seeds in 1 cup of milk for 10 minutes. Drink it once per day.
- Take 8–10 pieces of saffron and mix into a cup of warm milk. Drink daily, or every few days.
- Eat 1 tbsp of aloe vera gel once or twice a day.

Exercise

Fresh air and regular exercise (*yoga*, walking, swimming, jogging, cycling) is recommended.

Other

Fasting for 1–2 days every 3 months, with lemon water or a fruit diet, removes toxins. Try to maintain a relaxed and positive attitude. Meditation can relieve stress. Massage, especially of the scalp and feet, can be rejuventaing and nourish the skin. Regular sleeping habits should be kept.

Medicines

Aśokārista, Śatāvarī ghṛta, Cyawanaprāśa.

Menstrual Disorders

Menstrual disorders such as painful cramps and irregularity are related to aggravation of all three *doṣas*. The main *doṣa* involved is *vāta*. The lower pelvis is the seat of *apāna vāta*, which is responsible for elimination of menstrual blood, stool, urine and reproductive fluids. At the commencement of menstruation, *apāna vāta* is increased. The symptoms of aggravated *apāna vāta* are disturbed digestion, constipation or diarrhea, flatulence and vomiting, cramps in the legs, pain in the lower pelvis and general weakness.

Diet

Sour foods, fried foods and beans should be avoided during menstruation. Foods that cause constipation or aggravation of *vāta* should not be consumed. Vegetables including pumpkin, potato, mushroom, cauliflower, peas and eggplant should be excluded from the diet. Papaya, cucumber, squash and zucchini are recommended. Food can be garnished with spices like cumin, asafoetida, fenugreek, black pepper, cloves, coriander and mint.

Herbs

- Crushed garlic can be taken twice a day. Up to 2 cloves may be taken for each dose. This may be added to meals.
- 1 tbsp of aloe vera gel mixed with a pinch of black pepper or cinnamon can be eaten. Take twice a day, or until cramps stop.
- A decoction of cumin seeds can be taken from the first day of menstruation. Add 1 tbsp of cumin seeds to 2 cups of water and simmer over a moderate heat until the mixture has reduced by half. Sieve, add raw sugar or honey, sieve and drink. This is one dose. Two doses daily for three days can relieve symptoms. Taken with each successive cycle, this remedy reduces the severity of symptoms.
- An infusion of fresh ginger or 1 tsp of dried ginger in 1 cup of water can relieve symptoms.

Exercise

Although the inclination may be to take complete rest, remaining active and taking regular exercise is beneficial. Walking is especially good for alleviating cramps. Simple stretching is also recommended.

Other

Taking purgatives (laxatives) for about 2 days before the scheduled start of menstruation can alleviate disturbed *vāta*. Massage of the lower abdomen with warm sesame oil for 10–15 minutes, followed by the application of a hot fomentation (such as a hot water bottle) while resting, can soothe cramps.

Medicines

Kumārī-āsava, Rajapravartanī vaṭī.

Obesity

Obesity or overweight is a condition characterized by deposits or storage of excessive fat. This health issue is becoming an increasing problem in the Western world. Āyurveda categorizes bodies into eight different shapes or types. Two of these body types are very unhealthy—very thin and very fat. *Caraka Saṁhitā* identifies those who are very fat as facing the most health problems. This is because the extra fat puts a strain on the heart, kidneys, liver and the joints such as the hips, knees and ankles. Overweight people are susceptible to diseases like coronary thrombosis, high blood pressure, diabetes, arthritis, gout, liver and gall bladder disorders.

Diet

Intake of fruits and vegetables should be increased. Bitter vegetables are recommended. Salt, dairy products, sugar products, potatoes, rice, alcohol and meat should be avoided. Fried, oily and processed foods should be minimized.

A sample diet: Drink a glass of warm water mixed with the juice of half a lemon or lime and 1tsp of honey upon waking. Breakfast can be cereal such as wheat or oats, and one cup of skimmed milk. At mid-morning a glass of orange, pineapple or carrot juice can be consumed if desired.

Lunch may be a fresh salad of raw vegetables (carrot, beet, cucumber, cabbage, tomatoes) or steamed vegetables, whole grain bread and a glass of buttermilk. Snacks in the afternoon can include fresh or dried fruits, herbal teas and vegetable soup. At dinner, whole grain bread, steamed vegetables and any seasonal fruits except bananas can be eaten.

Herbs

- Mint is very effective. Drinking mint tea, or eating mint chutney with meals may be helpful.
- Honey (1 tbsp with warm water) is an excellent remedy as it causes fat to be circulated and utilized as energy.

- In the morning, an equal quantity of unpeeled, grated carrot and apple can be eaten on an empty stomach. Do not eat anything for 2 hours afterwards.

Exercise

Physical activity is an important part of a weight reduction plan. It uses up calories stored as fat, and also relieves tension and tones muscles. Walking and *yoga* are the best types exercise to begin with, and may be followed by swimming, jogging and other outdoor sports.

Other

Fasting for one day every fortnight is beneficial. 1 tsp of honey and the juice of ½ a lime can be mixed in a glass of lukewarm water. This mixture can be taken several times during the fasting day. If necessary, fruit and vegetable juices and herbal teas can also be consumed.

Eat only when hungry and restrict eating to main meals. If hungry or craving snacks, eat fruits (fresh or dried), vegetables (carrot or celery sticks) or pumpkin seeds. Eat in a quiet, peaceful place and concentrate on the food you are consuming. Chew thoroughly and slowly.

Medicines

Triyūsṇādī loha, Medohara guggulu, Loha rasāyana.

Dear Dr Chauhan

...As for my health, although I don't seem to have lost that much weight, my shape is very different. I think that I have come down about 2 sizes in clothes since I started to follow your advice. I have a lot more energy and my complexion has improved. I am also calmer and less anxious. In addition, I just received the results from a blood test and the doctor told me that my blood sugar level is normal. Thank you so much for this. With deep respect, affection and gratitude,

Ms SC Latvia

Skin Disorders

The skin has six layers, and is formed from various tissues/*dhātus* including blood, fat, and muscles. The skin often displays symptoms of poor quality *dhātu* formation. One of the main contributing factors to the condition of the skin is inadequate or inappropriate diet. This is why limiting treatment to external application of creams or oils is usually unsuccessful in curing skin problems like eczema, psoriasis, rashes, pimples and acne. Although disorders of the skin are caused by an imbalance of all three *doṣas*, the primary *doṣa* involved is *pitta,* and symptoms of heat, redness and inflammation are often visible.

Diet

Any foods that aggravate *pitta* should be eliminated from the diet. This includes hot, spicy, acidic, sour, fried, oily and greasy foods. Drinking tea, coffee, alcohol or smoking can also aggravate pitta. White sugar and flour and their products should be minimized.

Drinking 3–4 quarts/litres of water a day is beneficial, as is wheat grass juice and milk. Intake of green, leafy vegetables, sweet fruits, nuts, seeds and grains should be increased. Corn, lentils and soy products are recommended.

Herbs

- Take ½ tsp turmeric powder twice a day with water.
- If neem (*nīma*) leaves are available, boil them in water, filter and wash the affected area. Products containing neem may be used instead, like creams or capsules.
- A juice made from apricot leaves can be applied to the affected area.
- The fresh gel of aloe vera can be directly applied to the skin, or the 1 tsp of gel may be consumed twice per day.
- Mix equal quantities of cucumber juice, rose water and lime juice. Apply after washing the skin and leave overnight.

- Take ½ cup of tomato juice and mix with 1 tsp of lemon juice. Apply to the affected area.
- Add 1 tsp of camphor oil to ½ cup of coconut oil. Put in a glass bottle and close with a lid or cap. Place the bottle in direct sunlight for two hours. Apply this oil to the affected area.
- Mix 5 tbsp of yellow sulphur powder with 1 cup of mustard or coconut oil. Apply this paste to the affected area daily, and wash after ½ hour. It is more effective if you sit in the sun or in a warm place after applying this oil.

Exercise

Try to get some fresh air and early morning sunlight every day.

Other

Soaps and shampoos should not be used on the affected area. Do not wear tight, restrictive clothing or synthetic fibres. Maintain regular bowel movements. Excessive exposure to the sun and heat should be avoided, as this aggravates *pitta*.

Medicines

Rasa-māṇikya, Nimbādi cūrṇa, Pancatikta ghṛta.

Dear Partap

I have been taking neem capsules for the last 3 months, and I am really surprised at the results. My skin has cleared up totally. I have had skin problems (adult acne) for many years, and neem is the only thing that has made a difference. I am curious about what it is that makes it so effective—but I know that is does work when nothing else has.

Ms MO South Africa

Part III

APPENDICES

APPENDIX 1

Reference Table of *Dosas*

DOṢA	*VĀTA*	*PITTA*	*KAPHA*
Definition	That which moves	That which digests	That which binds
Dominant Elements	Space *ākāśa* Air *vāyu*	Fire *agni*	Earth *pṛthvī* Water *jala*
Qualities	Rough, dry, light, fast, mobile, cool, subtle	Hot, sharp, acidic, intense, illuminating, transforming	Dense, heavy, firm, stable, slow thick, sticky, wet, clear, cold
Location	lower part of the body—Colon, rectum, bladder and urinary tract, spine, legs, thighs	middle portion of the body—Stomach, liver, duodenum, small intestine, eyes, skin, blood	upper part of the body—Head, nose, throat, chest, lungs, joints, fatty and connective tissues, ligaments, tendons
Governs	Nervous system, respiration, movement, circulation of fluids, excretion, stimulation of digestive juices and tract	Metabolism, digestion, bile, absorption, enzymes, hormones, sight, intelligence, comprehension	Mucus, saliva, cohesion of tissues, joints, lubrication, endurance and stamina, immunity, growth
Senses	Hearing and Touch	Sight	Taste and Smell
Related Emotions	Enthusiasm, flexibility, fear, tension, anxiety	Courage, willpower, anger, irritability, jealousy, envy	Love, patience, forgiveness, greed, possessiveness
Tastes that			
Aggravate	Pungent, bitter, astringent	Sour, salty, pungent	Sweet, sour, salty
Alleviate	Sweet, sour, salty	Sweet, bitter, astringent	Pungent, bitter, astringent
Increased by	• Traveling, activity, television, noise, late nights, excessive sexual activity • Windy, cold or dry weather • Prior to sunrise and sunset • Middle to old age	• Physical exercise, sports, stimulation of emotions, digestion or circulation • Exposure to heat and sun • Midday and midnight • Adolescence/adulthood	• Overeating, sleeping excessively or during the day, sedentary lifestyle • Cold and damp climates • Early morning and evening • Childhood
Symptoms of disturbance	• Conditions caused by dryness, dehydration, problems with mobility or movement • Insomnia, lack of appetite, tension, fatigue, restlessness	• Conditions with burning, acidity, or associated with fever, flushing, itching, perspiration, sight problems • Irritability, intolerance, anger, criticism, hot temper	• Conditions with heaviness, lethargy, excess mucus production, water retention, congestion, indigestion • Drowsiness, depression, slowness, stubbornness
Remedies to balance	• Dense, heavy foods containing fire, water or earth elements (sweet, sour, salty tastes) • Oil massage and steaming, detoxification of the colon	• Sweet, cold and light foods containing no fire element. Bitter, astringent tastes • Purgatives (laxatives) are considered the best therapy for excess *pitta*	• Light, dry, bitter foods, pungent and astringent (sharp) in taste, hot and spicy foods • Steaming and increased physical exercise, emetic therapy (supervised vomiting)

Appendix 2

Reference Table of Tastes

Taste: *Rasa*	**Sweet** *Madhura*	**Sour** *Amla*	**Salty** *Lavaṇa*	**Pungent** *Kaṭu*	**Bitter** *Tikta*	**Astringent** *Kaṣāya*
Examples	Sugar, milk honey, melon, potato, rice bread	Lemon, lime grapefruit, yogurt, cheese vinegar	Salted nuts, sauces, salt, processed foods, kelp	Ginger, onion, garlic, chili, radish, most spices	Tumeric rhubarb barberry aloe, neem	Unripe fruit, tea, alfalfa, raspberry, quince, plums
Elements: *Mahābhūtas*	Earth *pṛthvī* Water *jala*	Earth *pṛthvī* Fire *agni*	Water *jala* Fire *agni*	Air *vāyu* Fire *agni*	Air *vāyu* Space *ākāśa*	Air *vāyu* Earth *pṛthvī*
Aggravates	*Kapha*	*Kapha* *Pitta*	*Kapha* *Pitta*	*Vāta* *Pitta*	*Vāta*	*Vāta*
Alleviates	*Vāta* *Pitta*	*Vāta*	*Vāta*	*Kapha*	*Kapha* *Pitta*	*Kapha* *Pitta*
Qualities *Guṇas*	Cold Heavy Moist/oily	Hot Light Moist/oily	Hot Heavy Moist/oily	Hot Light Dry	Cold Light Dry	Cold Heavy Dry
Vīrya	Cooling (least)	Heating (moderate)	Heating (least)	Heating (most)	Cooling (most)	Cooling (moderate)
Vipāka	sweet *madhura*	sour *amla*	sweet *madhura*	pungent *kaṭu*	pungent *kaṭu*	pungent *kaṭu*
Action: *Karma*	+ weight + strength + toxins	+ appetite + acidity – libido	+ digestion + elasticity – *śukra*	+ metabolism + thirst/temp – *āma*	+ coldness – fever – toxins	+ stiffness + emaciation + contractions
Main organ	Pancreas	Liver	Kidneys	Lungs	Heart	Colon
Disorders	Diabetes Cough Asthma	Hyperacidity Jaundice Ulcers	Infertility Baldness Wrinkles	Weakness Vertigo Joint pains	*Dhātus* Dehydration Immunity	Stomach ache Colitis Angina
Emotions	Love Attachment Satisfaction	Envy Irritation Pessimism	Greed Self-pity Obstinacy	Hatred Anger Resentment	Grief Sorrow Despair	Fear Anxiety Asceticism

APPENDIX 3

Yoga Exercise

Salute to the Sun—*Sūrya Namaskāra*

Sūrya means "sun" and "*namaskāra*" is "salutation", or a form of greeting. This exercise is ideal to perform in the morning, greeting the sun as it rises. The movements of this *yoga* exercise prepare you for the day ahead. It stretches, tones and invigorates all the muscles, joints and organs of the body. The twelve postures described below are performed in rhythmic succession twice, to complete a sequence of 24 movements.

1. With eyes closed and feet together, bring the palms together in front of your chest. Relax the body and breathe normally.

2. Raise both arms above your head while inhaling. Stretch them back, while bending the upper part of your body back. Keep your arms shoulder width apart.

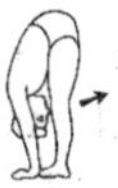

3. Exhale while bending forward from the waist. Try to touch your knees with your forehead, and the floor on either side of your feet with your hands.

4. Put both palms on the floor and right leg back with the knee on the ground. Bend the left leg, with the foot between the hands and inhale.

5. Move the left leg back, beside the right foot, while exhaling. Form a "triangle" position by raising your buttocks/hips. Keep legs and arms straight.

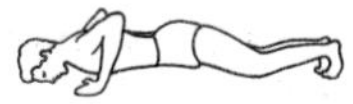

6. Lower the knees, chest and chin to the floor. The hips and abdomen should be raised from the floor. Hold the breath.

7. Lower the hips to the floor. Straighten the elbows, push the chest forward, arch the back and inhale. Your arms will be slightly bent and thighs on the floor.

8. Repeat position 5. Exhale as you raise your hips. Keep the feet on the floor and the chin close to the chest.

9. Repeat position 4. Inhale as you bend the left leg and bring the left foot between your hands. Lower your right knee to the floor and bend the head back.

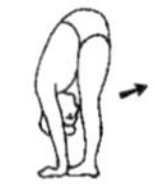

10. Repeat position 3 while exhaling. Bring the right knee forward next to the left foot and straighten both knees. Bend from the hips and bring the forehead to the knees.

11. Repeat position 2. Straighten your back and stretch your arms above your head. Keep them shoulder width apart. Bend the head and upper body back while inhaling.

12. Repeat position 1. Bring the palms together in front of the chest. Close the eyes and exhale.

This is half a round. Repeat these steps to complete a full round. In the second half of the sequence, stretch the left leg back instead of the right (step 4) and bend the right leg with the foot between the hands (step 9). Complete 3-12 rounds per day. This exercise benefits all internal systems including digestion, circulation and respiration. It assists in deep breathing and increases oxygen intake and the elimination of toxins. It stretches major muscle groups and improves flexibility, posture, balance and strength.

APPENDIX 4

Common Herbs and their Uses

HERBS are plants (or parts of them) that have a medicinal or culinary use. Their use has a rich tradition over millennia, and thousands of recipes and remedies have been devised using them as principal ingredients. Their medicinal value is still being explored today, often with remarkable results. Modern science cannot replicate many of the therapeutic wonders of the plant world.

Āyurvedic philosophy considers herbs and plants as living entities, and accords them due respect. The traditional methods of harvesting, processing and using herbs acknowledges their sacred nature. Plants are not picked carelessly, but are gently tended and maintained and only the specific portion of the plant required is taken. As they are picked for the purposes of healing, they are carefully selected with sensitivity.

Herbs and components of plants are picked at specific times to maximize their potency. Branches and leaves are collected when it is rainy or in spring, roots in summer or winter, bark in autumn, stems in winter, and flowers or fruits when they are in season. Usually, stone or clay pots are used to prepare herbs for internal use. This bowl should only be used for herbs, and cleaned with hot water after use. Glass or metal utensils are also suitable. If metal is used, copper is considered appropriate when preparing remedies for *kapha* conditions, silver or bronze for *pitta* and iron for *vāta*.

Mixtures of herbs are usually used, and they are consumed with the aid of an *anupāna* (the vehicle for administration). This can be hot or cold water, milk, honey, *ghī* or the juice of herbs or fruits. The *anupāna* augments the effect of an herb, and makes it palatable. The choice of *anupāna* can significantly alter the internal action of the herb and its potency.

The dosage prescribed varies, depending upon the person and condition treated. Factors like age, weight and constitution are important considerations. Herbs are generally non-toxic, and side effects from their use are normally not experienced. However, common sense and caution are required. The use of herbs should not substitute professional medical consultation and advice. An Āyurvedic doctor or health care professional should be consulted before administering any internal herbal remedies to children, pregnant women, the elderly and the very weak.

ALOE VERA

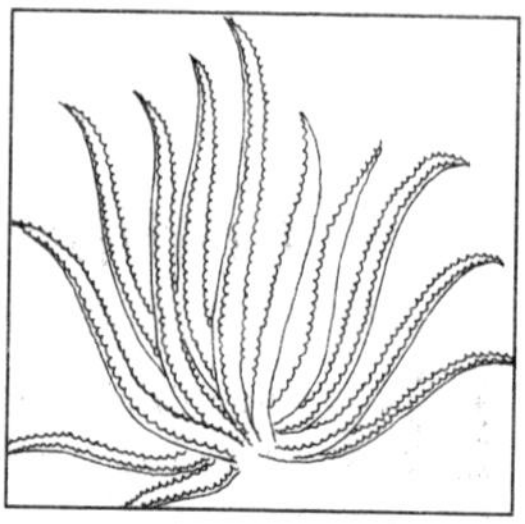

Botanical name : *Aloe Vera*
Sanskrit name : *Kumārī, Gṛhakanyā*
Taste/*Rasa* : Bitter, sweet
Quality/*Guṇa* : Heavy, oily, viscous
Potency/*Vīrya* : Cold
Vipāka : Bitter
Alleviates : *Pitta, Kapha*

Appearance : Aloe Vera is 1–2 feet high. The leaves are succulent, broad at the base and pointed at the tips, with spines along the edges.

Habitat : It is native to hot, dry regions and is originally from North Africa and Spain.

Medicinal part : Gel from the leaves, which is extracted when they are peeled or split open.

Remedies

Abscess/boil
- Peel a leaf on one side. Sprinkle it with 1 tsp of turmeric. Apply the leaf to the area and cover with a bandage.

Burns/wounds
- Skin is soothed and heals quickly when fresh gel applied.

Constipation
- Eat 1 tbsp of aloe gel every morning on an empty stomach.
- Boil ¼ cup of aloe pulp with ½ cup of castor oil, ½ cup finely chopped onion and ½ cup raw sugar. Simmer over a low heat until it becomes a thick paste. Cool and place in an airtight container. Take 1–2 tsp before bed.

Debility
- Take 1 cup of aloe gel, 4 finely chopped garlic cloves, and 1/4 tsp each of black pepper, asafoetida, cumin, turmeric and fenugreek. Mix together with ½ tsp of *ghi* and 1 tbsp of sesame oil. Take 1tsp every day with water or milk.

Dyspepsia
- Take 1–2 tbsp of the gel twice daily.

Rheumatism
- Apply warm gel to the affected areas.

Skin disorders
- External use: apply fresh gel to the area.
- Internal use: take 1–2 tsp of fresh gel daily.

Other uses: Aloe Vera pulp has healing properties internally and externally. It is moisturizing and anti-aging, so is often used in lotions for the skin. Internally, it benefits the circulatory system, liver and spleen. It is also effective in a variety of stomach or digestive disorders. Pregnant women, or children below the age of five years should never take aloe vera internally.

BASIL

Botanical Name : *Ocium sanctum*
Sanskrit Name : *Tulasī, Surasā*
Taste/*Rasa* : Pungent, bitter
Quality/*Guṇa* : Light, dry
Potency/*Vīrya* : Hot
Vipāka : Pungent
Alleviates : *Kapha, Vāta*

Appearance : Basil is 2-4 feet high. Leaves are oval shaped, with smooth or toothed edges depending on the variety. The flowers are small and whitish-purplish, growing on an upright stem.

Habitat : It grows well in most habitats and is found throughout the world.

Medicinal part : Leaves, flowers, seeds, roots.

Remedies

Coughs, cold, flu

- Take 10-12 washed, crushed basil leaves and 1 tbsp finely chopped fresh ginger. Fry in a pan over a low heat until the ginger has browned. Add 1 cup of water and boil for several minutes. Strain, add 1 tbsp of honey and drink.
- Make a decoction by boiling 10-15 leaves in 2 cups of water. Drink warm.
- Extract the juice of 10-15 basil leaves; add 1 tsp of ginger juice and 1 tsp of honey. Mix and take in the morning and evening.
- A powder of dried basil leaves can be used as a snuff to clear nasal congestion.

Digestive problems

- Boil 10–20 basil leaves in water and drink.

Fever

- Grind 7 basil leaves, 4 peppercorns and 2 tsp of raw sugar and mix with 1/3 cup of water. Take on an empty stomach.

Longevity or Loss of appetite

- Chew 2–4 leaves on an empty stomach in the morning.

Skin disorders

- Make a paste with fresh leaves and water. Apply to the affected area.
- Take 1 tsp of juice daily.

Other uses: Basil is a natural air freshener and insect repellant. It is used in cooking, especially Italian food, soups and pasta sauces. It is considered one of the sacred plants of India, and is grown in most households. Orthodox Hindus worship a variety of basil known as Holy *Tulasī* daily by watering it, offering leaves to God and walking around the base of the plant four times.

CINNAMON

Botanical Name : *Cinnamomum zeylanicum*
Sanskrit Name : *Tvaka, Utkaṭa*
Taste/*Rasa* : Pungent, bitter, sweet
Quality/*Guṇa* : Light, dry, sharp
Potency/*Vīrya* : Hot
Vipāka : Pungent
Alleviates : *Kapha, Vāta*

Appearance : The tree can grow 20–25 feet high. The bark is rough, brown and brittle. Leaves are glossy and dark-green, 4–7 inches long with several veins running parallel along them. The flowers are small and grow in hairy clusters.

Habitat : Cinnamon grows in tropical or sub-tropical environments. It is native to Asia.

Medicinal part : Inner bark, powder from dried leaves and oil from leaves, roots or bark.

Remedies

Cough/bronchitis
- Mix 1 tsp each of cinnamon, turmeric, ginger, black pepper, cardamom and clove. Add 3 tbsp of raw sugar and grind together to make a fine powder. Take ½–1 tsp of this powder mixed with honey twice per day.

Cold/flu
- Boil 1 tsp of cinnamon in 1 cup of water. Simmer until it is half the volume, strain, add honey and drink warm.

Diarrhea
- Mix 1 tsp each of cinnamon, ginger and cumin powder with honey to make a paste. Take 1 tsp three times a day.

Insomnia
- Add ½ tsp of cinnamon powder and 1 tsp of honey to 1 cup of warm milk. Drink before bed.

Mouth purifier
- Boil 1 tsp of cinnamon in 1 cup of water. Cool and use as a gargle.
- Mix equal parts of cinnamon, cardamom and dried bay leaf. Mix 1 tsp of this powder in 1 cup of hot water and drink twice daily.

Nervous tension
- Take a pinch of cinnamon powder mixed with honey before bed.

Skin disorders
- Apply a paste of cinnamon and lime juice daily.

Toothache
- Put 1–2 drops of cinnamon oil on a cotton ball and press around the tooth.

Vomiting/Nausea
- Eat a pinch of cinnamon powder.

Other uses: Cinnamon is used for flavoring cakes, breads, desserts, drinks and confectionary. It is also used for making incense and perfumes. Taking cinnamon once a day (mixed with warm water, milk or eaten directly) can assist in milk secretion for nursing mothers'.

CLOVES

Botanical Name	:	*Syzygium aromaticum*
Sanskrit Name	:	*Lavanga, Devakusuma*
Taste/*Rasa*	:	Bitter, pungent
Quality/*Guṇa*	:	Light and oily
Potency/*Vīrya*	:	Cool
Vipāka	:	Pungent
Alleviates	:	*Pitta, Kapha*
Appearance	:	This evergreen tree grows 30–40 feet tall. The bark is smooth and gray; leaves fragrant and grow in pairs; flowers are pink when mature and in small clusters at the end of branches.
Habitat	:	Hot, tropical environments.
Medicinal part	:	The dried, unopened flower buds (cloves), oil made from them.

Remedies

Asthma
- Mix 4–5 drops of clove oil with 1 tbsp of honey and 1 clove of crushed garlic. Take before bed.
- Boil 6 crushed cloves in ½ cup of water. Add 1 tsp honey. This mixture can be taken 2–3 times per day.

Bad breath
- Chew 1–2 cloves twice a day.

Fever
- Add 3 crushed cloves, 2 cardamoms, 2 tbsp of aniseed, 6–7 basil leaves and 1 tsp of cinnamon to 2 cups of water. Boil and then simmer until it has reduced by half. Drink this herbal decoction, once or twice a day.

Indigestion/nausea
- Fry 2 tsp of cloves and add to 1 cup of boiling water. Steep for 30 minutes. Drink 1 tsp of this solution 3–4 times a day.

Muscle cramps or Painful joints/back
- Apply warm clove oil on the affected area and massage gently.

Sore gums/throat
- Gargle an infusion made from cloves and warm water.
- Chew 3–4 cloves.

Toothache
- Apply clove oil to the surrounding gum or the cavity.

Vomiting
- Fry ½ tsp of clove powder, mix with 1 tbsp of honey and eat.

Other uses: Cloves are used to flavor foods, and are mixed with turmeric, cinnamon and chilies in curries. In India, they are mixed with other herbs and eaten with betel leaf as a breath freshener and digestive aid.

CORIANDER

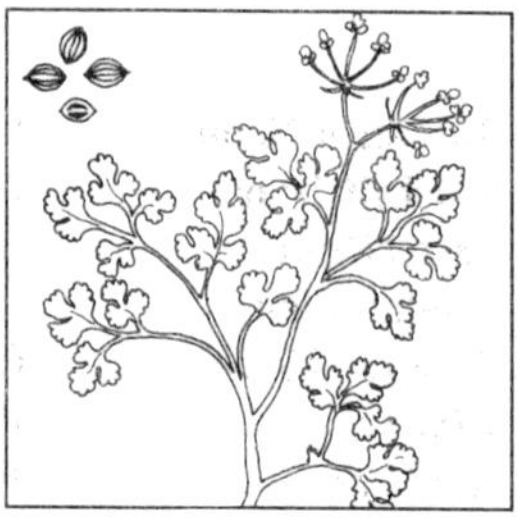

Botanical name : *Coriandrum Sativum*
Sanskrit name : *Dhānyaka, Kustumbrū*
Taste/*Rasa* : Astringent, pungent, bitter
Quality/*Guṇa* : Light and oily
Potency/*Vīrya* : Hot
Vipāka : Sweet
Alleviates : *Vāta, Kapha*

Appearance : The bush is 1–3 feet high, with many branches. The leaves are soft and small with a fragrance. Flowers are white and appear at the end of winter. Seeds are round, yellowish brown and divided into two.

Habitat : It is grows in temperate climates. It is native to the Mediterranean region.

Medicinal part : Roots, leaves, seeds, flowers and fruits, oil extracted from plant.

Remedies

Conjunctivitis
- To soothe the eyes, use 1–2 drops of diluted leaf juice.

Coughs, cold, flu
- Crush 2 tsp of coriander seeds. Add 2 tsp of chopped, peeled ginger. Put the mixture into a frying pan over a low heat. Stir to prevent the mixture from burning. Add 2 cups of water. Cover the pan to retain the fumes. Boil for a few minutes. Filter the liquid. Mix in 1 tbsp of honey and drink warm.

Headaches
- Make a paste of the dried seeds and water and apply to the forehead.

Nose bleeds
- Put 5–6 drops of the oil or juice in each nostril.

Pitta disorders
- Add 1 tbsp of crushed seeds or leaves to 1 cup of water. Soak for at least 3–4 hours. Drink twice a day.

Sinus problems
- Inhale the steam from a few tbsp of coriander seeds boiled in 4 cups of water.

Swellings
- Apply a compress of damp, crushed coriander leaves to the swelling.
- Drink a coriander tea infusion made from 1 tsp of seeds and 1 cup of hot water.

Other uses: Coriander is used in cooking a variety of recipes. The powdered seeds can be added to vegetables while cooking. A paste or chutney containing coriander is used as an appetizer before meals. To make chutney, grind a medium bunch of coriander leaves and a small bunch of mint leaves together with a little water, lemon or lime juice and a pinch of salt. For variations, mango pulp, grated coconut, chopped nuts, natural yogurt or sour cream can be added. Serve as a sauce for vegetables.

CUMIN

Latin name : *Cuminum cyminum*
Sanskrit name : *Jīraka, ajājī*
Taste/*Rasa* : Pungent
Quality/*Guṇa* : Light and dry
Potency/*Vīrya* : Hot
Vipāka : Pungent
Alleviates : *Kapha, Vāta*

Appearance : Cumin is an annual herb with branched stems. The leaves are bluish green and grow to around 2 inches long. The white or rose-colored flowers appear in late spring. The seeds are yellow-brown when dried.

Habitat : Hot, dry climates in sandy soil (Iran, North Africa, Middle East, India).

Medicinal part : The fruits, which are dried and commonly referred to as seeds.

Remedies

Diarrhea
- Roast 2/3 tsp of cumin seeds and powder them. Add a pinch each of ginger powder, cinnamon powder and black pepper. Mix in 1 cup of yogurt. Eat twice a day.
- Mix 1 tsp each of cumin, ginger, cinnamon and honey. Eat ½ tsp 3 times a day.

Digestive disorders
- Boil 1 tsp of cumin in 1 cup of water. Add 1 tsp of juice from coriander leaves and a pinch of salt. Drink after meals for several days.

Fatigue
- Add ½ tsp each of cumin, coriander, black pepper and lentils to 1 cup of water and boil. Add salt and drink.

Flatulence/Gas
- Mix an equal quantity of crushed cumin seeds, black pepper and ginger. Make an infusion by mixing it in hot water. Drink warm twice a day, for several days.

Insomnia
- Sprinkle 1 tsp of cumin on a sliced banana. Eat at night regularly.

Lactation
- To increase lactation, mix 1 tsp of cumin and 1 tsp of sugar and drink with warm milk each evening.

Prickly heat
- Crush 1tbsp cumin seeds with coconut milk and apply frequently.

Other uses: Cumin is used to flavor bread, pastries, cheese, pickles and chutneys. It is widely used in Indian cooking and is an ingredient in curry powder and mixed spice.

GARLIC

Botanical name : *Allium Sativum*
Sanskrit name : *Rasona, Ugragandhā*
Taste/*Rasa* : Pungent
Quality/*Guṇa* : Heavy, oily, sharp
Potency/*Vīrya* : Hot
Vipāka : Pungent
Alleviates : *Kapha, Vāta*

Appearance : The plant has long, narrow, flat leaves. The bulb consists of up to 10–25 cloves, which are covered in a whitish, thin, papery outer layer. White flowers grow from a long stem in the center of the plant.

Habitat : Garlic grows easily in dry environments. It is native to Asia.

Medicinal part : Bulb (cloves), oil

Remedies

Arthritis, Sciatica
- A paste made of crushed cloves and water is applied to the affected part, or a cut clove rubbed directly onto the area.
- Fresh cloves may be eaten (1–3 per day).

Asthma
- Boil 3 cloves of chopped garlic in 1 cup of milk and drink before bed.
- Peel and crush 1 clove of garlic. Boil in ½ cup of malt vinegar. Cool and then strain. Take 1–2 tsp each evening.

Digestive disorders
- Crush 1–2 cloves of garlic and take with warm water or milk.

Fever
- Mix 1 tbsp of crushed garlic and ¼ cup of finely chopped basil leaves. Add 1 cup of water and boil until ½ cup remains. Take 2 tsp twice per day.

Insect bites
- Dab garlic paste on the affected area and leave for 5–10 minutes.

Rejuvenation
- Eat garlic cloves (1–3 per day), or use garlic in cooking.

Sinusitis
- Mix 1 tsp of crushed garlic, 1 tsp of turmeric and 2 tbsp of honey. Take 1 tsp daily.

Skin problems
- Eat 1–3 garlic cloves or take a garlic oil capsule daily.
- Rub a cut clove or the paste onto the affected area several times a day.

Other uses: Garlic is mainly pungent but represents five tastes (all except sour). It is widely used in cooking, especially Mediterranean cuisines. Garlic is considered to be a natural aphrodisiac, and stimulates the reproductive system. Those devoted to spiritual growth usually avoid garlic for general consumption, as it is considered *rājasic/tāmasic*.

GINGER

Botanical name : *Zingiber Officinale*
Sanskrit name : *Śuṇṭhi, Nāgara*
Taste/*Rasa* : Pungent
Quality/*Guṇa* : Dry ginger is light and oily; Fresh is dry and heavy
Potency/*Vīrya* : Hot
Vipāka : Dry ginger is sweet; Fresh ginger is pungent
Alleviates : *Kapha, Vāta*
Appearance : Ginger is a perennial herb that grows up to 6 feet high. The roots are known as rhizomes, and are around an inch in diameter. When fresh, the rhizome is white or yellow. It becomes darker when dried.
Habitat : It grows in damp, hot and humid environments.
Medicinal part : Root (rhizome)

Remedies

Arthritis
- Mix 6 tsp of ginger powder, 6 tsp of caraway seeds and 3 tsp of black pepper. Take ½ tsp of this mixture twice a day with water.

Cough, cold
- Mix ½ tsp of ginger powder and ½ tsp of turmeric with 1 tbsp of honey. Take twice a day.
- Take 1 tsp of ginger juice mixed with 1 tsp honey 2–3 times per day.
- Boil 1 tbsp chopped ginger in 1 cup of water. Strain, add sugar or honey and drink warm.

Loss of appetite
- Put 5 tbsp of chopped, fresh ginger in a glass jar. Cover the ginger with lemon juice, add a pinch of salt and 1 tbsp of cumin seeds. Put the jar in the sun for 2 days in summer, or 3–5 days in winter. Eat ½ tsp before meals.

Nausea, flatulence
- Mix ½ tsp of ginger juice, 1 tsp of lime-juice, 1 tsp of mint juice and 1 tbsp of honey. Take twice per day.

Stomach ache
- Boil 1 tsp of chopped ginger in 1 cup of water, add a pinch of salt and drink.

Vāta disorders
- Drink warm water mixed with ½ tsp of ginger powder and ½ tsp of turmeric.

Other uses: Ginger is used in either fresh or powdered form in many recipes. In addition to flavoring vegetables, soups, pickles and chutneys it can be used in cakes, biscuits, and drinks. To make a rice dish seasoned with ginger: cook 1 cup of rice. Put the cooked rice in a dish and add around 2 tbsp of butter or ghee and 1 tsp of salt. Mix and cool the rice. Prior to serving it, mix through 1¼ cups of natural yogurt and 1 tbsp of finely chopped fresh ginger.

MINT

Botanical name : *Mentha spicata*
Sanskrit name : *Pūtihā, Rocanī, Pudinā*
Taste/*Rasa* : Pungent
Quality/*Guṇa* : Light, dry, sharp
Potency/*Vīrya* : Hot
Vipāka : Pungent
Alleviates : *Kapha, Vāta*

Appearance : Mint is a bushy, perennial shrub that grows 1–2 feet in height, with a strong aroma. The leaves are dark green and oval shaped, ribbed on the underside and slippery.

Habitat : Mint is native to Europe. It is a hardy and fast growing plant that can adapt to most environments. There are a number of varieties around the world.

Medicinal part : Leaves, seeds, oil extracted from the entire plant.

Remedies

Digestive disorders including indigestion, flatulence, nausea and diarrhea
- Wash a medium bunch of mint leaves. Shred and place in a bowl. Add a pinch of salt, 1–2 tsp of lemon juice and 1 tsp each of coriander and cumin seed powder. Add some water and grind to a paste. Take 1 tsp of this paste twice a day prior to meals, or with meals.
- Chew ¼ tsp of the seeds, swallow with water.
- Mix 1 tsp mint juice with 1 tsp of lime juice and 1 tbsp honey. Take 3 times a day.
- Drink mint tea (1 tbsp of leaves, 1 cup of water), or warm milk and mint.

Bad breath
- Mix 1 tbsp of mint juice in ½ cup of water. Use as a gargle.
- Chew a few mint leaves.
- Use dried mint powder to clean the mouth and teeth.

Nausea
- Mix 1 tsp dried mint, ½ tsp ginger, ½ tsp of black pepper and 2 tsp of raw sugar with 1 cup of water. Boil and drink warm.
- Boil 1 tsp of dried mint and ½ tsp of cardamom in 1 cup of water.

Pimples and acne
- Put some mint paste on affected area. Leave overnight.

Other uses: Mint flavors many dishes. In India, mint chutney is used as an appetizer before meals. A traditional Indian recipe that is easy to make is mint yogurt or *raitā*. To make mint yogurt, take ½ cup of mint leaves and grind with a little water. Add 1 tbsp of this paste to one cup of natural yogurt. Mix well. Add a pinch of salt and some roasted cumin seeds. Serve chilled with vegetables, bread or rice.

TURMERIC

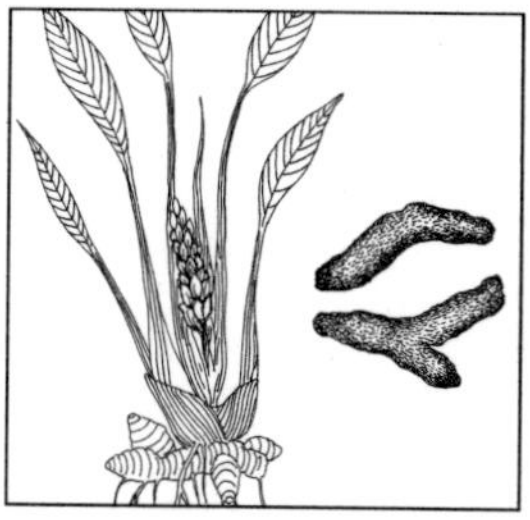

Latin name : *Curcuma longa*
Sanskrit name : *Haridrā, Gaurī*
Taste/*Rasa* : Bitter, pungent
Quality/*Guṇa* : Light and dry
Potency/*Vīrya* : Hot
Vipāka : Pungent
Alleviates : *Kapha, Vāta, Pitta*

Appearance : It is 2–3 ft tall and consists of several stalks that support up to 6–7 large, oblong shaped leaves. The pale yellow flowers are clustered in spikes. The yellow root is the source of the spice and is graded by color.

Habitat : Humid conditions with rich soil. It is native to South East Asia.

Medicinal part : The root (rhizome), which is boiled, dried and cleaned.

Remedies

Anaemia
- Mix 1 tsp of turmeric juice with honey and take daily.

Asthma
- Boil 1 cup of milk with 1 tsp of turmeric powder. Drink warm.

Burns
- Mix 1 tsp of turmeric with 1 tsp of aloe gel and apply.

Conjunctivitis
- Mix 1 tbsp of crushed, raw turmeric in 1/3 cup of water. Boil and sieve. 2–3 drops of this mixture may be used in each eye up to 3 times per day.

Complexion
- Apply a paste of turmeric on the skin before bed, and wash off after a few minutes. In the morning, remove any remaining yellow tinge with a paste of chickpea flour (*besan*) and oil.

Dental problems
- Mix 1 tsp of turmeric with ½ tsp of salt. Add mustard oil to make a paste. Rub the teeth and gums with this paste twice daily.

Diabetes
- ½–1 tsp of turmeric should be taken 3 times per day.

Diarrhea
- Take ½ tsp of turmeric powder or juice in water, 3 times per day.

Pain
- Mix 1 tsp of turmeric and 2 tsp of ginger with water to make a paste. Spread over a cloth, place on the affected area and bandage.
- Add 1 tsp of turmeric to 1 cup of warm milk and drink before bed.

Other uses: In cooking, turmeric provides a yellow color to food. It is an important herb in *Hindu* rituals. It is also an ingredient of cosmetics as it is beneficial for the skin. Burning turmeric can repel insects. Inhaling the smoke can assist in coughs, asthma and congested nasal passages.

Appendix 5

Recipes

Āyurveda advocates foods that are fresh, simple to prepare and easy to digest. Some commonly used items, like *ghī*, buttermilk and *khicaḍi* may not be widely available or normally used in the West. However, they are easy to make at home and you can enjoy the pleasure of making and eating some of these tasty foods yourself. The recipes for some basic dairy products (butter, buttermilk, cheese, cream, *ghī* and yogurt) and *khicaḍi*, are listed below:

Khicaḍī

Khicaḍi is easy to digest and stimulates the appetite. It balances all three *doṣas*. It is considered excellent for patients suffering from digestive disorders, fever, diarrhea and chronic diseases that have weakened the *dhātus* or decreased *ojas*. It is good to eat when you feel tired, weak or after fasting. The recipe below is for basic *khicaḍi* , but there are many variations of this, using different combinations of vegetables and spices.

Ingredients

- ½ tsp cumin seeds
- 3 bay leaves
- 1 tsp coriander seed powder
- ½ tsp turmeric
- ½ tsp salt
- 1 tsp grated, fresh ginger
- 4–6 cups of water
- 2 tbsp *ghī* or sunflower oil
- ½ cup *bāsamatī* rice
- ½ cup of split mung beans/*dāla*
- OR—1 cup of mung beans (for a lighter recipe)

Method

- Put the rice and mung beans in a bowl. Fill with water until the mixture is covered. Rub the mixture between your hands for about 30 seconds. Drain the discolored water and repeat. When the water remains clear, it is ready for preparation.
- Warm the *ghī* or oil in a saucepan. Add cumin and bay leaves, and lightly fry. Add the turmeric and coriander and stir well.
- Add the water, rice, mung beans and ginger. Bring to the boil and then simmer covered for 10–15 minutes or until the rice is cooked. Add salt to taste.
- A teaspoon of *ghī* can be added on top prior to serving.

Buttermilk

Buttermilk increases the digestive fire/*jaṭharāgni*, and balances *vāta*, *pitta* and *kapha*. It is helpful in various digestive disorders like constipation, indigestion and loss of appetite. According to Āyurvedic lore, a person who drinks buttermilk will never fall ill, and a disease cured with buttermilk will never reappear. It is considered a "wonder drink" and is consumed daily in most Indian households.

Ingredients

- 1 cup of natural yogurt
- 3 cups of water

Optional: Honey
Raw sugar
½ tsp black pepper
½ tsp ginger powder
Grated fresh ginger
Fresh coriander leaves
1 tsp of roasted cumin seeds
Salt according to taste

Method

- Mix the water with the yogurt. You can use a mixer or blender.
- Skim off any oil that floats to the surface.
- Add black pepper, roasted cumin seeds, salt or ginger for flavor. Honey or raw sugar may be added instead for sweetness. Your own combination of herbs and spices can also be used.

Yogurt

Yogurt is heavy to digest and heating in nature. It decreases *vāta* and increases *kapha* and *pitta*. It has a binding quality and is used as a supporting medicine in diarrhea and dysentery.

Ingredients

- 4 cups milk
- ½ tsp natural yogurt in summer
- OR—1 tsp natural yogurt in winter

Method

- Heat the milk until is lukewarm. In winter, heat it slightly more.
- Add the yogurt to the milk and keep it at room temperatures in summer. In winter, keep the mixture in a hot place or in the oven. Or, a cloth can be wrapped around the container to retain the heat.
- Check after 5–6 hours. It should be thick and firm. If it is has not set, check every hour for up to 12 hours. If it has still not set, the temperature of the milk or the surroundings, or the amount of yogurt used may not have been sufficient.
- Refrigerate until use.

Ghī

Ghī (ghee) is considered useful for cooking as well as medicinal purposes. In cooking, it is used for lightly frying vegetables, as a substitute for butter in some cases, and in place of oil. It alleviates *pitta* and *vāta* but increases *kapha*. It stimulates digestion and metabolism, and improves memory, strength and intellect. Regular use of *ghī* is a *rasāyana*. It is also used to treat burns, as a massage lubricant and in many home remedies.

Ingredients

- 1 pound of unsalted butter
- OR—use your own homemade butter.

Method

- Melt the butter in a saucepan over a medium heat. Stir occasionally so that it does not stick to the bottom of the pan.
- Once all the butter has melted, simmer for about 10–15 minutes until the mixture starts bubbling and becoming frothy.
- Stir gently and reduce to a low heat.
- Once the mixture separates into a transparent yellowish liquid and solids at the bottom of the pan, remove from the heat immediately. The solid part should be whitish in color.
- Let the mixture cool slightly, and then separate the solids by pouring the mixture through a metal sieve into a metal or glass container. This liquid portion is the ghī, and the solids can be discarded. It can be stored at room-temperature, or refrigerated.

Cream

Home-made cream is not as fatty as commercially produced cream, and is delicious with fruit or sweet dishes. Cream increases *kapha* and alleviates *pitta* and *vāta*. It can block the channels if taken in excess. In small quantities, it acts as a *rasāyana* and lubricant, and can be used externally for skin care and massage.

Ingredients

- Around 2 quarts (2 litres) fresh milk (quantity can be varied according to amount of cream required)

Method

- Bring the milk to boil and then simmer. Repeat this 3 times. Cool to room temperature.
- Refrigerate for 4 to 5 hours.
- Skim all the cream off that has floated to the top. The remaining fat free milk can be used for drinking.

Cheese (*Panīra*)

Fresh cheese is known as *panīra*, and is rich in calcium, protein and fats. In small quantities is easily digested and alleviates *pitta* and *vāta*. However, as it is heavy and cooling, in larger quantities it can increase *kapha*. It is beneficial for weak people as it provides energy, increases strength and encourages *dhātu* growth.

Ingredients

- 2 quarts (2 litres) of milk
- 2 tbsp of lemon juice
- Porous cloth

Method

- Heat the milk in a saucepan over moderate heat. When it starts boiling, add lemon juice.
- Lower the heat and stir the mixture continuously. The milk will curdle and separate into a white liquid and solids. Keep stirring for 5–6 minutes.
- Pour the mixture through a metal sieve and discard the liquid.
- Place the solid residue into the cloth and tie into a tight bundle.
- Put on a flat plate with a heavy weight on top for 5–6 hours, while refrigerated. This squeezes out any remaining liquid.
- Remove the cloth and keep the cheese refrigerated, in a bowl.

Butter

Fresh homemade butter is the highest quality butter. It helps in *pitta* and *vāta* disorders, especially skin diseases and blood impurity. It has a binding quality, so eating an excessive amount blocks the circulatory channels (*srotas*). It improves memory, increases immunity and enhances reproductive fluids (*śukra dhātu*).

Ingredients

- 1 quart (1 litre) of cream OR
- Your own home-made cream
- A few ice-cubes or iced water.

Method

- Put the cream in the bowl of a food processor or mixer fitted with a blending blade. Mix the cream for 10 to 15 minutes. If the weather is hot, add a few ice-cubes or a few tablespoons of iced water when it starts separating. The mixture will convert into a thick butter, with some watery residue.
- Drain off any water residue and put the fresh butter in a sealed container.
- Keep the butter refrigerated.

Glossary

Sanskrit Pronunciation Guide

Vowels

a	around, but	o	go, stone
ā	tar, father, far	u	push, pull, full
e	they, prey	ū	rule, rude, crude
i	pin, fill	ai	aisle
ī	police, pique	au	how, house

Consonents

b	bear, bird	ñ	singe, canyon
bh	abhor	p	paper, sip
d	the, than	ph	father
ḍ	drum	r	ring, rim
dh	adhere	ṛ	grit, writ
c	chair	s	sun, sound
ch	pitcher (ch-h)	ś	sure, sugar
g	dog, gun	ṣ	shun, bush
gh	ghost	t	tub, toe
h	heart, harm	ṭ	ta with tongue against front teeth
k	seek, kite		
l	like, lake	th	thermal, thunder
ṁ	French word bon	ṭh	anthill
n	nut, now	y	yes, yellow
ṅ	sing	v	sweet, wind
ṇ	say r and then na		

Abhyanga : to smear, anoint, oil massage.

Ācāra : good conduct, an established rule of conduct.

Agada tantra : toxicology; a branch of Āyurveda dealing with poisons.

Āgantuka : external, stranger, incidental.

Agni : fire, light, heat.

Ahaṁkāra : conception of one's individuality; egotism; pride; haughtiness.

Āhāra : food, anything ingested into the body, that which goes in.

Āhāra rasa : the juice of food, essence of food, nutrient plasma.

Ajāsṛika : activities that promote positive health.

Ajīrṇa : indigestion, weak digestion.

Ākāśa : free open space, ether, sky, atmosphere.

Ākṛiti : physical appearance, external shape.

Alābū : a vessel made of dried gourd.

Ālocaka (pitta) : a type of *pitta* governing vision, causing to see.

Āma : uncooked, raw, undigested, a toxic material produced from undigested food.

Āmavāta : a disease caused by *āma* and *vāta*, comparable to arthritis in modern medicine.

Amla : sour taste.

Āmalā (*Āmalakī*) : an Āyurvedic herb—*Emblica Officinalis.*

Añjana : black pigment applied to eyes and eye lashes.

Anna-vaha srotas : the channels transporting grains or food, the digestive system, alimentary canal.

Anupāna : a fluid vehicle for medicine; drink taken with or after medicine; drink after eating.

Anurasa : a secondary flavor, a subordinate feeling.

Anuvāsana (*basti*) : enema given with an oily substance.

Apa : the element water, water.

Apāna (*vāta*) : one of the five types of *vāta*, which governs expulsion of faces, flatus, urine, menstrual blood etc.

Apara-ojas : one of the less important of two types of vital fluid (*ojas*) present in the body, inferior, lower.

Aparādha : offence, sin, wrong action, misuse.

Ardhāvabhedaka : A kind of migraine affecting half of the head or skull.

Ārśa : saintly, pious, sacred.

Artha : economy, money, object.

Āsana : posture, seat, position.

Asātmya : unwholesome, bad, improper.

Asātmendriyārtha saṁyoga : improper contact of senses with their objects.

Aṣṭānga Hṛdaya : an ancient Āyurvedic text written by *Vagabhaṭṭa.*

Asthi : bone.

Asthi-vaha srotas : channels that carry nutrient material for bones.

Asura : demon, an evil spirit, opponent of God.

Ātapa : heat, sunlight.

Atiyoga : excessive use, over-use.

Ātmā : soul, spirit, true Self.

Aum : name of God.

Avalambaka (kapha) : one of the five types of *kapha*, which gives strength to heart.

Āvaraṇa : cover, layer.

Avedhya : that which should not be pierced or punctured.

Avidāhī : does not produce acid or burning.

Avipattikara Cūrṇa : an Āyurvedic medicine popularly used to treat hyperacidity.

Āyus : combined form of soul, mind, body and senses, life span.

Āyurveda : the knowledge of body, mind, senses and soul; the science of life.

Basti : herbal enema.

Bheda : division, variety, distinction.

Bhrājaka (pitta) : a type of *pitta* that gives color or lustre to the skin.

Bhutāgni : the fire (enzyme) that digests elements (*bhūta*).

Bhuta-vidya : the science dealing with microorganisms and evil spirits, demonology.

Brahma : study of the *Vedas*, study of spirit, the absolute, self-realized soul.

Brahmacarya : disciplined routine followed while studying for spiritual enlightenment.

Brahma-muhūrta : time period (two hours) preceding sunrise.

Brāhmi : a herb popularly used for enhancing memory, Latin Name: *Centella asiatica*.

Bodhaka (kapha) : one of the five types of *kapha* that helps to determine various tastes in mouth.

Buddhi : intelligence, intellect.

Cakra : a circular structure or plexus formed by intersection of many energy carrying *nādis*.

Cakśu : eye.

Caraka (Charaka) : a respected authority in the history of Āyurveda who wrote *Caraka Saṁhitā*.

Caryā : routine, practice.

Cikitsā : treatment, a therapy to retain balance, practice or science of medicine.

Citraka : name of a herb, Latin name: *Plumbago Zeylanica*.

Citraka-mūla : the root of the herb citrak (*Plumbago Zeylanica*); used for increasing digestive strength.

Citrakādi vatī : an Āyurvedic medicine made using *citrak* as the main ingredient.

Dantī mūla : root of the herb *danti* (Latin name: *Baliospermum montanum*).

Deśa : region, country, area, kingdom.

Dhāraṇā : concentration of mind combined with controlled breathing.

Dhātrī : a synonym of *Amalaki* (*Emblica Officinalis*).

Dhātu : tissue element that sustains the body, layer, stratum.

Dhātu-agni : the fire (enzyme) that converts juice of the food into tissue.

Dhyāna : meditation.

Dinacaryā : daily routine.

Drava : liquid.

Dūṣya : that which is contaminated or adulterated, seat of disease manifestation in the body.

Doṣa : fault, deficiency, that which contaminates.

Gandharva : celestial musicians, Heavenly singers.

Ghī (Ghee) : clarified butter.

Gokśuru : puncture vine, Latin name: *Tribulus terrestris*.

Gudūci : name of a herb : Latin name: *Tinospora cordifolia*.

Guggulu : a gum from the herb called Indian bedellium, Latin name: *Commiphora mukul*.

Guṇa : quality, peculiarity, attitude, characteristic.

Guru : heavy, weighty, great, large, respectable, teacher.

Harītakī : Chebulic Myrofalan, Latin name: *Terminalia Chebula*.
Harṣaṇī : delightful, pleasant.
Hīna yoga : insufficient, deficient.
Indriya : faculty of sense, organ of sense.
Īsabgol : a herb commonly used as a laxative. Latin name: *Plantago ovata*.
Jala : water, fluid.
Jalaukā : leech.
Jaṭhara : stomach, abdomen.
Jātī : jasmine.
Jaṭharāgni : fire located in stomach, digestive fire, gastric juices, digestive enzymes.
Jivhā : tongue.
Jīva : the living soul, alive, life.
Jñānêndriya : knowledge perceiving senses or organs.
Kājala : a black pigment applied to eye lashes and inner coat of eye lids.
Kāla : time period, season.
Kāmya : desirable, amiable, action to fulfill a desire.
Kapha : phlegm, mucus, one of the three main biological energies of the body.
Karaṇa : doing, making, effecting, causing.
Karañja : Indian beech, Latin name: *Pongamia pinnata*.
Karavīra : Indian oleander, Latin name: *Nerium indicum*.
Karmêndriya : an organ of action, the working sense.
Kaṣāya : astringent taste or flavor.
Kaṭu : pungent taste or flavor.
Kaṭukā : a herb (picrorhiza), Latin name: *Picrorhiza kurroa*.
Kaṭhina : hard, firm, stiff, harsh, inflexible, cruel.
Kaumārabhṛtya : the branch of Ayurveda that deals with child-care, pediatrics.
Kāya : body, habitation.
Kāya-cikitsā : treatment of body diseases, internal medicine.
Kedāri Kulyā : a rule of tissue formation using the analogy of the irrigation of a field. Each tissue receives nutrition in a specific order like each section of the field (*kedāri*) is irrigated through specific channels (*kulyā*) one after the other.
Khara : hard, harsh, rough.
Khale Kapota : the rule of tissue formation which states that, like each pigeon (*kapota*) picks up the grains for its nourishment from the field (*khale*), each tissue takes its nourishment separately.
Khicaḍī : a recipe made by cooking rice and mung beans together, with some spices.
Kledaka (*kapha*) : one of the five types of *kapha* that helps moistening the food and digesting it in the stomach.
Kriyā : action, practice, applying a remedy.
Kriyākāla : duration of an action.
Kṣīra Dadhi : a rule of tissue formation which states that, like milk (*kṣīra*) converts to yogurt (*dadhi*), food directly transforms into each tissue.
Kubera : the God of riches and treasure.
Kuṭī : cottage, hut.
Kuṭīprāveśika : entering or living in a cottage for the purpose of rejuvenation.
Laghu : light, small, minute.
Lavaṇa : salty taste of flavor.
Lavaṇa-bhāskara : an Ayurvedic powder popularly used to enhance digestion.

Madakāri : that which causes intoxication.
Madanaphala : emetic nut, Latin name : *Randia spinosa*.
Madātya : effect or disorder resulting from intoxication.
Madhura : sweet taste of flavor, pleasant, charming, delightful.
Madya : any intoxicating drink or substance.
Mahābhūta : gross or physical elements, being great.
Mahad tattva : intellect, great principle.
Mahendra : a great king or leader.
Majjā : bone marrow.
Majjā-vaha srotas : channels transporting bone marrow.
Mala : impurity, dirt, filth, wastes excreted out of body.
Malinīkaraṇa : the act making impure, staining.
Māṁsa : muscles, flesh, meat, fleshy part (pulp) of a fruit.
Māṁsa-vaha srotas : channels transporting muscles.
Manas : mind.
Manda : slow.
Mandāgni : weakened state of digestive fire.
Mantra : *Vedic* hymn, sacred or mystical verse, a prayer.
Matasya : fish.
Meda : fatty tissue.
Medhā : mental power, intelligence, wisdom, prudence.
Medo-vaha srotas : channels transporting fatty tissue.
Medhya : enhancing wisdom, mental power and intelligence.
Mithyā-yoga : wrong use, wrong employment.
Mokśaṇa : to let flow, liberating, losing, releasing.
Mṛdu : soft, delicate, tender.
Mudrā : position, image, gesture.
Mūnga dāla : a variety of green dry beans (mung beans) used for cooking or making sprouts.
Mūtra : urine.
Mūtra-vaha srotas : channels transporting the urine.
Nāḍī : pulse, any tubular organ such as vein or artery.
Naimittika : a cause to achieve a specific result.
Nānātmaja : a disease caused by a single *doṣa*.
Nasya : administering a remedy through the nose.
Nīma (*Neem*) : Margosa tree, Latin name: *Azadirachta indica*.
Netra : eye.
Nidāna : cause of disease and investigation of it.
Nidrā : sleep.
Nija : innate, one's own, internal.
Nirūha (*basti*) : an enema not of an oily kind.
Niyama : restrain, regulate, to fix upon, control, check.
Ojas : vigor, strength, vitality, the essence of all tissues (*dhātūs*).
Pācaka (*pitta*) : one of the five types of *pitta* that governs digestion of food.
Paiśācika : demonical, related to ghosts or evil spirits.
Panca : five.
Panca karma : five types of elimination therapies to clean the body.
Panīra : a type of fresh cheese made by curdling milk.
Para-ojas : high quality or superior vital fluid located in the heart.
Paramparā : an authentic teacher-disciple lineage.
Parīkṣā : examination, inspection, investigation.

Pariṇāma : result, consequence, transformation.
Pāśava : animal type, belonging to cattle or animal family.
Paścāta karma : post action, therapies induced after the primary therapy.
Peyā : rice gruel or any drink mixed with a small quantity of boiled rice.
Picchila : slimy, slippery.
Pippalī : long pepper, Latin name: *Piper longum.*
Pitta : fire, bile, one of the three main biological energies in the body.
Prabhāva : effect, prominent, peculiar or special action of a herb.
Prajñā : wisdom, intelligence, knowledge.
Prajñāparādha : misuse of intellect, offending the wisdom.
Prakṛti : nature, constitution, natural form, and original nature.
Prakopa : vitiation, aggravation.
Prāṇa : the breath of life, life air or life force, energy, power.
Prāṇa-vaha srotas : channels carrying breathing air, the respiratory system.
Prāṇa-vāta : one of the five types of *vāta*, which governs respiration and sensory functions.
Prāṇāyama : to control the breath, controlled breathing techniques.
Prāpti : obtaining, attaining.
Prasara : spreading, extension.
Pratyāhāra : withdrawal (especially of senses from external objects).
Praveśa : to enter, go into.
Preta : spirit of a dead person, wandering spirits, ghosts.
Pṛthvī : earth, world.
Pūga : betel nut, Latin name: *Areca catechu.*
Purīṣa : faces, stool, waste matter.
Purīṣa-vaha srotas : channels transporting faecal matter, excretory system.
Puruṣa : human being, person, often used for man.
Pūrva : prior, preceding, former, earlier.
Pūrva-karma : prior action, preparation for the primary treatment.
Pūrvarūpa : the preliminary symptoms of disease.
Raitā : yogurt mixed with herbs or vegetables.
Rajas : passion, action.
Rakta : blood.
Rakta-mokśaṇa : blood letting, letting the blood flow out.
Rakta-vaha srotas : channels carrying blood, circulatory system.
Rājasic : passionate, active, sharp.
Rākśasa : demon, an evil, infested by demons, demonical.
Rañjaka (pitta) : one of the five types of *pitta* that governs blood formation.
Rasa : juice, taste, flavor, essence, liquid, fluid.
Rasa-vaha srotas : channels carrying plasma or lymph.
Rasa śāstra : alchemy, the processing of mercury.
Rasāyana : things (herbs, foods, activities) that prevent aging and promote longevity.
Rāśi : quantity, a measure for quantity, a heap, a pile, mass.
Rātricaryā : routine to be followed in night or evening, night regime.
Ṛṣi : a saint, learned person.
Ṛtucarya : seasonal regimes, routine to be followed in various seasons.
Rūkśa : dry, arid, not greasy, emaciated, thin.

Rūpa : sign, symptoms of disease.
Śabda : sound, tone, voice.
Ṣaḍa : six.
Ṣaḍavidha : six types.
Sādhāka (pitta) : one of the five types of *pitta* that governs mental functions.
Śākuna : relating to birds, having the nature of a bird, bird catcher.
Śalya tantra : science of surgery.
Śālākya tantra : science using probes or cylindrical sticks for investigation and treatments, branch dealing with eyes, ears, nose and throat.
Sama : balanced, equal, even.
Samādhi : profound or abstract meditation, intense contemplation.
Samāgni : balanced state of digestive fire.
Samāna (*vāta*) : one of the five types of *vāta* that assists in digestion and assimilation of food.
Śamana : suppression, alleviation
Sāmānya : similar, identical, like.
Sāmānyaja : a disease caused by two or three *doṣas*.
Saṁhitā : methodically arranged collection of verses, texts.
Samprāpti : pathogenesis, the complete route of manifestation of disease.
Saṁsarjana (*karma*) : diets and activities practiced after a treatment to get back to normal routine and food.
Samyaka : accurate, proper, correct.
Saṁyoga : combination, connection, conjunction.
Sancaya : accumulation, collection, gathering.
Sāndra : dense, thick, solid, compact.
Śankhapuṣpī : a herb used as a tonic for nervous system: Latin Name: *Convolvulus pluricaulis*.
Sanskrit : purified, sanctified, an ancient language of India.
Sapta : seven.
Sapta-dhātu : the seven constitutional elements or tissues of the body.
Sara : liquid, fluid, moving, wandering.
Sarpa : snake, serpent.
Sarpagandhā : name of a herb used for lowering high blood pressure, Latin name: *Rouwolfia serpentina*.
Śarīra : body, physical body.
Sarvāngāsana : a yoga posture.
Śāstrīya : according to original texts (*śāstra*), confirmable to sacred precepts.
Sattva : spiritual essence, quality of purity or goodness.
Sattva-vajaya : a therapy that increases the mode of goodness (*sattva*).
Sāttvic : pure, genuine, spiritual, honest.
Śavāsana : dead body posture of *yoga*.
Śilājīta : a black sticky mineral similar in appearance to bitumen.
Sirā : any tubular vessel in the body—a vein, nerve or artery.
Śira (Śiras) : the head, skull.
Śirodhārā : pouring oil or any other liquid on forehead from a special pot.
Śīrṣāsana : head stand posture of *yoga*.
Śīta : cold, chilly.
Ślakśhaṇa : smooth, polished, soft, tender, gentle.
Ślesaka (*kapha*) : one of the five types of *kapha* that provides lubrication to various joints.
Snehana : lubricating, anointing, rubbing with oil.
Snigdha : sticky, viscid, unctuous, smooth, adhesive.
Śodhana : cleaning, purifying, refining.
Sparśa : touching, sense of touch.

Sṛṣti Utpatti : creation of the universe
Srvaṇam : transportation, carrying.
Śṛnga : horn.
Srotas : channels, tubes, hollow vessels carrying substances.
Sroto-duṣṭi : impurity of channels.
Sthāna saṁśraya : location in a place, relocation of *doṣas*.
Sthira : firm, hard, solid, compact, strong, immovable, fixed.
Sthūla : large, thick, big, gross, massive, stout.
Śukra : reproductive tissue.
Śukra-vaha srotas : channels transporting the reproductive tissue or fluid.
Sūkśma : minute, small, subtle, short, fine, feeble.
Sūrya namaskāra : saluting the sun, a set of exercises popularly used in *yoga*.
Suśruta : author of *Suśruta Saṁhitā*, pioneer of surgical techniques.
Suśruta Saṁhitā : a text of Āyurveda that deals mainly with surgery.
Svābhāvika : belonging to or arising from one's own nature, natural.
Sveda : sweat, perspiration, warmth.
Sveda-vaha srotas : the channels carrying the sweat.
Taitreya Upaniṣada : part of the *Vedas*
Takra : buttermilk, a drink made by mixing water in yogurt and churning it
Tamaka śvāsa : a kind of asthma.
Tamas : ignorance, darkness, delusion.
Tāmasic : ignorant, lazy, dark, stale.
Tanmātrā : un-manifested form of the five elements, seeds for element.
Tarpaka (*kapha*) : one of the five types of *kapha* that nourishes the sense organs.
Tejas : fire, light, clearness of eyes, glow, glare, top of a flame.
Tīkśṇa : sharp, hot, fiery, pungent.
Tīkśṇāgni : strong digestive fire, increased activity of digestive fire.
Tikta : bitter taste or flavor.
Tri : three.
Tridoṣa : the three *doṣas* (*vāta, pitta, kapha*).
Tridoṣic : relating to *tridoṣa*.
Triguṇa : the three qualities of Nature (*sattva, rajas, tamas*)
Triphalā : an Āyurvedic recipe made by mixing equal quantities of fruits of three particular herbs.
Trivṛta : a herb (Indian jalap) used for purgation, Latin name: *Operculina turpethum*.
Tulasī : Holy Basil. Latin Name: *Ocimum sanctum*.
Udaka-vaha srotas : channels transporting water or watery liquids in the body.
Udāna (*vāta*) : one of the five types of *vāta* that governs speech and voice, breathing upwards.
Upa-dhātu : not a main tissue, a secondary tissue that supports the main tissue.
Upaśaya : the allaying of disease by suitable remedies, advantageous medicine, diagnosis by the effect of medicines or food items.
Upastambha : supporting pillars, sub-pillars.
Upyoktā : User
Upyoga-saṁsthā : using method, user manual, instructions to use or practice a technique.
Uṣṇa : hot, warm, passionate, sharp.
Uttānapādāsana : a *yoga* posture (*āsana*).
Uttara basti : a special type of enema given through the urinary tract.
Vāgabhaṭṭa : a respected authority in Āyurvedic theory who wrote *Aṣṭānga Sangraha* and *Aṣṭānga Hṛdaya*.

Vaidya : Āyurvedic doctor.
Vājīkaraṇa : the science of aphrodisiacs, producing virility.
Vānaspatya : a tree, shrub or plant.
Vamana : the act of vomiting, emesis.
Varuṇa : God of waters, sea, rivers.
Vāta : wind or air as one of the three main biological energies of the body.
Vātā-tapika : exposed to air and heat (sun), outdoors.
Vāyu : air, wind, one of the five elements.
Veda : ancient books of knowledge, sacred knowledge.
Vibhītaka : Belliric Myrobalan, Latin name: *Terminalia bellirica.*
Vidāhī : heat, burning, inflammation, acid.
Vikṛti : sickness, alteration, change, imbalance, agitation.
Virecana : purgation.
Vīrya : potency, power, vigor, semen.
Vipāka : ripe, mature, state of food after digestion.
Viśada : clear, pure, spotless, shining.
Visrāvaṇa : to let flow, to let spread.
Viṣamāgni : irregular digestive fire, unstable digestive fire.
Viśeṣa : opposite, different.
Vyāna (*vāta*) : one of the five types of *vāta* helps the function of circulation in the body.
Vyakta : visible, specific.
Yama : rules, instructions, guidelines.
Yāmya : one who takes initiative, is courageous and has leadership qualities.
Yaṣṭīmadhu : licorice, Latin name: *Glycyrrhiza glabra.*
Yoga : to link, to add, to join, a progressive method to become self-realized and link the soul to Universal consciousness.
Yūṣa : soup generally made from various kinds of pulses.

Bibliography

Abdul, H. & Saheb, H. *The Complete Book of Home Remedies.* 6th edn, Orient Paperbacks, Delhi, India, 1999.

Atreya. *Practical Ayurveda—Secrets for Physical, Sexual and Spiritual Health.* 1st Indian edn, Jaico Publishing House, Bombay, India, 1999.

Babu, S. *A Treatise on Home Remedies.* Pustak Mahal, Delhi, India, 2000.

Bakhru, H. *Herbs That Heal.* Orient Paperbacks, Delhi, India, 1990.

—— *Foods That Heal.* Orient Paperbacks, Delhi, India, 1990.

—— *A Complete Handbook of Nature Cure.* 2nd revised edn, reprint, Ashwin J Shah, Bombay, India, 1995.

Chaturvedi, S. *Ayurveda for You.* Bharatiya Vidya Bhavan, Bombay India, 1998.

Chopra, D. *Quantum Healing—Exploring the Frontiers of Mind/Body Medicine.* Bantam Books, USA, 1990.

—— *Perfect Health—The Complete Mind/Body Guide.* Harmony Books, New York, USA, 1991.

Dasa, S.N. *The Yoga of Dejection—Self Beyond Identity Crisis.* Jiva Institute Vrindavan India, 2000

Dash, B. & Sharma, R. *Caraka Samhita—Text with English translation and critical exposition based on Cakrapani Datta's Ayurveda Dipika.* vol.I (4th edn, 1995), vol.II (2nd edn, 1985) & vol.III (1st edn, 1988) Chowkhamba Sanskrit Series Office, Varanasi India, 1985.

—— *Ayurvedic Cures for Common Diseases.* 4th edn, Hind Pocket Books Ltd, 1991.

Dash, B. & Junius, M. A *Handbook of Ayurveda.* Naurang Rai Concept Publishing Company, Delhi India, 1983.

Davis, R. *An Easy Guide to Ayurveda—The Natural Way to Wholeness.* 1st Indian edn, B. Jain Publishers Ltd, New Delhi, India, 1997.

Deshpande, R., Qutab, A., Ranade, S. & Ranade, S. *Health and Disease in Ayurveda and Yoga.* Revised edn, Anmol Prakashan, Pune, India 1999.

Dev, C. *Beauty and Body Book—The Natural Way.* Reprinted edn, Hind Pocket Books, Delhi, India, 1999.

Frawley, D. *Ayurvedic Healing—A Comprehensive Guide.* 1st Indian edn, Motilal Banarsidass Publishers, Delhi India, 1992.

—— *Ayurveda and the Mind—The Healing of Consciousness.* 1st Indian edn, Motilal Banarsidass Publishers, Delhi India, 1998.

Frawley, D & Lad, V. *The Yoga of Herbs—An Ayurvedic Guide to Herbal Medicine.* Lotus Press, Santa Fe, New Mexico, 1986.

Godagama, S. *The Handbook of Ayurveda—India's medical wisdom explained.* Kyle Cathie Ltd, London, Great Britain, 1997.

Goldberg, B. *Look Younger, Live Longer.* 1st Indian edn, Pustak Mahal, Delhi, India, 1998.

Grace, K. *Aromatherapy Pocketbook.* Llewellyn Publications, Minnesota, USA, 1999.

Green, A. *Principles of Ayurveda.* Thorsons, London, Great Britain, 2000.

Gupta, L. & Guru, L. *Positive Health Through Ayurveda.* Chaukhamba Sanskrit, Pratishthan, Delhi, India, 1989.

—— *Essentials of Ayurveda.* Chaukhamba Sanskrit Pratishthan, Delhi India, 1996.

—— *Biogenic Secrets of Food in Ayurveda.* Chaukhamba Sanskrit Pratishthan, Delhi India, 1999.

Jenson, B. *Foods That Heal—A Guide to Understanding and Using the Healing Powers of Natural Foods.* Reprint edn, B. Jain Publishers Ltd, New Delhi India, 1998.

Johari, H. *Dhanwantari.* Rupa & Co, New Delhi, India 1992.

Joshi, S. *Ayurveda and Panchkarma—The Science of Healing and Rejuvenation.* 1st Indian edn, Motilal Banarsidass Publishers, Delhi, India, 1998.

Krishnamurthy, K. *Outlines of Ayurveda.* Books For All, Delhi, India, 1997.

Kutumbiah, P. *Ancient Indian Medicine.* Reissued edn, Orient Longman Ltd, Chennai, India, 1999.

Lad, V. *Ayurveda: The Science of Self-Healing, A Practical Guide.* 1st Indian edn, Motilal Banarsidass Publishers, Delhi, India, 1994.

Lal, H. *Health Through Raw Eating.* Preem Chand, UP, India, 1990.

Monier-Williams, W. *A Sanskrit-English Dictionary.* New enlarged edn, Marwah Publications, New Delhi, India. 1986

Morningstar, A & Desai, U. *The Ayurvedic Cookbook—A Personalized Guide to Nutrition and Health.* 1st Indian edn, Motilal Banarsidass Publishers, Delhi India, 1994.

Murthy, N & Pandey, D. *Ayurvedic Cure for Common Diseases.* 5th Revised & Enlarged edn, Orient Paperbacks, Delhi, India, 1995.

Ram, A. *Herbal Indian Perfumes and Cosmetics.* Sri Satguru Publications, Delhi, India, 1997.

Ranade, S. *Natural Healing Through Ayurveda.* Motilal Banarsidass Publishers, Delhi India, 1994.

Rhyner, H. *Ayurveda—The Gentle Health System.* 1st Indian edn, Motilal Banarsidass Publishers, Delhi India, 1998.

Sachs, M. *Ayurvedic Beauty Care—Ageless Techniques to Invoke Natural Beauty.* 1st Indian edn, Motilal Banarsidass Publishers, Delhi, India, 1995.

Sairam, T. *Home Remedies—A Handbook of Herbal Cures for Common Ailments,* vol.1 (1998) & vol.2 (1999) Penguin Books, India, 1998.

Sarma, K. & Swaminathan, S. *Speaking of Nature Cure—Regain, Retain and Improve Health the Drugless Way.* Sterling Publishers Private Ltd, Delhi, India 1993.

Sharma, L. *Yoga for the Cure of Common Diseases.* Hind Pocket Books, Delhi, India, 1987.

Sharma, R. N. *Arogya Prakash—A Practical Handbook of Ayurvedic Health Rules and Diagnosis & Treatment of Diseases.* 1st English edn, Baidyanath Ayurved Bhawan Ltd, Nagpur, India, 1983.

Sharma, R. *Herbal Beauty Care.* Pustak Mahal, Delhi, India, 2000.

Singh, R. & Udupa, K. *Clinical and Experimental Studies on Rasayana Drugs and Pancakarma Therapy.* Central Council for Research in Ayurveda and Siddha, New Delhi, India, 1993.

Svobada, R. *Prakriti—Your Ayurvedic Constitution.* 1st Indian edn, Motilal Banarsidass Publishers, Delhi, India, 1994.

Swami, Krsna B. *The Healthy & Wise Choice—Vedic Vegetarianism.* Swami, K, India, 1993.

Swami, Prabhupada A.C. *Bhagavad-gita As It Is.* Complete edn, Collier Books. New York, USA, 1972.

Swami, Satyananda S. *Asana Pranayama Mudra Bandha.* Enlarged and revised edn, Bihar Yoga Bharati, India, 1996.

Tarabilda, E. *Ayurveda Revolutionized—Integrating Ancient and Modern Ayurveda.* 1st Indian edn, Motilal Banarsidass Publishers, Delhi, India, 1998.

Weil, A. *Spontaneous Healing.* Fawcett Columbine/Ballantine Books, New York, USA, 1995.

BIBLIOGRAPHY

BOOKS IN HINDI

Acarya, D. *Aasana—Pranayama* (Yoga Postures—Breathing Techniques). 6th edn, Bhagwati Prakashan, Delhi India, 1997.

Atri, D. *Susruta Samhita* (Commentary on *Susruta's* work). 5th edn, Motilal Banarasi Das, Delhi India, 1975.

Chhanganee, G. *Astanga Sangraha* (Commentary on *Vagabhatta's* work). 7th edn, Chaukhamba Sanskrit Sansthan Varanasi India, 1991.

Desai, R. *Ayurvediya Kriya Sarir* (Ayurvedic Physiology). 6th edn, Shri Baidyanath Ayurveda Bhavan Limited Nagpur India, 1982.

Ghanekara, B. *Vaidyakiya Subhashita Sahityam* (Useful Quotes on Health). 7th edn, Chaukhamba Sanskrit Sansthan Varanasi India, 1999.

Mehata, A. *Swadesi Cikitsa ke Camatkara* (Wonders of Ayurvedic Remedies). 1st edn, Kalyan Chikitsa Prakashan Delhi India, 1991.

Pandey, P. *Swasthya-Raksaka* (Self Health Care). 4th edn, Niroga Dham Prakashan Indore India, 1991.

Parashar, R. *Sarangdhar Samhita* (Commentary on *Sharangdhar's* work). 3rd edn, Shri Baidhyanath Ayurveda Bhavan Limited Nagpur India, 1984.

Pathak, R. *Padartha Vijnana* (Metaphysics). 7th edn, Shree Baidyanath Ayurveda Bhavan Limited Nagpur India, 1984.

Sharma, H. & Pal, S. *Kashyapa Samhita* (Commentary on *Kashyapa's* work). 4th edn, Chaukhamba Sanskrit Sansthan Varanasi India, 1994.

Sharma, P. *Dravyaguna Vijnana* vol. II (Description of Herbs). 7th edn, Chaukhamba Bharti Academy Varanasi India, 1983.

Shastri, K. & Chaturvedi, G. *Caraka Samhita* (Commentary on *Caraka's* work). 13th edn, Chaukhamba Bharti Academy Varanasi India, 1986.

Shukla, V. *Kaya Chikitsa* (Internal Medicine). 3rd edn, Chaukhamba Subharati Prakashan Varanasi India, 1995.

—— *Ayurvediya Vikrti Vijnana* (Ayurvedic Pathology). 4th edn, Chaukhamba Sanskrit Pratisthan Delhi India, 1997.

Uniyal, M. *Jadi Butiyon ka Krsikarana* (Agriculturization of Medicinal Plants in India). 1st edn, Baidhynath Ayurveda Shodha Sansthan Patna India,1998.

Upadhyaya, Y. *Madhava Nidanam* (Commentary on Diagnostic Methods of *Madhav*). 26th edn, Chaukhamba Sanskrit Sansthan Varanasi India, 1996.

Vaidya, L. *Astang Hridayam* (Commentary on *Vagabhatta's* work). 1st edn, Motilal Banarasi Das Publishers Private Ltd. Delhi India, 1963.

Vaidya, L. *Bhava Prakasa* (Commentary on *Sri Bhavamisra's* work). 3rd edn, Motilal Banarasi Das Delhi India, 1968.

Verma, O. *Ahar Cikitsa* (Food Therapy). 1st edn, Narayan Prakashan Jaipur India, 2000.

About Jiva

Jiva Institute (founded in 1992) is a non-profit research and development organization that aims to revive traditional Indian sciences and culture with the use of modern technology. Jiva has three divisions working to achieve this objective—Education, Health, and Culture. If you are interested in learning more about the Jiva Institute, visit www.jiva.org

Other Jiva Publications

Srimad Bhagavata Mahatmyam

In Vaikuntha not even the Leaves Fall

Sri Tattva Sandarbha of Srila Jiva Gosvami

The Hitopadesa of Sri Narayana Pandita

The Yoga of Dejection—Self Beyond Identity Crisis

A series of audiotapes on philosophy and religion.

A variety of computer education resources: student textbooks and software; teacher training manuals and programs; and educational Internet content.